The Migration Apparatus

The Migration Apparatus

SECURITY, LABOR, AND POLICYMAKING

IN THE EUROPEAN UNION

Gregory Feldman

Stanford University Press
Stanford, California

Stanford University Press
Stanford, California

Printed in the United States of America on acid-free, archival-quality paper

Library of Congress Cataloging-in-Publication Data

Feldman, Gregory, 1969- author.
  The migration apparatus : security, labor, and policymaking in the European Union /
Gregory Feldman.
    pages cm
  Includes bibliographical references and index.
  ISBN 978-0-8047-6106-2 (cloth : alk. paper)--ISBN 978-0-8047-6107-9 (pbk. : alk. paper)
  1. European Union countries--Emigration and immigration--Government policy. 2. Foreign
workers--Government policy--European Union countries. 3. Illegal aliens--Government
policy--European Union countries. 4. Internal security--European Union countries. I. Title.
  JV7590.F455 2011
  325.4--dc23   2011023762

Typeset by Bruce Lundquist in 10/14 Minion

To Ilo and Uku. May your hearts always be this migrant's home.

Most of what matters in our lives takes place in our absence . . .

Salman Rushdie, *Midnight's Children*

CONTENTS

PREFACE

This book aims for two goals. The first goal is to capture how the European Union's emerging migration management apparatus interfaces with the contemporary global political and economic order. The book's operative questions are how the apparatus's various parts articulate without a centralized authority, and how a normative policy subject is conjured up in its whirlwind of disparate policy processes. It focuses less on the questions of how well the apparatus works "on the ground" and whether migrants "really" conform to the demands pushed upon them. While crucially important, these questions do not necessarily point the investigator to the myriad routines of scattered technocrats whose work enables this apparatus, synergistically and perhaps unwittingly. Regardless of the degree of the apparatus's success, literally millions of migrants and travelers around the world must deal with its convergent strength, generated from the otherwise unrelated effects of external border control, biometric information technologies, and circular migration programs. Though large, it would be misleading to describe such a social construction as "large-scale." This tag suggests that it rests loftily above real people and acts independently of them. It does neither. Rather, it results from the situated practices of technocrats, officials, and experts who often do not know each other and conduct much of their work virtually in cyberspace. If local rituals organize people by establishing *direct connections* between them, then apparatuses destroy those mechanisms, individualize people, and create *indirect relations* between them so that they, or their labor power, can be processed to an enormous degree. Grand moral statements make up for the social breakdown. They integrate policy experts, policy targets, and the apparatus that relates them into a common, if vacuous, ethical frame: "A migration policy that works for everyone," as EU officials are known to say. Put starkly, however, the strange effect of this social situation is that there is no "social" in the substantive sense of the term.

The book's second goal is to deploy a suitable ethnographic methodology for achieving the first goal. Like globalization, an apparatus poses obvious challenges to participant-observation, anthropology's signature field method, which was designed to map direct social and ecological connections. Ethnographers' responses to the shattering of fixed place share a commitment to tracing tangible connections across the globe, establishing an in situ presence in as many nodal points as possible, and filling in the gaps with keen theoretical insights. This book offers a vital complement to these important responses: specifically, a methodology for studying highly mediated social relations and the veritable absence of connections between actors who are nevertheless absorbed in the same processes, though often from radically different positions. If alienation, estrangement, and objectification are hallmarks of mass capitalist society, then we should consider a nuanced understanding of "connections" as a methodological and theoretical construct. How do we study amorphous systems of population regulation—under which we all increasingly live—that rely on countless educated laborers who lack serious influence as particular individuals, ongoing ties to each other, and direct contact with the masses of people whom their labor indirectly regulates? I hope that what I call "nonlocal ethnography" will help us to examine how these (non)connections specifically take their shape, and their toll. It also acknowledges another hallmark of mass society, whether one is a poor Southern migrant or a wealthy Northern citizen, or any combination thereof: as we lack control over the most important conditions of our lives, so these conditions are rarely formulated in our midst. This point does not require us to abandon in situ field research, which places the ethnographer "there" in the actor's midst. Rather, it requires us to continue to complicate how we identify and access the elusive "there" where we need to be to understand what made that actor's midst possible.

ACKNOWLEDGMENTS

Producing this book quickly became both a great challenge and a sheer pleasure. Many people helped significantly with the former and hopefully shared with me in the latter. Of course, none of them share the blame for the pages that follow! I apologize if I have accidentally omitted any of their names below.

Michael Jandl played a crucial role in getting my fieldwork started. His colleagues and many others located at different places around the EU were extremely generous with their time, space, and attention. This book would not have materialized without their support. Many of these individuals appear in the book, though their names have been changed or left unmentioned for reasons of confidentiality. I hope that the final product wins their respect.

At various stages in the project, the manuscript benefited from the encouragement and feedback of Joe Heyman, Cris Shore, Susan Greenhalgh, Hugh Gusterson, Paul Silverstein, Bill Beeman, Don Brenneis, Paul Spoonley, Robert Rubinstein, Dan Hiebert, and Pablo Mendez. Alexia Bloch and Neil Guppy provided helpful comments on the grant proposal. At the University of California, Irvine, Susan Greenhalgh and her graduate Anthropology of Public Policy class (particularly Adonia Lugo, Connie McGuire, and Shaozeng Zhang) gave their class time and comments on a book chapter titled "Illuminating the Apparatus: Steps Toward a Nonlocal Ethnography of Global Governance." That chapter appears in the edited volume *Policy Worlds: Anthropology and the Anatomy of Contemporary Power*, published by Berghahn Books (2011) and edited by Cris Shore, Susan Wright, and Davide Però. With permission of the publisher, parts of it also appear in Chapters 1, 3, 4, 6, and 7 of the present book.

Various pieces of the book were delivered as papers at different universities since 2005. These include Brown University's Watson Institute for International Studies and Brown's Working Group on Anthropology and Population in the Population Studies Training Center. I would like to thank Winifred Tate, Nicholas Townsend, Marida Hollos, Kay Warren, and Inna Leykin for invitations and stimulating discussions. During the workshop "Migration in a Neoliberal Age," hosted by the University of Florida's Center for European Studies, I received helpful feedback from Maria Stoilkova, Monika Salzbrunn, Ayse Parla, Paul Silverstein, Cristiana Giordano, Laurie McIntosh, and Esther Romeyn. I thank Maria and Esther for the invitation to participate. I would also like to thank Ann-Cathrine Jungar at the Centre for Baltic and East European Studies at Södertörns Högskola, Stockholm, for hosting me as a visiting fellow, and Pat Cavendish for inviting me to deliver a keynote lecture for the Northeast International Education Association at Pierce College, Puyallup, Washington. Both opportunities offered useful input and engaging discussions, which further refined the present argument. At the University of British Columbia (UBC), the manuscript benefited from a number of workshops as well. These included the graduate student methods seminar in the Department of Geography; the research methods colloquium sponsored by the Interdisciplinary Studies Graduate Program; and Catherine Dauvergne's law workshop on "Challenging Sovereignty."

I have benefited tremendously from Dan Hiebert's insights during countless open-ended conversations on global migration. So-called working lunches were made for these kinds of conversations. Gogi Bhullar provided early and helpful assistance in orienting me through a maze of online EU documents. Two excellent doctoral candidates in UBC's Department of Geography provided crucial research assistance by sleuthing out and organizing various literatures, policy updates, and reports of all kinds. Luna Vives provided support midway through the project, particularly on matters pertaining to external border control. Sarah Zell took the baton for the final lap, which also included formatting and proofreading the entire manuscript twice. Amazingly, she completed much of this work between chemotherapy sessions. Francesco Brardinoni provided translation for the Italian language monologue in Chapter 4.

The research for this book was financed almost entirely through a Standard Research Grant from Canada's Social Science and Humanities Research Council, with extra support coming from UBC's Department of Geography and Office of the Dean of Arts. Though very pleasant and engaging on an individual basis, my time at UBC has been challenged by the increasing neoliberalization of the academy. Specific senior colleagues nevertheless made strategic moves to help me sustain a vibrant research trajectory against the structural odds. I am grateful to Mike Bovis, Graeme Wynn, David Ley, and Darrin Lehman for their interventions on this front. The editorial team at Stanford University Press has been highly supportive ever since the project's beginning. In particular, Joa Suorez, Mariana Raykov, and Jeff Wyneken handled each and every step with professionalism and aplomb. Year after year, Paul and Kathy Feldman have backed everything I've done and in ways that can only be repaid by doing the same for the next generation. Last, but not least, the influence of Merje Kuus is present throughout the text.

ABBREVIATIONS

3MP	Mediterranean Managed Migration Project
ALDE	Alliance of Liberals and Democrats for Europe
ANAPEC	Agence Nationale de Promotion de l'Emploi et des Compétences
APS	Arab partner states
BEG	Biometric Expertise Group
BORTEC	technical surveillance of Southern maritime borders of European Union
CIGEM	Migration Information and Management Centre
CIRAM	Common Integrated Risk Analysis Model
CNAI	Centro Nacional de Apoio ao Imigrante
DRC	Democratic Republic of the Congo
EBF	European Biometrics Forum
EBP	European Biometrics Portal
EC	European Commission
ECDC	European Centre for Disease Control
ECOWAS	Economic Community of West African States
EDA	European Defence Agency
EMN	European Migration Network
EMPO	European Migration Policy Organization
EMSA	European Maritime Safety Agency
ENP	European Neighbourhood Policy
EPS	European partner states
ESA	European Space Agency
EURODAC	European Dactyloscopy

EUROPOL	European Police Office
EUROSUR	European Border Surveillance System
EUSC	European Union Satellite Centre
FISO	Frontex intelligence support officer
GCIM	Global Commission on International Migration
IATA	International Air Transport Association
IBM	integrated border management
ICAO	International Civil Aviation Organization
ICMPD	International Centre for Migration Policy Development
ICONet	Information and Coordination Network
IDOM	Prevention of Irregular Migration Project (Egypt)
IGO	intergovernmental organization
ILO	International Labour Organization
IMF	International Monetary Fund
IMIS	Integrated Management Information System
IOM	International Organization for Migration
IPAD	Portuguese Institute for Development Support
ISO	International Standards Organization
IT	information technology
JHA	Justice and Home Affairs
JTC	Joint Technical Committee (of the International Standards Organization)
LIMES	Land and Sea Integrated Monitoring for European Security
MARISS	European Maritime Security Services
MEDSEA	Mediterranean Coastal Patrols Network
MEP	member of European Parliament
MIDA	Migration for Development in Africa
MPG	Migration Policy Group
NCP	national contact point
OECD	Organisation for Economic Co-operation and Development
OSCE	Organization for Security and Co-operation in Europe
PEP	Portuguese Electronic Passport
RABIT	rapid border intervention team

RAU	Risk Analysis Unit
RFID	radio frequency identification
RT	registered traveler
SIS	Schengen Information System
TEU	Treaty of the European Union (also called the Maastricht Treaty)
TREVI	Terrorisme, Radicalisme, Extremisme et Violence Internationale
UAV	unmanned aerial vehicle
UNHCR	United Nations High Commissioner for Refugees
UNODC	United Nations Office on Drugs and Crime
VIS	Visa Information System
WTO	World Trade Organization

The Migration Apparatus

1 UNCONNECTED IN THE ACEPHALOUS WORLD OF MIGRATION POLICYMAKING

What makes mass society so difficult to bear is not the number of people involved, or at least not primarily, but the fact that the world between them has lost its power to gather them together, to relate and to separate them. The weirdness of this situation resembles a spiritualistic séance where a number of people gathered around a table might suddenly, through some magic trick, see the table vanish from their midst, so that two persons sitting opposite each other were no longer separated but also would be entirely unrelated to each other by anything tangible.

Hannah Arendt 1958, 52–53

EYES ASKANCE

Officials from the immigration office of a wealthy European Union country's interior ministry have organized a field trip to one of its holding centers for "illegal" immigrants.[1] They are giving this tour to some sixty of their counterparts from European and North African states. Together, they are trying to establish common migration policy guidelines through the Mediterranean Managed Migration Project (3MP). Visiting officials can compare their host country's practices in the reception and detention of illegal migrants to their own. "Residents," as the center's staff calls them, number up to 160 at a time and stay an average of thirty-five days before they are returned to their countries of origin. A green, metal, double-layer fence encloses the facility. The outer ring reaches about six meters high while the inner ring climbs to five meters. The center sits peacefully in a green leafy suburb, looking safe, secure, and humane even though its functionalist architecture differs awkwardly from that of the surrounding neighborhood.

On a warm, sunny day the center's staff greets these officials (plus one anthropologist) with a wine and cheese reception in a grassy space next to the main entrance. As the fortified center incarcerates mostly darker-skinned migrants from

---

1. "Illegal," of course, is a relational status, not an objective descriptor. The use of scare quotes situates the term historically to avoid naturalizing illegality as a timeless attribute of the person to whom it is ascribed. The remainder of the text will refrain from using scare quotes now that the point has been made.

1

much poorer countries, this odd moment seems to fit Luis Buñuel's satirical film *The Discreet Charm of the Bourgeoisie*. Buñuel juxtaposes in a single frame polite members of the upper middle class, who enjoy fine dinners, teas, and other pleasantries, against an assortment of characters marginalized by global capitalism, Cold War geopolitics, and the French mainstream. The surreal and awkwardly close proximity of such disparate souls, like those gathered in and around the holding center, prompts reflection on how people who do not encounter each other *immediately* in their normal daily circuits are linked in unequal, far-flung, and highly *mediated* global power relations.

"What does the fence make you think of?" I ask an official, Maria, from a southern EU member state. "At least the surroundings are nice. In [my country] they are in tents," she replies regretfully. After this remark our hosts move us inside to the foyer, which features a portrait of the royal couple positioned on the wall slightly higher than eye level and facing the rows of chairs awaiting us. We are shown the same video that residents see upon their arrival at the center. It presents the state's options on how to "return" illegal migrants to their countries of origin. (As a Dutch official explains later, the term "deport" is not used in continental Europe, unlike in Britain, Canada, and the US, because of its association with Nazi deportations of Jews to concentration camps.) Each option involves increased levels of force. On one end of the spectrum is assisted voluntary return, in which removal is cooperative, comfortable, and comes with logistical and financial support from the International Organization for Migration (IOM). In some instances, IOM provides returnees with financial assistance to start up new businesses back home. On the other end is a forced return for uncooperative migrants that could involve handcuffs, ankle cuffs, straightjackets, soft helmets, and police escorts on chartered flights with other illegal migrants. In between these two extremes, migrants might be kept in light restraints while seated between two security guards on commercial flights. The video concludes with the narrator clearly enunciating that one way or another, "you will be returned."

After the presentation, our guide leads us down a corridor to the main security control center, which is encased in thick, shatterproof glass and located at the intersection of the facility's two main residence halls. We pass through a double-doored air-locked chamber that separates the security center from one of the residence halls. Our group experiences a moment of claustrophobia when the opposing doors lock us inside the transparent glass. We comfort ourselves with nervous laughter until the doors open and we are let to pass into the residence hall. The residents' rooms are enclosed with heavy metal doors purposely designed like those used in prisons. While these doors cannot be locked, they do have a small viewing slot that can be opened from the outside to look in. Residents sleep four to a room on two bunk beds. Our guide explains that the staff chooses the roommates and tries to avoid creating "ethnic ghettoes" on the one hand and "cultural clashes" on the other. Residents' money is kept separate, though they can request it twice a week. They are allowed outside for just two hours a day within a fenced courtyard where they can play football, basketball, or just breathe fresh air. Volunteer "educators" organize leisure activities such as arts and crafts. A ping-pong table, foosball table, and punching bag are found in a recreation room. Instant coffee and a small, old television set are available in the cafeteria. Peering into this room, one cannot help but notice an English-language curse about the host state, beginning with F, carved into a Plexiglas window.

Residents get an identity badge containing a photograph and other personal information. When it is time to shave, they can exchange the badge for disposable razors, which are numbered and stored in the control center. If off-site medical attention is required, then a resident would be transported to the hospital in handcuffs and remain handcuffed during the visit. During the night prior to their removal, residents are kept in a separate medical wing in a locked room lest they make a last-ditch effort to escape. The security guards—one of whom has followed us throughout the tour—carry no weapons, but helmets and shields are available to them if necessary. Discipline is effected much more through containment than force, as our guide explains. Unruly residents can be placed in an isolated holding cell for up to twenty-four hours at a time. Most residents are men between twenty and forty years old. If appearances and statistics are reliable, then the residents mainly originate from sub-Saharan Africa and Muslim countries; a few individuals are from the former Soviet Union. While some residents ignore us, many stare at us with indecipherable smiles as we peep into their sleeping rooms and recreation room and shuffle past them in the corridor en masse. Others look on contemptuously. Yet, in contrast to the frequent stares from the residents themselves, the interior ministry officials in our group make no eye contact whatsoever with the residents. They quietly pass through the center and diligently study its infrastructure. Only the representative of the United Nations High Commissioner for Refugees (UNHCR) examines it with a methodical eye. At one point, as our group is crammed in the medical wing, he whispers to me to check if the bathroom in the isolated holding cell has a toilet. I cautiously stick my head in the door while no one is looking, then glance back at him to nod in the affirmative. He nods back, indicating that this center meets international standards.

BEHIND THE ETHNOGRAPHIC SCENES

This visit to the holding center offers rich leads for an ethnography of migration management. Readily available are the questions of how the residents negotiate their status as illegals while they face imminent return, or how residents and staff manipulate each other to work the center's regulations to their own advantage. Indeed, the center could show how the ascribed status of illegal migrant is performed and contested, as suggested by the migrants' glances, the curse carved into the cafeteria window, and the regimented daily routines. We see the Foucauldian details through which docile bodies are produced as well as the tactics with which residents resist the center's technologies of rule. Assuming long-term access is granted, the center offers the logistical benefit of providing a manageable space in which to conduct extended ethnographic fieldwork and the ethical opportunity to give voice to people marginalized by capitalism and the security state.

While these matters remain vitally important, this book's point of departure is found not in a moment of direct, tangible social engagement but rather in one of banal, aloof, social indifference and disconnection, which, arguably, are more common in the contemporary world order. The policy officials' strenuous efforts to avoid eye contact with the migrants are palpable, not to mention curious, as the latter are precisely the same people whom the former are paid to regulate and about whom they ostensibly possess expertise. Why do they pass up the opportunity to keep their expert knowledge up to date? Why don't they talk to residents and ask them about their lives if they are in fact there to see the proverbial "situation on the ground"? Why don't they even look at them? Their object of ethnographic expertise—the illegal migrant—is *immediately* available to them. These officials, of course, have nothing to gain by engaging the migrants face to face or by acknowledging their glances, sneers, and mysterious smiles. To establish contact with them would only expose to attack the moral arguments underpinning the officials' power position and that of the judicial, political, and economic systems they represent. They must instead maintain an invisible wall of silence.

Focusing on these nonconnections between people nevertheless bound up in the same social processes, this book's basic ethnographic questions are as follows: Where do these officials' moral arguments come from? How do they pertain to ongoing social, political, and economic processes? What assumptions do they hold about citizenship, territory, the individual, and the economy? How does today's European political economy make it convenient for them to construct migrants as particular problems requiring particular policy solutions? Most significantly, how do the myriad processes involved in these officials' daily work converge so as to form a decentralized apparatus of migration management composed of disparate migration policy agendas, generic regulatory mechanisms, and unconnected policy actors and policy "targets"? Ethnographers rightly stress the importance of face-to-face experience and tangible connections and conflicts in ethnographic fieldwork. Nevertheless, how do we deal with a situation in which policy officials patently ignore the migrants in their immediate presence? How do we manage a case where unconnected policy domains and sundry regulatory mechanisms fuse together but human connections (and conflicts) are rarely forged, are tenuous at best, or are structurally discouraged?

Herzfeld's (1992, 5–10) "secular theodicy" might explain the social indifference. Some officials blame the bureaucratic system in which they work for harmful decisions that they themselves must reluctantly make. The official at the outdoor reception, Maria, illustrated the point with the wistful remark that illegal migrants in her country are kept in tents. She expressed her regret about the effect of her own work on migrants, with whom she personally sympathizes (see Chapter 4). However, most officials (and particularly those who move high up the bureaucratic ranks) speak confidently about the moral clarity of the laws they uphold and the migration policies they develop. As one project officer for 3MP noted:

> What I find normal is that if you break the law, then it's a problem. Since states have existed, they have guarded their borders. If [migrants] are recognized as guilty, the consequences should be applied. Of course, there should be proportionality and human rights, but in any case, [consequences] should be the case.

This frank remark suggests that something more than a helplessness to help must explain the indifference witnessed at the holding center. Moreover, a simple avoidance relationship like those described in classic social anthropology is an insufficient explanation because a ritual avoidance assumes a prior social connection and comes with the expectation of its restoration. In this case, no such connection existed before, during, or after the trip to the center.

Therefore, this book explores bureaucratic indifference by asking what *mediates* the policy official's view of the migrant; and what organizes people who are now "unrelated to each other by anything tangible" (Arendt 1958, 53).

It starts from the position that modern mass society is held together by indirect human relations more than direct, organic connections between people. People historically have been connected through locally formed practices such as the exchange and barter of tangible goods; rituals and rites of passage involving social and bodily contact; visible acts of obeisance to elders; and public torture—a ritualized assault on the body—as a spectacular display of ancient, sovereign power. These types of connections are being replaced by relations that are indirectly mediated through abstract third agents such as: policy representations of the public; social norms against which we measure ourselves and our relevance to others; mathematical formulas that objectify populations in the course of public administration and corporate marketing strategies; and, of course, money, signifying exchange value.

In the context of EU migration management, I seek to understand how large systems of population regulation both constitute and materialize out of highly mediated relations and the near absence of connections between people. That exploration leads us to an ethnographic terrain, so to speak, that features much less of the face-to-face interaction among and between migration officials and migrants and much more of the vast, acephalous, and decentralized world of policymaking. In that world, most of the relevant policymakers, technocrats, and experts barely know each other yet speak a common language of migration management. Their policy terrain is where the migrant emerges as a knowable problem, thus sparing the official the discomfort of listening to migrants tell their stories in their own words. Policy officials do not learn what they must about the migrant through *immediate* personal engagement; instead, they "see" migrants through the *mediated* practice of policymaking, rendering the migrant an "object of information, never a subject of communication" (Foucault 1977, 200). Hence, the "migrant" is not policy officials' primary interest qua policymakers but rather is the object of the political economy that their policy efforts serve. Similarly, poverty and hunger are not the primary interests of World Bank officials but rather their primary business; as loan officers they do not fly around the world to meet itinerant laborers and street dwellers but rather ministers of industry and high-level corporate executives (Goldman 2005, xvi). In both cases, connection with the policy object—the migrant or the poor—is neither established nor desired.

This book is thus necessarily concerned with how a dynamic living person is converted into a static policy object and with how we study the relevant policy processes ethnographically. The issue actually has less to do, per se, with places like the holding center than it might seem. The center, along with the roles performed by the people inside it, is only a temporary manifestation—an objectification—of deeper mediated social processes, or as Debord (1994) would see it, a spectacle concealing the struggle to organize the disunity and contingency of structural processes and conflicts (see also Wacquant 2002). The book focuses on the integration of three particular migration policy domains: circular labor migration, border control, and biometric information systems. Other migration issues, such as refugee flows, asylum claims, and family reunification, are interwoven, but the bulk of cross-border flows (both legal and illegal) is captured in labor circulation, which is also ordered significantly through enhanced border control and biometric information systems. Positive decisions on asylum claims are declining, and family reunification presupposes another individual's legal entry into an EU member state.

While much academic and policy discussion considers the difficulties that the EU member states have had on reaching common agreement on particular migration issues—for example, the maximum length of detention for illegal migrants, the limits on sharing visa application information among member states, and common criteria for admitting labor migrants—migration management is overall moving toward convergence. This point holds true particularly with regard to matters of border control and biometric information systems (Peutz and De Genova 2010, 2). Moreover, this convergence comes with a certain contradiction, which nevertheless encourages the very apparatus managing it. Many Southern countries have become increasingly reliant on immigrant remittances since the 1980s. This dependence results from the devastating effects on household, government, and enterprise income from restructuring programs channeled through the International Monetary Fund (IMF), the World Trade Organization (WTO), and the World Bank. Simultaneously, population decline and liberal economic restructuring in the Northern countries have increased earnings inequality and created a demand for low-wage jobs having few possibilities for advancement (Sassen 2008). The liberalization of the global economy has thus expanded the number of Northern, low-end, impermanent jobs and of cash-deprived Southern laborers to fill them. This situation makes it "rather surprising to see our powerful states reorient large parts of their state apparatus so as to control, detect, stop, detain, and deport basically vulnerable and powerless migrants" (ibid.). The phenomenon, however, is not so new. As Cresswell (2006) shows, modern mobility has always been inextricably linked to efforts to control, restrict, and regulate it.

RATIONALES OF GOVERNANCE IN THE AGE OF RIGHT VERSUS RIGHT

Like any other subject-position, the "migrant" does not exist ontologically but rather as someone who is enticed into a social role and negotiates it in a historically constituted field of political, economic, and social relations. The "migrant" therefore might not exist as such in other times, places, and contexts even if human movement has always been a regular feature of daily life. In this vein many anthropologists correctly argue for the need for "research on 'illegality' and hence 'legality' qua sociopolitical condition, in contrast to research on undocumented migrants qua 'illegal aliens'" (De Genova 2002, 423; see also De Genova and Peutz 2010; Coutin 2000, 23). To do so, we must focus primarily on the fluid and ephemeral processes that conjure up subjectivities, rather than offloading such processes as merely the context in which discrete objects move and events happen. Or as Comaroff and Comaroff (2003) put it, "the job of the social scientist is to construe the *processes* by which realities are realized, objects objectified, classes of persons and things classified, and so forth" (155, emphasis original). Much of this objectification occurs through simplified policy understandings of migration processes, which in turn offer up simplified understandings of migrants themselves: "the unfortunate poor," "economic migrants disguised as refugees," "freeloaders on the welfare system," "entrepreneurs wanting to develop their home countries." These simplifications establish an ostensible moral relationship between otherwise *unconnected* migrants and policy officials as part of a state effort to project a coherence onto unruly circulations. More specifically, they feed policy narratives, shape policy problematizations, and point to particular policy solutions in domains as different as biometric information technologies, refugee policy, circular migration policy, and border security practices (Shore and Wright 1997; see P. Silverstein 2005 for a comprehensive review of the anthropological literature on the problematization of migrants in Europe).

European Union migration policies, and their associated migration management apparatus, are inseparable from the contemporary European political spectrum, which has arrived at its narrowest span in the modern era (Mazower 2000). Whereas Europe once saw a rivalry among three ideologies—fascism, communism, and liberal democracy—for the prize of mass support, World War II and the subsequent Cold War reduced the competition to two primary antagonists. Western liberal democracies at this time developed their welfare systems to appease socialist-inspired opposition politics. The Western state mediated between the demands of labor (the traditional left) and of capital (the traditional right), but both sides of this equation were contained within the same national frame. Internationalism never sufficiently took hold outside (or ultimately inside) the Soviet sphere of influence. By the late 1980s, the collapse of socialism in eastern Europe, the liberalization of national economies, the forging of an EU common market, and the reduction of the welfare state to divert capital to the private sector had begun to erode leftist politics in Europe in favor of liberal politics celebrating the virtues of individualism. Simultaneously, the far-right in Europe surged, largely as a reaction against the subsequent increase in migration, the destabilization of traditional social and economic structures within the national territory, the ceding of state authority to Brussels, and the building of the common European project more broadly. Neo-nationalism, or at least neo-nationalist policies, attracted many of the constituencies abandoned by the political left as it accommodated a liberalizing global economy. Those citizens now seek protection within a national frame but in a populist form since, they charge, the state is no longer loyal to the nation.

These broad political dynamics have now created a situation where the state mediates tensions between the economic right and the nationalist right. Likewise, the right contains the debate on EU migration management as it negotiates the differing needs of the territorialized national state (or group of states) and deterritorialized global capitalism (Arrighi 1994, 33–34; 2005, 28; Harvey 2003, 26–33; Steinmetz 2003, 327). On the one hand, the economic right (neoliberals) demands a "flexible" labor supply for economic growth and quite readily turns to the global labor pool for it. On the other, the nationalist right (neo-nationalists) demands that the state resume its role as protector of the national interest: of its workforce, its collective identity, and its sovereignty.

These two sides have more similarities than their more vociferous proponents would admit. Both share a strong desire to crack down on illegal immigration and (with some exceptions) push to dismantle the welfare state (Gingrich 2006, 36). Both share a concern for a strong security establishment, even though neoliberals want it to clarify the circuits through which discrete and mobile individuals move and neo-nationalists want it to protect a more rooted and well-defined national (or local) collective. It is thus no coincidence that the EU has had more success in reaching agreements on the negative aspects of migration management, for example border security and migrant return, than in other migration policy domains (Samers 2004). If liberals push for the human rights of all people, neo-nationalists—in a distillation of their various arguments—push for cultural fundamentalism, which defends the moral integrity of any culture and insists on cultural relativism (Stolcke 1995). Cultural fundamentalism does not identify problems in the simple existence of other cultures or races per se (in contrast to interwar fascism), but rather in the mixing of people of different cultures. It maintains that moral judgments cannot be issued across cultural-cum-territorial lines and that all people are naturally xenophobic. Therefore, too much contact results in conflict, and separation is in everyone's best interest (Stolcke 1995). Cultural fundamentalism bears an uncomfortable familiarity with both the history of multiculturalism in liberal thought (Kymlicka 1995) and the concept of national sovereignty in the liberal post–World War interstate system (Feldman 2005a) as both also assume discrete cultural groups entitled to a space free of contact from "others." The pivotal disagreement between neoliberals and neo-nationalists on migration matters is over the length of time that migrants should be allowed to stay on national soil: neoliberals would have migrants stay as long as their labor is needed while neo-nationalists would try to restrict those stays in any case on the grounds that their presence jeopardizes the nation. The two sides settle their dispute rather easily through circular migration policy (Chapter 6), which allows migrants to return again to work in the host country as long as they leave when their visas expire. (The majority of illegal migrants simply overstay their visas.) This compromise satisfies both neoliberals and neo-nationalists: economic growth through cheap labor for the former and the monitored and restricted presence of migrants for the latter. This particular dynamic is the scaffolding of the emerging EU managed migration system: circular migration programs are the main legitimate portals for legal (temporary) entry while external border control and biometric information systems are the fences obstructing illegal entry.

Out of this historical trajectory emerge three key rationales that help to sustain, organize, and animate EU migration policy convergence. First, there is the isolation and securitization of the individual, or processes whereby people are recognized by bureaucratic systems as discrete individuals void of any inherent, direct, or organic social connection to any another individual (Poulantzas 1973; Trouillot 2001). The holding center showed how individuals are identified, recorded, separated, observed, and regulated through the architecture of the center itself. Visa applications, while often soliciting family information, are adjudicated as individual cases. Individualization also appears in many other parts of the EU's migration agenda, from expediting business travel through registered traveler programs, where affluent travelers receive highly personalized services, to prescreening visa applicants on the basis of large amounts of personal information, to more invasive biometric identification techniques at entry points and soon exit points as well. All of these personal and biometric data are instantly transferable across EU space through such law enforcement channels as the Schengen Information System (SIS) and European Dactyloscopy (EURODAC). The state can play this rationale in two ways, regarding the individual as either a security threat to be repelled or as a self-starting entrepreneur whose identity needs protection from transnational criminal organizations.

In contrast to the first rationale, which assumes active subjects, the second rationale assumes passive objects of humanitarian care. Here, the state may alternate between an altruistic and a paranoid stance toward the individual, sometimes leading to bizarre policy results. The point is exemplified by the fact that medical care is available to residents in the holding center, even if it requires their shackling to a gurney. Anthropologists have noted how this schizophrenic discourse plays out more systematically in refugee and asylum policy. For example, Miriam Ticktin (2006; see also Fassin 2005) demonstrates how the reliable (and harrowing) route to legal residency for undocumented immigrants in France (*sans papiers*) is to turn to physical injury and infection, which then obligates the state to place them in its care. As a result, an ethical configuration is now emerging "in which people end up trading biological integrity for political recognition" (33). What Ticktin identifies in France speaks to a broader ambidexterity in the state's management of migrants, namely that compassion is extended when the state can take for granted the migrant's political neutrality. On the one hand, dying migrants might be granted citizenship, while on the other, healthy illegal migrants can have their return trips home laced with humanitarian provisions, particularly in the case of the IOM-sponsored program of assisted voluntary return. As shown in Chapter 4, Frontex (the EU external border patrol agency) also deploys a humanitarian narrative about saving migrants from dangerous illegal journeys, only to return them to the lives of poverty they were fleeing. In all cases, humanitarianism is extended only when the migrant is removed from the body politic or when the migrant's body becomes incapacitated to the point of political impotence.

The migration policy processes examined throughout this book, and particularly in Chapter 5, will highlight the production of individualized subjects but will also show the concomitant rise of the police state in the modern, negative sense of the term. As individuals qua individuals become the locus of liberal governmentality so they also become suspect. Burgeoning surveillance capabilities have joined forces with this enhanced suspicion of individuals as would-be aliens, criminals, terrorists, and other clandestine border-crossers. These characters' invisibility, mobility, and unaccountability gnaw at the conceptual foundation of the international architecture of the national order of things (Löfgren 1989; Malkki 1995).

This fact leads to the third rationale, which territorializes and collectivizes policy subjects. It appears in such EU border control measures as coastal radar surveillance, sea patrol maneuvers, satellite imagery, and land-based rapid response teams. These types of efforts proliferate despite the fact that illegal border crossings account for only an estimated 5 percent of illegal immigrants. The European Commission (EC) raised the stakes when identifying EU territory as an "Area of Justice, Freedom, and Security" in need of special protection (Chapter 3). In the past, such words would conjure up mass support against the meddlesome militaries of nearby nation-states. Today they generate support against the prospect of a single migrant's entry—one whose individuality is washed into an imagined sea of alien faces.

These rationales of governance show liberalism as not only an ideology but also what Foucault (2008, 318) describes "as a principle and method of the rationalization of the exercise of government, a rationalization which obeys . . . the internal rule of maximum government." Contemporary governance shifts the responsibility of public order away from the classic centralized administrative state—the *raison d'état*—and toward a plethora of other agencies that encourage individual productivity, normality, and entrepreneurialism. With no serious alternative in sight, liberal ideology is now transforming into technologies of rule, thus reducing the politics of government to the policies of administration as many poststructural scholars have argued. One might add that as a consequence the suggestion box is replacing the ballot box.

Ethnographic research on structures of global governance must account for rationales of governance that play organizing roles both within and between *disparate* policy domains, migration or otherwise. Such research is not primarily a matter of tracing direct connections from one particular policy location to another, though significant research is available, for example, on the capacity of transnational networks to effect neoconservative agendas (Glick Schiller 2005) or to squander billions of dollars resulting in the disenfranchisement of millions of people (Wedel 1998). The production of vast inequality on a global scale takes more than particular social networks, and we should recognize that a handful of individuals are not easily capable of orchestrating large-scale social exclusion on an ongoing basis. Such exclusion primarily demands the ubiquity and banality of certain discourses of social order that, lying beyond the realm of critical reflection, easily legitimize the actions of particular networks (cf. Arendt 2006).

POLICY, THE APPARATUS, AND THE NETWORK EFFECT

This book joins a new front in the anthropology of globalization, which asks how sovereign nation-states interface with international organizations, global corporations, and each other to facilitate global governance, global security, and global capitalism (Comaroff and Comaroff 2001; Heyman and Campbell 2009; Ong 1999; Perry and Maurer 2003; Turner 2003; Weldes et al. 1999; see also Cowan 2003 for a historical view). The recent growth of anthropology of policy moves in a similar direction (Moore 2005, 13; Greenhalgh 2008; Riles 2006b; Shore and Wright 1997; Wedel and Feldman 2005; Wedel et al. 2005). Equally important, even if focusing on national rather than international contexts, is the growing interest in auditing practices, which organize the institutional processes that render information useful and manageable (Power 1997; Strathern 2000). Collectively, the above work explores the global as the interplay between organic, unpredictable social processes and authority's attempts to establish a method to regulate the apparent madness of it all. Chalfin (2006; see also 2010), for example, focuses not so much on the palette of colors composing transnational flows, or Appadurai's (1991) ethnoscapes, but rather on how international customs standards channel and facilitate the global circulation of commodities. Lea (2008) exposes how the organizing logics and cultural assumptions behind indigenous health care policy in Australia's Northern Territory steer it toward failure despite its practitioners' good intentions. Schwegler (2008) explores how neoclassical economics contains policy debates among Mexican technocrats thus channeling economic policy processes in particular directions despite their differences. Demonstrating the importance of dispersed and diffused connections among actors and institutions, Goldman (2005, xviii) mercilessly shows how the World Bank has established a global "knowledge bank" that "uniquely and effectively produces the research institutes, ideational frameworks, data sets, professionals, networks, government and nongovernment agencies, and policies that are influencing the trajectory of North-South relations today." This apparatus props up far-removed bureaucrats with the power to make life-and-death decisions over hundreds of thousands of people (xviii–xix). Studies on systematic efforts to control global processes also correct for an imbalance in the critical literature inspired by Foucault's dual notion of biopower. The disciplining of the individual receives far more attention than the regulation of the population, as the former lends itself better to location-specific field research than the latter (Greenhalgh 2003, 210). Emerging studies on population regulation complement the rich and numerous studies on how "local" people manipulate the global processes that arrive on their doorstep (cf. Inda and Rosaldo 2002).

Moving forward in this trajectory, this book's object of study is the de facto apparatus of migration management forming through countless policy processes and regulating ex post facto what the EU now identifies as the "Area of Justice, Freedom, and Security" (Chapter 3). This "area" exemplifies what Lefebvre (1991) calls a representation of space, or a conception of space, imagined by technocrats, administrators, planners, and so on. It conveys a certain vision of social order and economic efficiency within the EU that depends on highly regulated labor circulation and advanced police and surveillance measures. The realization of such a vast policy vision requires a wide array of largely unconnected specialists, including budget experts, social scientists, electrical engineers, digital technology experts, administrators, speech writers, and so on. It is through their work that migrants (and border-crossers in general) emerge as objects in the state's systematic efforts to regulate global circulations. Policy officials abstract an ideal "migrant" out of these flows and then codify it in policy writing, establish it as normal, and reassess its value in relation to changes in the processes to be managed.

However, these processes of abstraction do not end once an ideal migrant has been defined. Rather, policymakers must modify these abstractions as circumstances change. Foucault defines the work of constant adaptation rather literally as "normalization" (2007, 63). He indicates the sheer pragmatism of the reassessment when he notes that "the operation of normalization consists in establishing the interplay between these different distributions of normality and [in] acting to bring the most unfavorable in line with the more favorable" (63). Given its sheer pragmatism, the apparatus is not beholden to a higher purpose, despite its technicians' claims to the contrary. Instead, normalization keeps it perpetually in line with the contingencies and practicalities of history. Adaptability is perhaps the apparatus's most crucial feature, and high-level officials are wise enough to match a persistent doubt toward their policy successes with their full confidence in their policy rhetoric. For example, speaking at a conference celebrating the European Day for Border Guards and the fifth anniversary of the founding of Frontex (Chapter 4), Cecilia Malmström, European commissioner for home affairs (European Commission 2010), warned:

> It would not be credible to say that all the right tools are here and all the right laws are in place even if we have achieved a lot. The EU needs to commit even more to continue its improvement and be ready to adapt to new challenges in an ever changing reality. Travel flows are changing. Security threats are evolving.

Several developments in the anthropological literature help to conceptualize these kinds of policy processes into an object of study. These provide opportunities not only to trace global relations but also to identify the specific mechanisms through which they are maintained, regulated, and mediated. These mechanisms do their work by actually separating people. One direction is to ground globalization in transportable and abstract forms that get concretized in particular contexts. These "assemblages," then, "define new material, collective, and discursive relations" (Collier and Ong 2005, 4). In this usage, the concept of assemblages emphasizes the appropriation and reinvention of dominant forms of organization by actors in diverse situations. Anthropologists focusing on policy formation examine how expert knowledge functions in matters of public administration. In her lucid monograph on China's One Child policy, Greenhalgh (2008) develops a methodology for studying policy that looks at the interaction of policy problematizations (which pertains to how policymakers identify and calculate the significance of policy problems) and policy assemblages (which refers to the heterogeneous associations of policy elements like actors, institutions, and knowledges). Policy problematizations mobilize and also are mobilized by the "micropolitics of sciencemaking and policymaking," the interplay of which results in a concrete public policy (9–10). Greenhalgh speaks to the generative capacity of policy discourses, and identifies the varied elements composing assemblages that offer a rich perspective for studying population regulation in separate locations.

Similarly, Rabinow (2003, 49–55) develops Foucault's concept of the apparatus, which is a device of population control and economic management composed of otherwise scattered elements—discourses, architectural arrangements, laws, scientific statements, and so on—that coalesce in particular historical conjunctures usually identified as "crises." As Rabinow describes it, "the apparatus embod[ies] a kind of strategic bricolage, bricolage articulated by an identifiable social collectivity. It function[s] to define and to regulate targets constituted through a mixed economy of power and knowledge" (52).

In essence, the apparatus is the "network" that holds these elements together (Foucault cited in ibid.; see also Riles 2000, 3). It is not centrally controlled but rather instantiated in different parts at the level of "tactics," or the specific actions that technical experts make to control the object of regulation (53).

But what exactly is the ghost in the machine—what Foucault calls a network—that pulls an apparatus together while simultaneously separating, homogenizing, and/or collectivizing individuals? (see Trouillot 2001). What specific devices make the sundry "tactics" work in awesomely synergistic ways to encourage a global mobility regime built on what Shamir calls a "paradigm of suspicion"? (2005, 200). The devices that enable the network effect vary widely, but they share a certain abstract, generic, and highly rationalized quality that allows for their easy application to new social "problems." This book will focus on four in particular. A key device is rationales of governance that policymakers, technocrats, analysts, speechwriters, public officials, politicians, and many others deploy on a regular basis. These rationales succeed because of their simplicity and plasticity. On the one hand, they are technically convenient, allowing their users to deploy them as an obvious solution to an obvious problem without need of central command. On the other, they encourage rhetorical tropes that exemplify what Heyman (2000) calls "high-scale morality," or the sentiments and ideas applied to large numbers of unconnected people dispersed across geographic space in order to establish coherence among them. Examples include such phrases as "a migration policy that works for everyone"; "humanitarian approaches to border control"; or "enabling migrants to help themselves." The effect, of course, is not to create a moral world but to shut out alternative moral positions.

Other devices include "nonce bureaucrats," which refer to experts who are assembled temporarily on specific projects, experience a sense of community and fulfillment, and then disassemble when the job is done. "Shifters" are linguistic devices that can move across and integrate disparate policy domains because of their generic quality. Finally, technical standards create a common mode of processing information that enables the integration of separate information technology (IT) systems. Shifters and technical standards in particular work as "boundary objects," given their malleable character and their power to integrate disparate policy and social domains (Bowker and Star 1999, 15–16).

All of these devices create a network effect throughout the apparatus as they can be adopted in countless different contexts and obtain a tremendous power of synthesis. They are general without being vague and are utterly convenient to operationalize. They require no abstract thinking to be understood, which allows for their easy application in disparate policy settings. Since no central command is necessary, local actors become agents in their deployment. Given their work in multiple locales, they help to create a plurality of policy results, each varying according to context but all sharing an inherent family resemblance that facilitates their convergence. These devices are critical to the proliferation, expansion, and refinement of the apparatus because they serve both technical and moral purposes.

It is worth pointing out that the migrants whom the apparatus targets likely understand its network effect better than the isolated technicians who assemble its particular parts. The former confront it in its totality unlike the latter who are quarantined in a particular domain by virtue of the division of labor. No less important to recognize is that the use of the term "apparatus" and the attribution of agency granted to it should not be interpreted to mean that humans themselves lack agency. Instead, it is to show that the apparatus, rather than conquering individual initiative, makes it utterly reasonable to accept the choices it presents and offers few discernible targets of resistance. Conformity and agency combine to create hegemony. The effect is to render the language of "common sense" and technical administration interchangeable. To go against the grain requires that people make their own lives more difficult, which is always possible but discouraged at every turn.

A NONLOCAL ETHNOGRAPHY OF EU MIGRATION POLICY

Grasping how an apparatus—like the EU's migration management regime—emerges historically requires more than the ethnographer's direct, experiential encounters with particular people in particular places. Policy formation does not necessarily follow a trail of connecting dots. Its processes are highly diffuse, which either robs the ethnographer of a critical policy moment to witness or does not offer a clear singular chain from policy conception to policy implementation. The problem is more than a logistical one that could otherwise be fixed with a large travel budget and the access befitting a senior official. It is a problem of how to conceptualize global configurations of institutionalized power that absorb disparate policy domains, policy actors, and policy targets without central control or even a conspicuous desire to control in the maniacal sense of the term. In this case, ethnographers of policy processes should be careful not to fetishize policy officials' daily routines but rather should focus on how they reproduce rhetoric, sense current political leanings, and craft documents. These officials are not incandescent sources of policy power but rather administrators of policy rationales that operate in larger, looser constellations of government agencies, NGOs, intergovernmental organizations (IGOs), and EC institutions.

I suggest "nonlocal ethnography" as a methodological approach to such an empirical social construct that could be anywhere and nowhere at the same time (Chapter 7). It is designed to account for the fusion of an apparatus around the migrant qua policy problem and for the loosely organized policy networks that make it happen. Nonlocal ethnography tries to address a now established condition of global, neoliberal capitalism in which "the multiplication of profits will ultimately be brought about through the spontaneous synthesis of egoisms over the whole surface of the globe" (Foucault 2008, 301). Foucault observes that in this situation, "There is no localization, no territoriality, no particular grouping in the total space of the market." In a word, the situation is "nonlocal" (ibid.). This spontaneous synthesis is counteracted with a contradictory push of disassociation because the economic interests that create them ultimately destroy them as individuals seek security and abundance elsewhere. It follows that the basis of contemporary socioeconomic order is inherently unstable (ibid. 302–3). The apparatus, therefore, must be composed of generic elements that its technicians can easily adapt to new situations; it must be designed with impermanence in mind. Accordingly, nonlocal ethnography attempts to account for more durable (but less tangible) rationales, discourses, and processes that help to generate an apparatus, rather than account for more tangible (but less durable) objects and social locations, which are effects of an apparatus (for example, the holding center). In this regard, nonlocal ethnography addresses a methodological question that Trouillot sees as insufficiently answered, particularly in the global era: "Can the object of study be reduced to the object of observation?" He responds that the "extreme empiricist answer to that question tends to be a naïve yes" (2001, 135; see also Comaroff and Comaroff 2003; Feldman 2008, 316; 2011).

Nonlocal ethnography may yield a written product that does not seem sufficiently "thick." This result does not necessarily reflect the quality of the field research itself. Instead, it reflects an amorphous object of analysis that is qualitatively different than that on which ethnography first cut its teeth (cf. Gupta and Ferguson 1997; Amit 1999; Riles 2000, 19–20). If a nonlocal ethnography does not seem to go "deep" enough into the lives and actions of the people involved, then this reflects the fact that policy work itself is an exercise limited to surface appearances as it manages people indirectly and as hollow abstractions—that is, through such thin representations as statistical figures, vacuous claims of high-scale morality, rhetoric about solutions that "work for everybody," and caricatured narratives of "real" migrants' lives. Nuanced and contextualized understandings require too much effort to obtain, and present too many idiosyncrasies to consider, on a mass scale. Policymaking is an exercise in superficiality. Furthermore, tenuous connections (at best) make up the relations between policymakers, technocrats, and various officials working on the full span of policies from biometric technologies to migration and development programs. Their occasions for direct contact are limited in number. Most of the time their contact is mediated through remote forms of communication and standardized through shared policy language and shared images of the policy problem.

Nonlocal ethnography allows us to marshal evidence from a wide range of empirical sources such as interpersonal engagement, policy documents, newspapers, interviews, video clips, and e-mail correspondence. Along with many forms of extended face-to-face interaction, the nonlocal ethnographer spends time reading documents, listening to public statements from politicians and high-level bureaucrats, interviewing officials and experts, and following the press releases. Utilizing Gusterson's (1997) "polymorphous engagement," the ethnographer interacts with informants in a number of sites and uses an eclectic mix of research techniques, as no single source can flesh it all out. Yet, nonlocal ethnography remains committed to the epistemological objectives that participant-observation serves for a traditionally designed ethnographic methodology. First, it *displaces* the ethnographer, though not necessarily in terms of a geographic removal from a familiar cultural location. Rather, it displaces by insisting on the ethnographer's adoption of counterintuitive standpoints, so that new possibilities for interpretation and action can emerge. Second, it foregrounds historical *contingency* so that what is recognized as hegemonic, dominant, and seemingly omnipotent can also be recognized as socially constructed, and thus socially contestable, processes.

Some of the fieldwork for this book involved participant-observation with the European Migration Policy Organization (EMPO), a pseudonymous Geneva-based international organization that works to harmonize migration policies among states in Europe, the Middle East, and Africa. The EU often funds its projects, and EMPO designs them in reference to the objectives spelled out in the Tampere, Hague, and now Stockholm Programmes. I spent much time with the officials working on its 3MP initiative, which featured regular meetings for officials from EU and North African countries to discuss their respective practices on combating smuggling and trafficking and on the interception, reception and detention, and return and readmission of illegal migrants. Frontex and EUROPOL (the EU agency for national police cooperation) also coorganized 3MP, bringing more experts into the frame. Many different officials circulated through its meetings, from where initial contacts then snowballed into others, including, among others, officers in transnational crime units in southern Europe, EU policymakers in central-eastern Europe, international migration conference delegates in Vienna, EC migration experts based in Brussels, and migration policy scholars based in universities across Europe. I found crucial data in diverse places—in video productions of illegal migration journeys, official documentaries on border control practices, migration documents of all kinds, trinkets given out at migration policy conferences, and quantitative analyses of financial and demographic trends, to name a few.

The nonlocal ethnographer eventually learns how policy actors create and reiterate a self-referential circle of policy phrases that become ever more resilient as they are repeated (Chapter 3). It becomes apparent that these phrases also synthesize modes of analysis across migration policy domains. Perhaps policymakers' greatest impact lies in how they represent the migration situation "on the ground." This often makes what they *write* in their policy texts, their media releases, and their communications with their counterparts in other offices and countries more important than what they *do* in an observable way. This point suggests why the officials visiting the holding center did not look at the migrants in detention. The former do not "see" the latter through purely empiricist eyes (or through direct, *unmediated* sensory perception) but rather interpret them through bureaucratic "canons of relevance" (Sahlins 1995, 155) that organize the experience of sensory intake into a selective, *mediated*, and culturally specific framework of understanding. The purpose of that field trip was not to reveal the migrants' experiences in their pure truth. Instead, it was to discern evidence that bodies are circulating in an orderly fashion.

THE IMPORTANCE OF PUBLIC ADMINISTRATION

It is important to clarify that a focus on administrative regimes that objectify, individualize, and isolate people does not disregard either people's agency or the fact that policy plans rarely materialize as coherently as they are written. Social scientists have made crucial contributions to illustrating how grand policy plans can drastically fail to deliver what they promise (Dunn 2003; 2004; Escobar 1995; Ferguson 1994; Goldman 2005; Hyndman 2000; D. Mosse 2004; Scott 1998; Vigneswaran 2008). Like other large-scale projects, the EU's harmonized migration policy is uneven in realization and subject to countless interruptions, interventions, and internal conflicts. However, the disjuncture between policy plan and policy outcome should not foreclose ethnographic research on the former, which structures governance practices even if it does not fully determine their results. Recognizing the generative force of ideal plans, Tsing (2005, 7) similarly and subtly argues that "To turn to universals is to identify knowledge that moves—mobile and mobilizing—across localities and cultures." James Scott (2005, 401) makes a poignant defense of studies of state policy against the criticism that what really matters is what happens "on the ground":

> [N]one of the projects reach the ground uncompromised. Yes, of course. But can there be much doubt about which players in this cultural encounter hold most of the high cards? There may be reverses and skirmishes lost, but their deep pockets and geopolitical advantages over the long run systematically push the game in their direction.

Scott further asserts, and this book pessimistically agrees, that the international model of governance emerging from the North Atlantic has been more successful than colonialism in the convergence of forces brought to bear on and through the population. Such convergence, therefore, requires explicit ethnographic attention precisely for that reason.

Migrants themselves are well aware that they do not hold high cards in the game of migration management, and they often command agency only in the nominal sense (Lutz and Nonini 1999, 104). Dr. Melek Doğru, a Turkish scientist working in the Netherlands, expressed the familiarity of marginalization in an e-mail sent to a listserv utilized by Northern leftist and liberal academics decrying stringent US visa policies in a post-9/11 world:

> I suffered myself at all European borders. I was once even asked to show my paper and presentation material which I prepared for a Conference in Cardiff in Heathrow Airport many years ago. You wait at the immigration office with all the drug smugglers and all, and try to prove that you are not a criminal but a scientist. I became so much used to the idea of having no privacy at all and being humiliated in the borders that I guess the idea of giving fingerprints at the US border [as opposed to the EU border] does not seem to be shocking to me at all. How does this feel? I don't want to bore you with my adventures but my point is, this paranoia has always been there and I think it is only getting worse and more widely known.

Though even worse migration stories are readily available, this tale still raises Giorgio Agamben's (1998, 8–11) salient question for our times: how is it possible that modern society can reduce entire groups to *Homo sacer*? This character, "sacred man," highlights the centrality of dispensable subjects in the modern polis. Any given subject may be killed or let to die, but dispensable subjects categorically cannot be sacrificed lest the polity collapse. Hence, the excluded must be included. Frighteningly, the simultaneous integration and degradation of people in contemporary mass society is a process advanced perhaps as much by the benign neglect of liberalism as the sting of nationalism.

OUTLINE OF THE BOOK

The following chapters lay out the political context of EU migration management, explore three migration policy domains in detail, describe how they fit together into an apparatus, and fully explain nonlocal ethnography. Chapter 2 unpacks how the EU migration policy imagination is contained by neoliberals (economic conservatives) on the one hand, and neo-nationalists (nationalist conservatives) on the other, rendering the migration policy debate and policymaking as a matter of right versus right. While each side casts the other as its ideological antithesis, their views are quite compatible given their shared commitment to such basic features of the modern polity as controlled borders, civic order, and national security. The chapter illustrates how the creation of a liberal migration policy community simultaneously alienates that community from the actual migrants whom they strive to integrate into mainstream European society. Structural relations mitigate good intentions. This chapter also discusses recent neo-nationalist events in the Netherlands, Denmark, and Italy to show how anti-immigrant sentiment can move seamlessly rightward from a neoliberal position.

Chapter 3 analyzes different knowledge practices that facilitate the fusion of the migration apparatus out of its disparate parts. This involves creating an image of the EU as bounded space in need of special protection from unidentified circulating objects and people. This chapter details some EU-level policy processes through which that image emerged. After that space found a fixed place in policy discussions, technical experts soon began to materialize it through specific knowledge practices on a wide variety of migration policy matters. The chapter examines the creation and function of the *Asylum and Migration Glossary* developed by the European Migration Network that helps disconnected migration officials speak a common policy language. It also examines the Interactive Map (I-Map) developed by 3MP to give border officials a shared visual representation of clandestine migration routes. The chapter then describes the process through which 3MP standardizes a migration policy framework between officials from EU member states and North African states to better control "mixed migration flows."

Chapter 4 examines both Frontex's strategies to fortify the union's external border against illegal migration en masse and how experts use constructions of "risk," "crisis," and "humanitarianism" to justify these measures. It also examines how Cold War systems of land, sea, and air surveillance have been repurposed and integrated to give security officials maximum possible coverage of the external border, the adjacent seas, and even the migrant disembarkation points in distant transit countries. Border control officials thus gain a comprehensive picture of the EU's neighboring physical space and the bodies and objects moving through it. Crucial to this integration are the standardization of policy outlooks and the ability of geographically dispersed actors to communicate spontaneously. This chapter also illustrates how actors located in different positions relative to the border control apparatus interpret what are identified as its humanitarian rationales.[2]

Chapter 5 examines how biometric information systems and electronic travel documents individualize migrants and other travelers for easy identification. This approach to migration management complements the totalization of the migrant population that occurs in the border control procedures described in the previous chapter. It explains how the collection, storage, and dissemination of biometric data through such large-scale systems as EURODAC or SISI (which is not yet a biometric system) not only alienate individual travelers from each other but also alienate the self *from* the self and *to* the state. It also shows how the work of loosely affiliated, decentralized networks of IT professionals has the effect of creating ever more rigid and pervasive EU surveillance capacity. Policy officials idealize these systems as the protectors of globally circulating, creative individuals from the threat of invisible transnational criminal networks. They also increasingly use them for registered traveler programs, which expedite the global circulation of individuals with high economic and educational capital. These biometric initiatives result overall in a strange marriage between liberalism and the advanced security state.

2. I submitted the copy edits for this book just as the events in Tunisia, Libya, Egypt, and other Middle Eastern and North African countries took hold. Now known as the "Arab Spring," they prompted thousands of migrants to seek access to Europe, particularly Italy via Lampedusa. Though these developments are directly relevant to this book, the production cycle was too far along to incorporate them.

Chapter 6 argues that the now ubiquitous policy priority on "circular migration" is the crucial concept that resolves the differences between neoliberal and neo-nationalist positions. Wedged between border control and biometric IT systems, the main portals of EU entry are circular migration programs for non-EU citizens. These programs limit visa length but allow for a possible future return if the migrant leaves by the visa's expiry date. Thus they permit the circulation of labor migrants (satisfying the neoliberal) but prevent migrants from remaining indefinitely (satisfying the neo-nationalist). Circular migration is also seen to fill the gaps in Europe's aging workforce without encouraging "brain drain." It furthermore justifies the transfer of funds away from development projects to these programs in the name of empowering entrepreneurial migrants who would return to develop their homelands equipped with the knowledge, skills, and remittances obtained in the EU. The resulting economic growth, organically generated by the circular migrant, ostensibly cuts off migration's root cause. Circular migration functions as the rhetorical lynchpin and the conceptual glue that holds together the EU's larger migration management system. For this reason, migration policy officials (particularly high-level officials) must reiterate its promise and feasibility even if many of them privately doubt its potential as a silver bullet to solve structural problems.

Chapter 7 summarizes how the disparate migration policy domains of border control, biometric information systems, and circular migration are fusing together to form a migration management apparatus that elicits an idealized migrant as a normative subject. This discussion focuses on some of the devices that give the apparatus its network effect, thus allowing its easy proliferation into new social venues. The chapter then further articulates "nonlocal ethnography" to show how it illuminates an object like an apparatus, which is not isomorphic with a particular place(s). It situates this methodology in the trajectory of anthropology's recent strategies for adapting ethnography to the global arena.

2 RIGHT VERSUS RIGHT
How Neoliberals and Neo-nationalists
Dominate Migration Policy in Europe

The Right and the Left, which today alternate in the management of power, have
for this reason very little to do with the political sphere in which they originated.
They are simply the names of two poles—the first point without scruples to
desubjectification, the second wanting instead to hide behind the hypocritical
mask of the good democratic citizen—of the same governmental machine.

Giorgio Agamben 2009, 22

TRIANGULATION:
THE COMMON GROUND OF NEOLIBERALISM AND NEO-NATIONALISM

If triangulation is the measuring of the distance to an unknown third point
based on the angles to it from two fixed points, then neo-nationalists and
neoliberals represent the fixed points from which the "migrant" is kept at a
marked and convenient distance. Migration policy debates are likewise contained within these two positions even if few officials and public figures purely
embody either one of them. Though always respectful of state sovereignty,
most officials in the EC and in international organizations emphasize such
liberal ideals as freedom of circulation, human rights, and helping poor migrants to help themselves, their home communities, and their home countries. They often implicitly accuse neo-nationalists of parochialism and xenophobia with disparaging remarks about populist politics and pandering to
the public. To be sure, liberal officials prefer "populism" or "public opinion" as
euphemisms for neo-nationalism and neo-right to avoid accusations of fore-
going administrative neutrality. Neo-nationalists cast themselves as defenders
of the autochthonous whom the state has abandoned to the EU and globalization. Political correctness, they also assert, mutes any voice arguing that
multiculturalism has diminished the life chances of the titular nation. State
and local officials fall anywhere between these positions depending on the
political climate. While the outward relationship between these two generic
actors—the neo-nationalist and the neoliberal—is antagonistic, they share
much common philosophical ground and a common interest in not having

the migrant speak for him or herself, or at least not in a way that substantially changes migration policy.

The triangulation metaphor might oversimplify the complexities of migration debates in any particular European locale, but it nevertheless captures the dominant logic through which particular actors engage that debate. It also suggests that the differences between the two sides are matters of degree, not kind, as Calavita (2005) demonstrates in a southern European context and Hage (2000), in an Australian one. After all, they stand in the same triangle. The sanctity and prosperity of the nation, not the needs of the migrant, shape the debates between the neoliberal and the neo-nationalist. Neoliberals are inclined to facilitate temporary migration as a means to fill gaps in the labor market and to increase economic growth. Neo-nationalists ultimately do not want migrants on the state's territory for the sake of preserving national identity and protecting the material interests of disaffected workers up and down the economic ladder.

This chapter begins with an illustration of how a major international migration policy conference creates a liberal policy community among public officials, academics, NGO workers, and IGO officials who otherwise find direct contact difficult to sustain. This community-building also segregates them socially and spatially from the migrants whom they study and regulate, even if they desire an immediate connection to and understanding of migrants. The chapter then compares some of the basic tenets of interwar fascism, contemporary neo-nationalism, and liberalism to explain how the first two movements draw from mainstream discourses and the third is not as distinct from them as its proponents insist. This comparison establishes how neoliberalism and neo-nationalism have emerged as the narrow parameters defining EU migration policy processes. This discussion also considers contemporary neoliberalism not only as an ideology but, more pervasively, as an analytical framework to make policy decisions in widely different contexts. The chapter lastly illustrates how migration politics can move both seamlessly and more violently from the neoliberal to the neo-nationalist position, with Dutch, Danish, and Italian examples. The point of this comparison is not to pigeonhole particular actors into particular political parties. To do so would offer only a narrowly conceived and overly formalized analytical schema. Rather, it is to show how as a function of their inseparability the harmonization of the EU's migration policy unfolds through the interplay of the economic right (neoliberals) and the nationalist right (neo-nationalists).

DENIAL

Policy officials with liberal or neoliberal leanings strongly deny any ideological affinity to neo-nationalists lest they appear tainted by xenophobia and unwelcoming of legal migrants. However, following Žižek (2002), this denial might betray a fundamental connection as the neo-nationalist agenda often results from the full, logical extension of the policies that neoliberals defend. The efforts of liberal-minded officials to separate themselves from neo-nationalists appeared repeatedly in interviews, informal conversations, and with more discrete language, in public statements designed to highlight their commitment to human rights. There is no reason to doubt their sincerity, but in other venues frustrated migrants themselves point to the ultimate similarities between the two positions. A few examples jointly illustrate the point. First, two border patrol experts working for the Organization for Security and Co-operation in Europe (OSCE) described their experiences training border officials in Balkan countries aspiring for EU membership. When I asked what makes migration a security issue, the first one intentionally ventriloquized the familiar right-wing explanations to convey their hold on public opinion:

> Easy. Fear of losing, xenophobia, criminality. . . . We call it a "subjective security feeling." A small town, a child is missing; after a few days the police find out that she or he was sexually molested and killed. Parents will become very protective; even though it is a very rare event, people feel very threatened. It is the same about crime committed by an immigrant. If people would look close to the statistics, then it would turn out very different.

His colleague, rolling his eyes and letting out a sigh, finished the point, seemingly on behalf of all his colleagues frustrated with right-wing politics: "Also, [certain] political parties have exploited this fear." The key move here, of course, is the denigration of parents' fear as "subjective," which diminishes the parents' worry as irrational and indicative of the broader neo-nationalist perspective. He separates himself from the neo-nationalist fear.

The same separation became apparent during a similar conversation with two 3MP officials responsible for developing a set of common migration policy guidelines for EU and North African countries. The first said, "[Migration is] related to security insofar as it is linked to a state's territory. A state is responsible for its citizens." The second brought in the problem of nationalist populism:

> I agree, but it's not [only that] state security and social security impact the public. It's a vicious circle. Public opinion causes states to react and tighten. There's

too much emphasis on the security aspect, which puts things negatively. I don't like to link it only to security . . . [the] so-called clash of civilizations . . . there are differences in income, illegality, 9/11.

Thus, she disassociates herself from another neo-nationalist argument that insists on seeing immigrant integration as a recipe for a clash of civilizations.

However, despite the liberal officials' impatience with neo-nationalism in these two illustrations, and their goodwill gestures, migrants themselves are apt to see an "axis" binding neoliberals and neo-nationalists together. One exemplary panel at a high-level policy conference featured white, Northern speakers pleading for a liberalized, humane, and more open labor migration policy. Unimpressed with their outreach, an immigrant from the French Caribbean stood up in the sea of white faces and angrily said, "We are not just objects. We are people with dignity. We are not here to fill your slots." An embarrassing silence followed: the soul that liberals wish they could save just accused them of taking advantage of him. His skepticism does not suggest that the neoliberal is a closet neo-nationalist merely pretending to be progressive. Instead, it indicates that neoliberals and neo-nationalists, and the variations on their positions, are cut from similar philosophical cloth and can only separate themselves from each other to a limited extent (see below). Both sides have a vested interest in keeping the migrant at arm's length from serious policy discussion.

The denial of the inherent connection between the neoliberal and neo-nationalist positions serves a political-economic function. Žižek's (2000) argument as to "Why We Love to Hate Jörg Haider" offers a useful interpretive cut on the moral indignation that liberals express toward neo-nationalists. Haider— and other neo-nationalist leaders—now represents those constituencies abandoned by the political left as economic liberalization dismantles the traditional welfare state. The charges against Haider of xenophobia and racism are not unfounded, but they are also a counterattack on neo-nationalist efforts to reinvent what remains of an older national form of working-class solidarity that threatens the liberal economic agenda. The Danish People's Party, for example, works harder to maintain the welfare state than parties closer to the center. It captured 30 percent of the votes in the 2001 election from unskilled workers under age forty compared to 25 percent for the Social Democrats. However, liberals have an easier time challenging neo-nationalism in terms of racism than over differences in economic policy, as the latter would force them to defend reforms in front of people who have not reaped the benefits. The state's role is now to mediate this relationship between the center-right and the far-right, whereas in the past it did so between the left and the right. As one Argentine political observer remarked, "You no longer have a left, just a left finger of the right hand."

"BOURGEOIS ENTERTAINMENT"

How does a liberal migration policy community form out of disparate policy actors and structurally segregate itself from the migrants whom it wants to uplift? The annual Metropolis International conferences provide insight into this question. They reveal the structural forces that impose on conference participants, that shape the character of their interaction, and that distinguish them from the migrants about whom they spend the week discussing. Metropolis International is a network of networks, that is, a network of twenty-two national Metropolis migration networks composed of migration policy officials, academics, and researchers. Officials and researchers from international organizations are also regular participants in the conference. NGO workers and migrant rights groups attend in lesser numbers as the registration fee exceeds €500. Self-formed migrant associations rarely, if ever, attend. Most participants are from Canada, New Zealand, Australia, and the EU countries. They produce and reproduce the type of knowledge upon which the migration management apparatus rests. Their politics, broadly speaking, range from center-left to center-right with policy officials adopting the latter stance and academics espousing the former. As in many policy networks, the participants are rarely in direct contact with each other. They familiarize themselves with one another mainly through publications, periodicals, e-mail listservs, and working papers posted on websites. They do not necessarily share a history through tight social networks formed in elite universities but rather through their technocratic knowledge (which implies a high level of education) on topics such as law, public administration, economics, urban geography, and demography. Most participants have at least master's degrees in related fields, if not doctoral or law degrees. While Metropolis is not an EU entity per se (in fact, the Canadian government has been its most active supporter), the work of its participants supports the EU's efforts to harmonize migration management, making it a key site where EU policy discourse is stabilized.

The chief organizer remarked during his 2008 conference introductory speech on the need to unify disparate migration policy officials into a policy community, and disparate policy domains into a coherent migration management regime. He described the enormous challenges that states face in managing migration: assessing their demographic needs, attending to their humanitarian interests, developing systems to adjudicate visa and refugee applications, controlling borders, and so on. Exasperated by this list, he half-jokingly implored the audience to "pity the policymaker," who tries so hard to achieve migration "policy coherence." After explaining that in his country, immigration policy cuts across fourteen departments and ministries and includes several others on an ad hoc basis, he added, "pity the academic," who has provided a theoretical structure to develop policy.

Metropolis International conferences offer opportunities to galvanize these indirect and amorphous networks through intensive, week-long series of plenary panels and workshops as well as a variety of social activities. Scholars discuss the pros and cons of new government migration policies. Research institute directors tune in to funding opportunities. NGO managers learn about new directions in migration research and in national and EU migration policy. All these conversations have the effect of regularizing a certain pattern of policy discussion. This pattern is contained, on the one hand, by a liberal push toward making the individual migrant's experience in the host country as comfortable as possible: supporting language training programs, providing information on social services, protecting migrant workers from exploitation by ruthless employers, preventing deskilling, ensuring that human rights are respected, and so on. On the other hand, these discussions pay due respect to nationalism by accepting the receiving country's tightly defined conditions of admission: short-term visas; few, if any, chances for permanent residency or citizenship; minimal time in the host country; substantial paperwork required to apply for the work visa. The situation prevents the emergence of any polarized debate that might seriously jeopardize the cohesion of the overall policy community. Moreover, it increases the organizers' chances of attracting high-level policymakers or politicians to the conference and ensures continued buy-in from national governments. How is the cohesion maintained? How does the migration policy conference keep the debates contained within manageable limitations? How do its many participants deal with the deeper structural inequalities behind global migration despite their own egalitarian sentiments? How is the formation of the migrant as a policy subject linked to the formation of a migration policy community?

A Peculiar Migration Policy Community

To understand the consolidation of this policy community and its social distance from migrants, consider the venues, locations, and accoutrements surrounding a Metropolis conference, which routinely takes place in wealthy Northern cities such as Vienna, Geneva, Toronto, Copenhagen, or Melbourne. Since Metropolis aims to influence high-level policy actors, its planning committee has an incentive to ensure that the conference offers a certain degree of pleasure, comfort, and at times extravagance. In a Northern context, participants are not mainly from the economic elite but rather from the educated middle class, a group that Bourdieu (1984) might describe as able to enjoy their cultural capital but constantly concerned with falling out of political favor. The conference's major sponsors include the municipal governments of the host city, national ministries of the host country, corporate sponsors, and charitable foundations. Participants receive such amenities as a conference bag and a small gift, for example a photography book of the city's natural surroundings or a box of locally made chocolates. (Chocolates provided at the 2010 conference in The Hague had the conference logo inscribed with icing.) Conference participants are encouraged to stay in particular hotels, ranging from three to five stars. Junior scholars and NGO managers lean toward the three stars while the more seasoned government officials and others who have been attending regularly over the years prefer the four- and five-star options. High-end hotels likewise generate a sense of entitlement and exclusivity through the arrangement of the smallest details. One Hilton selected by Metropolis for conference accommodations offered bottles of still water in the hotel room for €6, which was located next to a discreet advertisement for Martell XO, its logo reading "Martell—Cognac—Up-taste." More expensive European hotels provide buffet breakfasts with embarrassing abundance: at least three types of juice, rolls of all kinds, pastries, vegetables, omelets, sausages, cold meats, warm potatoes, breakfast cereals, fruits, and coffee and tea. One quickly learns to take the abundance for granted even if many conference participants point out the irony. "This is how Metropolis buys off lefty academics," quipped one migration scholar and conference veteran.

Along with a hotel experience that invokes luxury and exclusivity, participants are well entertained in the conference program: a welcome reception in a historic and elegant town hall is a staple feature of the conferences. Long buffet tables offer the participants everything from rolled meats to multiple types of salads to wine and beer. Tables full of chocolates and other sweets also dazzled the guests at the 2008 conference in Bonn. Live bands provide entertainment to loosen the atmosphere and encourage networking. The opening reception for the Copenhagen conference featured a live choir in the Town Hall, a full buffet dinner, and tea and coffee served in Musel-painted china produced by the Royal Danish China Factory. The concluding banquet also featured a three-piece jazz band, and a Kir Royale aperitif was placed in one's hand upon entry. (The proportion of champagne to cassis was noticeably altered, costing the mix much of its desirable kick.) Delegates sat at round tables to a salmon salad starter, a beef or vegetarian entrée, glasses of red wine, white wine, and a dessert wine, plus dessert. The restaurant sat by the water near the Castle Church with a view of the famous Little Mermaid statue.

Most of the 2003 Vienna conference took place in opulent imperial settings such as the ornate city hall (*Rathaus*) situated across the street from the National Theater and adjacent to the parliament building. They capture the luster, prestige, and grandeur of royal pastimes, which now symbolize the European nation-state's power. The social program of the 2006 Lisbon conference offered a cocktail reception at the national coach museum displaying the former Portuguese royal family's horse-drawn carriages; an organ concert at the twelfth-century Lisbon Cathedral; an evening of *fado* and Portuguese music at the Trindade Theater in Chiado Quarter; and a closing dinner at the conservatory in Edward VII Park. Onsite registration for the full conference reached €685 (US$913). This figure exceeds the 2007 average monthly salary of US$820 in Senegal, which had over 200,000 emigrants living in Europe as of 2004.[1] The pleasantries that embroider the conference program must feel alien—and alienating—to the many thousands of illegal migrants who confront life-threatening journeys and endure degrading social statuses. Most of the academic participants, at least, recognize this sadly ironic situation but either disagree as to how to rectify it or conclude that it cannot be rectified in any case, thereby leaving it intact.

Tours

Each Metropolis conference offers a selection of preconference tours that reveal both the nationalist frame around neoliberal views and the social distance between policy officials and migrants themselves. Many of these tours visit local NGOs working on immigrant integration: one NGO created social opportunities in Copenhagen, another organized community theater productions in Bonn, while another supported youth activities in Lisbon. These tours have a strict pattern to them, reflecting the well-defined ways in which migrants are

---

1. Income data from the World Bank at http://devdata.worldbank.org/AAG/sen_aag.pdf (accessed 18 February 2010). Emigration figure from Focus Migration at http://www.focus-migration.de/Senegal.2636.0.html?&L=1 (accessed 18 February 2010).

managed at the municipal level. The delegates on the tour ride on a bus to the office of the NGO that runs the particular project. Their spartan facilities are usually located in low-income areas. The group walks into a meeting room crammed with chairs and a table upon which instant coffee and prepackaged cookies are made available. Staff members welcome the group to the office and deliver a PowerPoint presentation on their latest project. The slides are invariably filled with dense text, which makes for difficult reading, and images of smiling people of color. The first part of the presentation describes the NGO's funding sources, the municipal departments to which it reports, its partner organizations, and its basic mission. Their mission, staffers routinely emphasize, does not involve telling migrants what to do, but is to help them help themselves and make their own choices. The presentation then describes the social problems that the migrants are confronting: drugs, lack of access to the job market, social alienation, gang formation and violence, feelings of insecurity in their neighborhood. The projects the NGO organizes follow fairly regular lines: provide social/sport clubs for the youth, computer training classes, homework assistance programs, theater groups, language training, and community outreach so that immigrant and host communities can get to know each other, often in the form of "ethnic" food days. The NGO staff routinely speak of funding cutbacks from municipal governments that they have endured over the years. The question and answer period after the presentation is frequently comparative. Delegates on the tour often remark, "In [my European city] we have a similar situation, but we've approached it like this." The response is usually, "We haven't been able to do that because of our particular history." The particulars differ, but the form of the problem remains constant.

The similarities among EU cities suggest the common structural position that these cities maintain over the sending countries from which many migrants hail. Nevertheless, structural issues are rarely addressed because sympathetic delegates feel they can do very little about them. At the tour of a Copenhagen NGO that supports migrants working in a wealthy suburb, a Norwegian delegate asked an unusually frank and left-wing question: "This is a posh neighborhood. How do you make a unity of the upper class [Danish host population] and the lower class [immigrant population]?" The answer came back no less directly: "It's like oil and water, so we can only deal with the smaller problems." Their efforts, of course, do not involve challenging any of the structural problems that the lower-class migrants face but rather helping them adapt better to the problems they confront. This strategy leaves the nation untransformed by the migrants' presence even if it acknowledges a limited degree of multicultural-ism on its soil.

These NGOs often have a difficult time distinguishing themselves, in the eyes of the migrants, from the state's police force. This Danish NGO had recently completed one project that installed lighting in public spaces and mounted public art to beautify those spaces. It also organized community breakfasts. However, explained one of its project directors, "When we got started, they said 'you are an arm of the police.' We said, 'In one way we are a component of the police. In another way, we are trying to help you.'" Similarly, his colleague told the visitors that migrants in the neighborhood would never wear the T-shirt bearing the project logo, because it would risk alienating their own neighbors who might interpret it as complicity with the state.

Community Building

Metropolis aims to create a feeling of community among these dispersed policy players that will endure over time, as opposed to a collection of people who only congregate at annual intervals. For example, the end of the 2008 confer-ence in Bonn set the tone for the 2009 Copenhagen conference. During the last session the delegation watched a video montage composed of photographs of conference delegates talking to one another over coffees, in workshops, and on the tours. The audience saw themselves listening to one another, laughing with one another, exchanging ideas, and so on. They saw themselves cast as a community of thoughtful global citizens. The video concluded with a view of Earth in outer space surrounded by a halo of sunshine, suggesting Metropolis's commitment to a common global cause. The image would serve as the logo for the 2009 Copenhagen conference. The audience clapped loudly at the end, though one skeptic next to me rolled his eyes with boredom. One veteran par-ticipant from the academy with longstanding ties to government characterized this policy community in more cautious and ambivalent terms:

> Communities have longevity, but if the plug were pulled [on Metropolis], then I'm not sure it would keep going. . . . Communities have resilience . . . well . . . maybe all communities lack resilience. One day this will all disappear. It's not sad. It's life. Life is a mixture of the fleeting and semi-permanent. To be brutally honest, I like to keep myself in circulation. People know who I am a little bit. It's a way of making my professional presence known. . . . I [also] prefer to get my information verbally, when I see the person and the emotive gestures. I find reading an isolating, not an affective experience.

His sentiments suggest the impermanence of social-cum-professional connections in policy circles, but do not address the question of the apparatus's own resilience. If the plug were pulled on Metropolis, the same individual doubted later in the conversation that it would slow down the EU's efforts to harmonize migration management. His colleague, also an academic veteran with strong connections to government policymakers, simply reasoned that "other avenues will be found for information sharing."

As in Bonn, the 2009 Copenhagen conference, held in the new Bella Center, prepared the delegates for the 2010 conference set to be in The Hague. The convention center's commons area featured a display booth the size of a ten-by-thirty-foot room with a wooden floor. The two walls creating this room featured a ceiling-length photograph of the Dutch parliament building (with a view of the prime minister's office) backed by an open sky. The image was well illuminated with overhead track lighting. Local authenticity was conjured up by a wooden kitchen table surrounded by wooden chairs, which invited the delegates to feel comfortable while perusing the preconference brochures. One brochure cover had an aerial photograph of The Hague's main beach filled with people sunning themselves and splashing in the sea. The Scheveningen Pier extended into the water, and streets along the beachfront building were buzzing with activity. Other handouts included a postcard-size brochure describing citizenship policy in corporeal terms: "The Hague is not by chance a collection of buildings and individuals. The city has a heart, to which all residents provide form and content. The stronger the bonds, the larger and more vital that heart." To contribute to the pleasurable anticipation of the next conference, a simple black Dutch bicycle with a wooden crate as a front-end basket provided free key rings with small stuffed storks, which is The Hague's emblematic bird. Elsewhere in the gathering hall, a similarly inviting brochure prepared delegates for the 2011 conference planned for the Azores islands. The front cover featured an image from the sea looking toward the shore with historic beachfront buildings and sunny green hills in the background. Next to it was a glossy tourist brochure thirty pages long called "Azores: closer to nature" with a cover photograph of a steep mountain soaked in sunlight, green with vegetation, and carved by waterfalls splashing into the sea. During The Hague conference, promoters from the Azores handed out packages of locally grown dried tea leaves as an incentive to attend the next year's conference.

Cities compete hard to host the Metropolis conference; The Hague put down over one million euro for the 2010 honors. In The Hague's case, the municipal

government wished to counteract the recent growth of anti-immigration politics in the Netherlands led by Geert Wilders's Party for Freedom. The conference's organizing committee entertained the 2009 Copenhagen delegation with
a "surprise," as the chair of the final plenary panel put it. Thunderous music
pumped through the speakers to introduce a video narrated by The Hague's
deputy mayor Rabin Baldewsingh. Dressed in a business suit, this Dutch politician, a "visible" minority himself, talked about the home of the royal family
and described The Hague as a "modern" and "civil" city where "lots of people
speak English." The music transitioned to soft, reflective melodies as the deputy mayor spoke. Against the backdrop of various scenes of multicultural life
in The Hague, he informed the viewers that "the Hague is *the* international city
of peace and justice" and that it "is a very vibrant mosaic society with an international status." Between cuts of the deputy mayor, the video featured scenes of
eclectic city life backed by a soundtrack of funky, upbeat, contemporary jazz.
The video presented The Hague as multicultural, environmentally progressive,
and leisurely; it showed the parliament engaged in civil debate and citizenry
celebrating cultural diversity. It concluded with the enthusiastic deputy mayor
asserting, "We will put on a great conference. Can we do that? In the words of
Barack Obama, 'Yes, yes we can!'"

The Metropolis delegation chuckled at his corny, though winning, presentation and were then surprised, as the chair promised, to see the deputy mayor
himself riding the same bicycle parked at the 2010 conference display down the
auditorium's center aisle right before their eyes. When he reached the front, he
tossed the toy stork key chains high in the air toward the delegates as token gifts.
The session chair then made some quick remarks concluding with, "We hope
you will think about your trip to Copenhagen as pleasurable and worthwhile."
After the Copenhagen audience had finished applauding and began to move toward the auditorium's exit, the loudspeakers played Frank Sinatra singing "My
Way." To be sure, many conference participants interpreted the choice of music
for such a conference as a bit unusual. Sinatra alone cannot forge lasting bonds
among policy players. However, the affective experience of hearing Sinatra reinforces the overall conference experience as one of style, pleasure, and self-ex-
pression, and of Northern middle-class, individualized living. Regardless of any
given delegate's personal viewpoint on the politics of migration, the aesthetics of
the conference and the sense of community it engenders make it easier to forget,
or at least not seriously challenge, the structural conditions that have generated
so much migration to the EU in the first place. (The spectacle continued next

year in The Hague. The same bicycle remained parked for the entire conference on the stage of the plenary auditorium. Showing a Dutch commitment to multiculturalism, the queen attended the opening ceremony while a Eurovision-style performance featured a white-robed diva ascending from the stage inside a globe and signing, "We, we are as one. We can make it happen.")

Plenaries

Hints of liberalism are found in the titles of the workshops and plenary panels. The 2006 Lisbon conference involved some nine hundred people attending the various plenary sessions—"Thinking About Migration in a New Age of Mobility," "Migration Challenges in the Western Mediterranean," and "Contemporary Migration Management: The Return to Temporary Programmes?"—and participating in a range of workshops such as "Immigrant Integration in Urban Centres," and "Multiculturalism and Education." The title of the Lisbon conference, "Paths and Crossways: Moving People, Changing Places," ethnocentrically suggests a Northern postmodern reflexivity, stressing the importance of personal journeys and a world of equally fluid and detached souls rather than rooted, parochial citizens. Indeed, the unequal conditions that drive migration in a South–North direction, and not the reverse, are missing from the image that the title evokes. Side conversations during the coffee breaks saw many academics and NGO workers arguing that if wealthy Northern states were to lower their own tariffs the monetary inflow to the South would do much to slash the root causes of migration. However, these remarks rarely surface in the conference's formal presentations, as they could lead to polemical arguments that would alienate the national governments that support and seek "practical" input from the conference.

Thus the internal disagreements heard at Metropolis conferences are contained within routine policy questions: What is an acceptable length of time for adjudicating a refugee application? Should temporary immigrant labor be allowed to move from job to job? How much paperwork should be required in a visa application? And in recent years: What is the best way to manage the interface between migrant communities and police forces? All delegates agree on the basic challenge, which is fundamentally liberal: how can states create the conditions for orderly, humane, and targeted labor circulation and immigrant integration? Those who seriously dispute this framing of the policy challenge find the conferences discouraging. They would be positioned on the left in the form of advocates for a borderless world, a position for which few delegates at a

Metropolis conference have any patience. They would also be found on the far-right in the form of advocates for very strict border control and entry requirements, a position with which delegates disagree only in degree, not kind. The few poststructuralist academics in attendance express surprise and dismay at the conferences' tightly defined discussions. They vow not to return. Explained one member of the Metropolis International Steering Committee:

> You don't get radical, Marxist academics here. You don't get cultural studies. You don't get post-modernists here. There is a sense of a disembodied migrant. We tend to talk a policy and academic language. Migrant stories need to be inserted into the conference. We don't get the far right here either. What point would it serve if we want to talk about migration?

The unseen interlocutor at a Metropolis International conference is not the migrant, whose views are never solicited and very rarely heard, but rather the neo-nationalist. This figure's concerns are often recognized either by reference to vague popular opinion or by delegates' reluctance to support further liberalization of migration policy on the grounds that it would be impractical or infeasible.

The conference organizing committee carefully vets the plenary speakers. Across four or five plenary panels, speakers include high-level policy officials (for example, a former European commissioner for justice, freedom, and security), notable migration academics, and IGO leaders. Plenary talks cover such topics as recent migration policy developments, if the speaker works in a bureaucratic capacity; the latest in comparative research, if the speaker is an academic; or a description of urban multiculturalism, if the speaker is a public figure. Plenary sessions, usually lasting about ninety minutes, are followed by a ten-to-fifteen-minute question and answer period.

Almost invariably, questions remain within the parameters described in the tour of the Copenhagen NGO. Occasionally, deviations from this norm emerge, which tend to highlight the norm's very strength. In one case, a session chair working for a national broadcasting corporation in Europe challenged the audience to answer an observation made earlier that white children in North American schools described black children as preferring to live parallel lives rather than integrate into mainstream society. The chair said the delegation resembled the white kids as they describe immigrants as folks they neither understand nor hear from. He asked the next plenary speaker, a migration scholar, to provide his point of view. That speaker, who had already written his presentation, had to respond that he unfortunately would not be able to do so this time around. In another example, a psychologist, visibly frustrated with an impersonal statistical presentation, asked for the microphone.

> I will try to use my mind and not my heart. I am very emotional. They [immigrants] are not "low-educated groups." They are high-educated even though they are a different color and they are invisible. We [Danes] have a nationalist party, which is the third biggest party. This is political discrimination. They [immigrants] are hidden in your statistics.

Weak applause followed her vigorous remarks. The regular absence of migrants from the conference again suggests the disjuncture between the migrant and liberal policy officials. It comes into relief in the rare moments when a migrant addresses the panel during the question and answer periods. At the Lisbon conference, one immigrant of African descent asked for the microphone. Utterly frustrated, he spoke at length in broken English about the needs of migrants themselves and the difficulties they face in getting people to listen to them. His commentary carried on well past the customary allotted time, but the moderator was reluctant to ask him to conclude. When he did finish, an uncomfortable silence filled the auditorium. Then the microphone was given to a woman of African descent whose accent suggested that she was from the Caribbean. She spoke of the hardships that immigrants have always faced, describing her own grandfather's work on a sugar plantation as an example. Her remarks also left the audience silent.[2] The structural gap between migrant and liberal policymaker also emerged when another Caribbean immigrant cornered a white, highly educated official working to achieve a United Nations agreement on global migration known as the Berne Initiative. The immigrant forcefully laid out all the problems that he and his acquaintances were experiencing while trying to integrate into a comparatively tolerant and open Northern country. His monologue lasted for several minutes, leaving the official to listen politely. In the end, she had nothing to offer him except the routine advice that he should take these matters to the immigration authorities in his receiving country. She of course spoke of her personal concern for his situation, but as is typical of policy officials, they cannot individually intervene on a migrant's behalf. Both the immigrant and the official wished for a direct con-

---

2. In similar situations, applause from the audience has also followed the migrant's public assertion of his or her identity and integrity. However, this show of appreciation from the policy community has not changed the substance of the conference's policy discussions, thereby leaving the migrant in the weakest corner of the triangular relationship with neoliberals and neo-nationalists.

nection but neither could establish it, as connections are instead obstructed and then mediated through migration bureaucracies.

Referring to the conference's pleasantries, a German sociologist with a lengthy track record of consulting for the EC referred to this event as "bourgeois entertainment," or a place where comfortable and well-groomed policy players can insist to each other that they have the migrant's best interest at heart. His point resonates on a number of levels. The conference theme in Lisbon, for example, emphasized narcissistic reflection on individual migration journeys and discovery of personal new worlds. It also followed a bourgeois tendency to emulate and valorize the aristocracy, hence the reception in the Royal Coach Museum. These conference features turn attention away from the systematic appropriation of migrant labor, either through an escape into individualized personal worlds or through the pleasure of past aristocratic glories. Many participants of course see past these surroundings, but the latter still function to obstruct efforts to address migration as a relational issue that affects migrants far more negatively than the participants themselves.

HISTORICAL ROOTS OF NEOLIBERALISM AND NEO-NATIONALISM

If the Metropolis example illustrates the creation of a liberal migration policy community, then how do the politics it represents (and often against individual participant's intents) relate to the politics located further right on the political spectrum? The frequent charge from contemporary liberals and leftists maintains that neo-nationalists are holdovers from a bygone era. In interwar Europe, socialists and other progressives criticized fascists on the same ground. What many critics in both eras refused to acknowledge is that interwar fascism and contemporary neo-nationalism drew and draw heavily on ongoing mainstream assumptions about national order. Through the idiom of national belonging and the sharing of an idealized history, national order offers a path to social unity as a remedy for contemporary anxieties. As George Mosse (1979, 2) explains, interwar fascists did not reject liberal democracy per se but only parliamentary democracy, which they accused of creating an elite class between government and the people that fractured national unity and local community. (This sentiment is commonly heard in the North today.) They pushed for direct democracy in order to create an unmediated link between the leadership and the masses, a link often performed through public rituals, ceremonies, and other gatherings. Fascism drew on earlier religious movements in Europe that found even Protestantism too detached to address common needs. For example, pietism of the German mystical tradition offered the individual a direct spiritual connection to the divine, which gave its followers a sense of control over their lives during tumultuous times. Pietism also inspired the nineteenth-century bourgeois code of manners, morals, and egalitarianism that later combined with Romantic nationalism (Mosse 1979). The common theme in this historical trajectory is the effort to create social unity through a cultural idiom of belonging that would ward off the modernist effects of individualization, alienation, and estrangement. As Holmes (2000) lucidly argues, this ideological-cum-aesthetic history has supported different movements, particularly in French and German history. Able to absorb both rightist and leftist features of political life, "integralism" in its contemporary form holds an "unsettling potential . . . to join, fuse, merge, and synthesize what might appear to be incompatible elements" (13).

For neo-nationalists, immigration, the transfer of sovereignty to the EU, and the liberalization of the national economy alienate the national community from the state. However, economic uncertainty alone cannot explain the rise of right-wing movements because it would not account for the failure of left-wing internationalist movements to achieve the same galvanizing effects over the long-term. Supporters of fascism also shared an existential fear of losing social status and an organic connection to community and place. They were not suspicious of capitalism per se but rather of finance capitalism as it encourages an acquisitiveness and selfishness, which have particularly destabilizing effects on social order. Interwar fascists appealed to a wide range of social segments, not just the disgruntled working class, because the existential threat to which they responded was felt across the political spectrum and up and down the economic ladder. Fascism promised a sense of organic community absent in a world of rapid change and eroding social meaning (Mosse 1979). The most available form of community then (as now) was the national community.

Therefore, the resonances between contemporary neo-nationalism and interwar fascism do not suggest the backwardness of the former. Instead, these two historical periods generate a similar sense of individual anxiety and provide the nation as the most available idiom through which it can be overcome. Gingrich identifies three general characteristics of neo-nationalism in western Europe that capture the variations among the numerous neo-nationalist parties (2006, 31; see also Messina 2007, 65, for a typology of neo-nationalist parties): (1) populist criticism of further EU integration for its transfer of power from national capitals to Brussels and for its increased financial burdens; (2) skepticism toward EU enlargement because of the low income and cheap labor markets of the new eastern European member states; and (3) a hard line against illegal immigrants already inside the EU and new immigration from outside that is often combined with an effort to reduce the state's expenditures in social services. Holmes (2000, 10) adds that contemporary neo-nationalists (similar to interwar fascists) disparage "fast capitalism" not just for the accelerated pace of life it injects into an organic community. Rather, they resist its "corrosive ethical, moral, and social" effects by a reassertion of populism, expressionism, and pluralism (Berlin, cited in Holmes 2000, 6–7). Accordingly, these tenets allow the community to live according to its own uniquely aesthetic forms of belonging that are essentially incongruent with those of other groups.

Neo-nationalists use another tripartite construction to describe their current political confines, which also reflects the interwar fascists' desire for direct democracy (Gingrich 2006, 45). The powerful and influential—including EU technocrats, trade union leaders, the supreme constitutional judge, and so on—stand at the top. At the bottom are immigrant advocates and immigrants themselves, ranging from the alleged drug-dealing African to the Slovene minority member. Sandwiched in between is "the nation," which is constantly endangered by aloof leaders who favor immigrants over the autochthonous. Emotionally provocative arguments in defense of the undefined "common man" against multiculturalism and perceived preferential treatment for immigrants and foreigners have worked well to galvanize support. Turner (1995, 17) explains neo-nationalism's plasticity and inclusiveness as follows:

> The new cultural nationalist movements cannot simply be understood as expressions of the political right, even though it is the right that has effectively co-opted them. What must also be accounted for is their populist character as the social and political protests of subordinate social strata against the dominant political-economic and cultural order that excludes them from full participation in national life.

Neo-nationalist parties have indeed attracted many former social democrats whose party profile has waned since the beginning of neoliberal restructuring in the 1990s. Gingrich (2006) points out that these parties appeal to more constituencies than the proverbial down-and-out because a much larger swath of the population feels *perennially insecure*. He reinforces the point by noting that neo-nationalist parties do well in small, wealthy European countries with low unemployment rates and draw much support from urban employed voters (such as Norway, Switzerland, Austria, and the Netherlands). Crucially, the term "employed" no longer signifies steady and secure income and social status. This category now includes temporary and part-time workers, many of whom work in the ever-growing but unstable services sector. This swath of the work-force includes educated workers struggling to start a career for the third time as well as young proletarians (41). These are not the individuals who have fallen out of the system, as it were, but rather individuals upon whom the system thrives. This situation differs from that of the classic welfare state, which caught in its safety net a predictable percentage of the unemployed while everyone else worked and earned with a relative sense of security. Now the entire population feels vulnerable in a shifting global economic arena, regardless of their position on the economic ladder, thus introducing a permanent sense of insecurity throughout the body politic. It offers neo-nationalist leaders a ready supply of supporters per Žižek's formula described above.

Gingrich's (2006, 42–43) explanation of the rise of Jörg Haider and the Freedom Party illustrates the point. This party captured only 5 percent of the national vote when he assumed leadership in 1986. This number reached 27 percent in 1999, making it the second strongest party in Austria and forcing Wolf-gang Schüssel's People's Party to accept it as a governing coalition partner in 2000. Supporters, however, were not exclusively the "regular guys on the street," as the Freedom Party liked to stress, but rather: young male workers disillu-sioned by the leftist politics of their socialist parents; small family-business owners, who identify with the Austrian national self-image; and single people and families from the lower middle class who hold ambitions of upward mo-bility. Like interwar fascists, these supporters cannot be hammered together in specific policy plans. Due to their sheer diversity, neo-nationalist leaders rely in-stead on charisma and grand rhetoric to capitalize on their supporters' shared sense of uncertainty. Hence, the EU has seen the rise of such charismatic lead-ers as Jörg Haider, former leader of Austria's Freedom Party (42); Jean-Marie LePen of France's National Front; the late Pim Fortuyn of Holland's Fortuyn List; Geert Wilders of the Party for Freedom; and similarly, Christopher Blocher of the Swiss People's Party.

Arendt's concept of the "mob" captures the deeper draw of neo-nationalism (1966, 107). Considering alienation in mass society, she argues that the mob is not composed of the "people" writ large but rather of the "residue" of all classes, whom society has marginalized and who thus have an estranged relationship with the body politic. Representing many different strata, niches, and backgrounds, the "mob" becomes easy to mistake for the "people." However, the mob is a more specific entity. It resents society, the parliament, and the state for rejecting its variety of needs, which explains why its unity is established negatively, through a common sense of loss, rather than positively, through specific interests. Arendt points out that the mob has impressive organizational features, is prone to "hero-worship," and is drawn to charismatic leaders often from a high level of society (112). Perhaps most crucially, Arendt's example of the mob in France during the height of the Dreyfus Affair shows that most important events—which included pogroms, among other acts of violence—occurred outside of parliamentary politics and with the aid of high-level leaders tapping into organic populist sentiment.

Neo-nationalism's fit with mainstream discourse appears in how its advocates refute liberal charges of racism. Stolcke (1995) explains that neo-nationalism posits that human beings are not stratified vertically by virtue of biologically determined traits, as in the nineteenth-century social Darwinism that inspired racism and interwar fascism. Instead, it claims that all individuals are biologically determined to be carriers of a particular culture and are xenophobic by nature. Hence, cultural groups should remain separated from each other for everyone's sake. Note here that the claim is not a vertical separation based on moral superiority but rather a horizontal one based on moral incommensurability. Furthermore, when cultural fundamentalists insist that "others" should remain in their original cultural homelands for fear that cohabitation would lead to conflict, they craft an argument homologous to the universally accepted tenet of state sovereignty, which formally denies one nation-state the right to meddle in the domestic affairs of another on the grounds that moral claims cannot be asserted across national-cum-territorial lines. Indeed, this tenet exemplifies liberal cultural relativism, which suits neo-nationalist needs (and also premised North American anthropology for nearly a century). Given cultural relativism's ambidextrous appeal to cultural fundamentalism and multiculturalism, Turner is correct to argue that their usage by rightists and leftists (or liberals) "should be understood as complementary refractions of the same conjuncture of social and political economic forces" (1995, 17). Marilyn Strathern (1995, 16) reinforces the point when noting that "one would not want to be carried (reassured?) by the idea that cultural fundamentalism is a right-wing plot. It may be useful for right-wing political language, but such politics also draw on usages more generally current."

In this vein, Gerd Baumann (1996, 24) well illustrates how a common discourse contains the spectrum of opinion on immigration and multiculturalism in London. He shows how particular ideological positions differ in degree, not kind, as they all utilize the same discourse of reified culture. Conservatives contend that immigrants are culturally unprepared to succeed in England, which makes integration structurally impossible and results only in social problems. Baumann notes the stereotypes of black communities as crippled by problematic family organization and Asian communities as sexist because of the practice of arranged marriage. What he describes simply as "conservative" neatly matches the culturally fundamentalist reasoning of neo-nationalists. Liberals retain the notion of reified cultures at odds with English society but attribute the problem to social disadvantages that keep immigrants—or more politely, "migrants," as Baumann points out—quarantined in their traditional lifeways. Proper social services, better education, and stronger integration programs would help "liberate" them so they could acculturate into English society, which itself would remain homogenous and unchanged. The discourse's left-wing version features an essentialized notion of the "Black community," composed of Africans, Afro-Caribbeans, and South Asians, when pushing for the improvement of immigrant communities' material conditions. Even the most committed neoliberal, claiming to see all newcomers only as radical individuals, cannot undo the discourse of reified culture, and must instead work within its parameters. Neo-nationalism's clean overlay with the full political spectrum serves as a reminder that it is a mainstream, not an extreme, ideology.

To be sure, neoliberalism requires a clear vision of civic order, which ends up rendering it compatible with neo-nationalism. Jamie Peck (2008) explains that with all its emphasis on a small state and individual liberty, neoliberalism must still establish a legal, judicial, and police infrastructure to ensure fair play among individuals. But what constitutes fair play? Will Kymlicka (1995), advancing a long line of liberal thinking on multiculturalism, shows that balancing individual needs against the needs of groups has always been liberalism's dilemma. As just one case in point, he notes that the roots of contemporary liberalism trace back to an assumed homogenous Englishness (and presumably Scottishness). The idea of liberal society hinging on a discrete individual's contract with the state has never fully severed itself from Hegel's notion that culture and similarity of taste are the prerequisite of state order. To be sure, while liberals profess the distastefulness of exclusions based on national criteria, they defend them nonetheless in migration policy. They cannot bypass the popular demand for a sense of community, which always entails exclusion to some degree. Furthermore, liberals actively support restrictions based on income (for example, registered traveler programs, discussed in Chapter 5) and on good manners (such as the use of cultural exams for Southern visa applicants, discussed later in this chapter). Two factors, then, make modern state society less individualistic than liberals can hope it will be: one, of course, is the idea of a shared national culture, and the other, no less significant, is the bourgeois concern, dating from the nineteenth century, with respectability and manners, a plastic enough term that can mark anyone as an outsider if necessary: blacks, Jews, Muslims, the poor, the homeless, the working class, the migrant, and so on. The desire to police borders, both physical and social, is hardly unique to the neo-nationalist.

However, neoliberalism functions both as an ideology and as a rationality of public administration. As pure ideology, it assumes that the state and individual exist in separate spaces, with liberals necessarily pushing back against a state that encroaches on individual freedom. In contrast to this characterization, Foucault (2008, 161) argues that the state itself creates the civic space that liberals need to make people economically productive and socially tranquil through a regime of laws, contracts, professional associations, banking, and so on. In short, the state guarantees the efficiency of the market while people arbitrate the price and values of the goods and services they exchange. The EU migration policy initiatives explored throughout this book are conceived through just such a neoliberal paradigm. Such a rationale appears in the form of conditions for participating in circular migration programs, for obtaining electronic travel documents and legally crossing borders, and for participating in migration and development programs. This neoliberal frame comes packed with its own assumptions of public order that cannot be separated from a concern with national order even if it appears to fully respect people as universally circulating laborers rather than particularized citizens.

TRIANGULATION'S IMPACT ON MIGRATION POLICY

To argue that neoliberalism and neo-nationalism share common ground is not to argue that mainstream Europe is essentially xenophobic. Rather, it is to show that the political discourse across the spectrum assumes the notion of reified cultural groups, fails to incorporate the migrants' own perspectives, and pulls the relevant policy processes in a conservative direction. As this happens, the politics of discrimination move from cultural fundamentalism, which seeks the migrant's removal from sovereign territory, to overt racism, which justifies the denigration of others on the grounds that they are categorically inferior. The following cases, drawing on examples of neo-nationalism from the Netherlands, Denmark, and Italy, illustrate how a shift from a neoliberal position rightward involves a continuous slide rather than discrete breaks.

The Netherlands

The popularity of the late Dutchman Pim Fortuyn exemplifies the insepara-bility of the (neo)liberal and neo-nationalist positions. Fortuyn was a former Marxist sociology lecturer turned populist anti-immigration leader of the self-named political party Pim Fortuyn List. His movement encompassed many different agendas, represented in his own eclectic profile. Fortuyn previously worked as a Marxist sociologist at the University of Groningen. He was elegant, flamboyant, and gay with outspoken views, particularly on sexual freedom. En-couraged by his media popularity, he entered the political realm even though no established party would incorporate him. Early in 2002 his party won over one-third of the vote for the municipal government of Rotterdam, tradition-ally dominated by Labour, acquiring seventeen of the city council's forty-five seats (Sunier and van Ginkel 2006, 107). Fortuyn was ultraliberal on social is-sues and played up his colorfully gay persona in the public arena. He supported gay rights and the legalization of soft drugs and prostitution, all of which are hallmarks of permissive Dutch society. He also called for a reduction in the numbers of immigrants and asylum-seekers, which dropped from forty thou-sand per year in the mid-1990s to ten thousand in "no time at all" (114). Taking advantage of Huntington's "Clash of Civilizations" metaphor, he argued that because of immigration civilizational conflict is now occurring within states, not just between them, as young homophobic Moroccans in Rotterdam had beaten up his gay friends. He also chastised Muslims for treating women as second-class citizens (114).

Fortuyn also boldly called for the first article of the Dutch Constitution, for-bidding discrimination, to be removed, as it was blocking the free speech of liberal, tolerant, and freedom-loving autochthonous Dutch citizens, which in-tolerant Islam threatened (114). His position spoke not to Romantic ideas about the collective Dutch nation but rather to the need to protect Dutch individual-ism from what he described as culturally conservative and backward Muslim fundamentalists. These views resonated with many Dutch citizens, as they reaf-firmed social liberties won from an austere Christian Church in the 1960s and are now seen as threatened by fundamentalist Muslim immigrants (van der Veer

2006). Fortuyn once declared that he liked fucking young Moroccan boys but did not want backward imams to restrain him (120). His statement is striking not just for its violent sexuality but also for its appeal to individualism with extreme self-indulgence. The riots that erupted by the parliament building after his murder (by a left-wing animal rights activist, not a Muslim) signified the resonance of his message. Van der Veer (2006, 115) explains that Fortuyn tapped into a public sentiment unreached by the staid politics of the Christian Democrat, Socialist, Labour, and Liberal parties. Like many populist leaders, he could excite people who felt that he could stand up to political correctness and say what they could not. A national poll voted him the greatest Dutchman of all time ahead of Erasmus and Rembrandt (115). Fortuyn List gained support not only from the traditional far-right but also from a broad range of people disaffected by back room politics of the center-left government. Supporters included the young and poorly educated as well as urban dwellers, suburban "white flight" voters, and even other non-European immigrants who themselves felt that more immigration would create job insecurity (Sunier and van Ginkel 2006, 116).

Per Arendt's mob politics, established Dutch politics, then, absorbed the populist concern with protecting liberal individualism back into national immigration policy. For example, applicants for Dutch residence permits from the global South (basically any country outside the EU, Norway, Switzerland, Lichtenstein, the Vatican, Monaco, the US, Canada, Japan, Australia, and New Zealand) must now pass tests on Dutch language and society at the cost of €350. The exam's preparatory materials include a video on Dutch culture featuring two men kissing in a public park and a topless woman emerging from the sea onto a crowded beach (MSNBC 2006). The exam must be taken in a Dutch embassy or consulate in the applicant's country of origin or residence (though not in Holland). The applicant submits proof of identity, sits for a photograph, and provides fingerprints before the exam. Then Dutch immigration minister, Rita Verdonk, argued, "It is important that you not be afraid to make clear demands of people—that they subscribe to our European values, that they respect our laws and learn the language" (Tape 2006). Verdonk's concern is essentially a mainstream one, as it underpins the objectives of naturalization procedures in most EU countries. Again, these objectives are themselves consistent with the post–World War I state system in which the citizenry embodies the putative national culture unique to the state's territory. Apart from tempering the excessive effects of a drive toward national homogenization, liberalism, in practice, is not fundamentally at odds with Verdonk's own position.

Denmark

The Danish parliament approved tighter regulations on marriage that also demonstrate the contradictions within liberalism itself. Passed in 2002 by a coalition of the Liberal and Conservative parties with support of the right-wing Danish People's Party, the law prevents Danish citizens who are twenty-four years or younger from marrying anyone from outside the Nordic countries (Denmark, Iceland, Norway, Sweden, and Finland). The law also requires that the spouse/partner reside permanently in Denmark, have adequate housing at his or her disposal, be self-supporting, and have no convictions of violent acts against a former spouse/partner within the last ten years. Couples—two people seeking marriage or a registered partnership—must live together at the same address, have entered into the relationship voluntarily, and have a combined attachment to Denmark that is greater than their combined attachment to any other country. "Combined attachment" is measured through specific criteria such as the length of time each person has lived in Denmark, the strength of family acquaintances in Denmark, whether the individuals have custody rights to a child living in Denmark, whether the individuals have completed an education program or have a solid connection to the labor market in Denmark, how well the individuals speak Danish, and whether the individuals have strong ties to other countries, which could be measured by the number of extended visits or the existence of children and family members abroad. The attachment requirement is waived if the spouse/partner has held Danish citizenship or has legally resided in Denmark for more than twenty-eight years. The law's passage led to a drop in the number of marriages of non–ethnic Danes to foreigners, from 62.7 percent in 2001 to 37.9 percent by 2005. One effect of the law has been a simultaneous rise in the number of non–ethnic Danes marrying other non–ethnic Danes, from 17.3 percent to 29.1 percent (Copenhagen Post, cited in Islam in Europe 2006). This shift could be read as a step away from immigrant integration and toward cultural segmentation.

This law coincides with the rising influence of Danish neo-nationalism, which made use of crises and sports to consolidate its movement (Hervik 2006). First, Danish voters narrowly decided against ratification of the Maastricht Treaty (Treaty of the European Union, or TEU) in June 1992, with 51 percent against and 49 percent in favor. Even though a second referendum would narrowly pass less than a year later, the first result ignited a fierce sense of national pride that was compounded by Denmark's surprise victory in the 2002 Euro Cup football championship ten years later. These events shaped an existential debate about the vulnerability of national culture in an age of globalization and European integration. This debate has intensified in western Europe since the end of the Cold War and the expansion of the EU. With half the Danish population actively concerned about immigration, the public greeted other events of the early 1990s with great controversy. Denmark received seventeen thousand refugees from the war in Bosnia-Herzegovina between 1992 and 1995. They were first given a two-year temporary refugee status, and then full refugee status equipped with access to an integration program. During the period of parliamentary debate, however, the opposition demanded that anyone fleeing "for their own convenience" be refused entry to Denmark, and that the country did not wish to be influenced by cultural and religious difference (Hervik 2006, 97). These events created an opening for an established neo-nationalist presence in public debate, which largely occurred through the newspaper *Ekstra Bladet*. Its editor launched a campaign about immigration and multiculturalism on the grounds that Danes were never asked if they would accept these immigrants and foreigners, invoking the image of the "people" sandwiched between an elitist government administration on one side and immigrants and NGOs on the other. They contended that distant politicians were responsible for the transformation of a hitherto peaceful society into a conflicted multicultural one. The newspaper and its main political affiliate, the Danish People's Party, could then claim the mantle of representing the ordinary Dane and fighting for the preservation of Danish culture. Not only rightist politicians supported this view but also traditional leftists among the Social Democrats (98–100).

These events together showcase the limits of Western liberalism in trying to accommodate multiculturalism on a global scale (see Cowan et al. 2001). According to the minister of integration, the marriage law was designed to prevent forced and arranged marriages between Danish children of immigrant parents and foreigners. This justification draws on a liberal charge of releasing the individual from traditional social obligations but manifests itself as culturally intolerant as it opposes an important Muslim practice. In another variant of the interplay between liberalism and neo-nationalism in Scandinavia, Unni Wikan (2002) argues that government multicultural policies in Norway favor the privileged members of immigrants groups while leaving other members of those groups unprotected from oppressive traditions such as forced marriages. Liberalism is thus sacrificed for the maintenance of non-European traditional social orders. Wikan herself is not advocating for harsh immigration restriction but rather for a more finely crafted multicultural policy that helps prevent immigrant girls (in this case) from becoming victims of gender discrimination as Western liberals would define it. Nevertheless, the fact that her views have been appropriated by Norway's neo-right and criticized by liberals defending government policy testifies to the complexity of separating these two positions in political debate. The result is that liberal positions get pulled toward xenophobic and nationalist ones.

Italy

The challenges confronting the Roma in Italy show the slippage from the neo-nationalist position of moral incommensurability to a racist position that treats nonnationals as morally inferior. As in Denmark and the Netherlands in 2006, the Italian interior ministry was given to a neo-nationalist politician in the form of Roberto Maroni of the Northern League, a collection of parties unified around an anti-immigration platform among other issues. The confluence of two events fostered a hostile attitude toward Roma. First, Maroni's interior ministry argued that the 10,600 illegal entries into Italy during the first half of 2008 constituted twice the number of entries during the first half of 2007, and that 350 clandestine immigrants had landed just days before the state of emergency was announced (Goldirova 2008). Second, this trend combined with a growing resentment toward Roma immigrants, which had been aggravated by a spike in Roma immigration from the former Yugoslavia beginning in the 1990s and another following Bulgaria's and Romania's 2007 accession to the EU (European Roma Rights Centre 2008, 4). A crystallizing moment came in November 2007 when Roma were publicly accused of killing an Italian woman. The government responded by increasing its expulsions of illegal immigrants, particularly Roma. Simultaneously, many Roma living in either government-authorized or makeshift camps became more vulnerable to attacks because of their dense living arrangements (European Union Agency for Fundamental Rights 2008, 8). Italian gangs set these camps ablaze with Molotov cocktails on at least eight occasions (European Roma Rights Centre 2008, 2). Roma account for only 150,000 of the people in Italy, with half holding Italian citizenship and 20–25 percent holding citizenship of other EU countries. They nevertheless loom large in the nationalist imagination as outsiders who occupy the dirty jobs, who are consummate thieves, and who have no compunction about using their children as beggars.

On May 10, 2008, police evacuated two Roma camps in a low-income suburb of Ponticelli in the aftermath of an alleged kidnapping of an Italian baby by a sixteen-year-old Roma girl. The mother grabbed the baby back from the girl who then fled the scene. However, she was apprehended by the mother's father who also shouted for help. A crowd gathered at the scene, and only a last-minute intervention by the police saved the girl, whom the crowd threatened to lynch. A judge placed her in precautionary detention, but backlashes came against Roma settlement camps in Ponticelli. Within three hours of the alleged attempted kidnapping, twenty Italians had beaten and stabbed a Romanian laborer. Two days later three Italian boys doused a Roma camp with gasoline and set it on fire. The next day over three hundred locals led by a group of Italian women staged an attack on a large camp that was home to forty-eight Roma families. Police evacuated smaller Roma camps, placing the residents in larger ones for protection. Many of the abandoned camps were torched as well (European Union Agency for Fundamental Rights 2008, 4–6). The under-secretary of state for the interior condemned the violence as did many others. However, the government's interest in the matter appears ambiguous. Referring to the publicly debated need to deal with the "Roma problem," Interior Minister Umberto Bossi, who once suggested shooting at boats carrying immigrants, added, "People do what the state can't manage" (Wilkinson 2008). On May 21, 2008, the Council of Ministers of the Italian government controversially declared a ten-day national state of emergency "with regard to nomad community settlements in the territories of Campania, Lazio, and Lombardia regions" (European Roma Rights Centre 2008, 7). According to the European Roma Rights Centre, the Italian government "refuses to acknowledge that Romani communities in Italy do not conduct a nomadic lifestyle" (n.7). The crisis was not that of an invading army, an organized challenge to the state, or even a natural disaster but rather the "exceptional and persistent influx" of irregular migrants.

The shift from the Dutch case to the Italian case signifies the shift from the politics of cultural fundamentalism to the politics of producing dispensable people, as best articulated by the Italian philosopher Giorgio Agamben (1998) in his writings on *homo sacer*. The government's state of emergency partially drew on Law 225/92, which allows public authorities to suspend various laws and regulations in the event of natural disaster crises. In other words, the "Roma problem" moved beyond a problem of supposedly incommensurable groups; the Italian government reframed the Roma as a product of nature and in effect as nonhuman, a degradation encouraged by mob politics. Safely protected by 225/92, Berlusconi's government passed a security package in response to the upheavals surrounding the Roma camps. This package included measures to deport illegal immigrants, to deploy the armed forces to help keep order in cities, to dismantle unauthorized Roma camps, and to regulate specifically the entry of Roma and Romanians into Italy. The last measure required a suspension of Italy's participation in the Schengen Agreement (European Union Agency for Fundamental Rights 2008, 11).

Berlusconi's measures shortly followed the passage of a law that makes undocumented migration in Italy a criminal offence that carries with it a penalty of six months to four years in prison. In June 2008, the Italian government began taking a census count in the Roma camps, with the commissioner for Rome announcing, "Gypsies would also be fingerprinted and photographed and this would allow the authorities to identify them" (European Roma Rights Centre 2008, 9). Maroni justified this measure by arguing that fingerprinting Roma children (over the age of fourteen) and adults would ensure that parents who send their children out to beg could be traced and punished (Pisa 2008). This measure, however, directly contradicts Article 8(1) of Council Directive 95/46/EC, an EU law prohibiting the collection of data based on racial or ethnic origin unless used for specific aims that do not result in the abuse of the target population. Maroni was given the power to move Roma camps and to keep Roma under legal surveillance. He explained that no new camps would be created as these could spark new protests (Adnkronos International 2008).

The presence of neo-nationalism in Europe, of course, does not mean that Europe is yoked to each neo-nationalist demand per se. Indeed, the Council of Europe, the European Parliament, and the center-left opposition in the Italian parliament condemned the Italian government's state of emergency in July 2008. The EC also investigated the legal maneuvers that enabled it. Nevertheless, the common ground beneath neo-nationalism and liberalism precludes the latter from ultimately dispelling the paranoia of the former even if it might mitigate its worst effects. The Italian case shows how the logic of anti-immigrant violence does not differ in kind from that of cultural fundamentalism but only in degree. The critical slip occurs when the claim that different cultures are equally valid though incommensurable transforms into the claim that some other cultures are either of lesser moral character or less than human (not even "cultural," as being cultural is an essential human trait according to the cultural fundamentalist argument). The danger of asserting the existence of fundamental differences between groups of people—even if that assertion is made with good intentions—is the ease with which it can be expanded into the argument that difference means inferiority and expendability. The point is often revealed in various neo-national leaders' offhand remarks. For example, Giancarlo Gentilini, a former mayor of Treviso in northern Italy, described immigrants as "slackers" and asserted, "We should dress [immigrant slackers] up like hares and bang-bang-bang" (Marrese 2002).

The overall movement rightward across the spectrum transpires seamlessly and approaches its zenith in the condemnation of entire civilizations. The Al-Qaeda attacks on September 11, 2001, provided such an opportunity to Pia Kjærsgaard (2001), leader of the Danish People's Party:

> It has been mentioned that September 11 became the beginning of a fight between civilisations. I don't agree about this, because a fight between civilisations would imply that there were two civilisations, and that is not the case. There is only one civilisation, and that is ours. Our opponents can't plead to belong to a civilisation, because a civilised world would never be able to carry out an attack which contains so much hatred, so much savagery, so much abomination. With this, I regard September 11 as an attack on civilisation itself. On the civilisation which decent people have built up during decades and centuries, and which is based on uprightness and freedom. The others want to implement ferocity, the primitive, the barbaric, the medieval.

Kjærsgaard did not limit these condemning remarks to terrorists but baldly expanded them to incorporate and essentialize an entire group of people implicitly identified as Muslim. Even if neo-nationalists do not determine the migration policy debate in particular EU member states, certainly neo-nationalist assumptions constrain the policy imagination of how to manage the movement of people from the global South to the European Union.

THE POLITICAL BOUNDARIES OF A
MIGRATION MANAGEMENT APPARATUS

The many facets of the EU's efforts to harmonize migration management discussed in subsequent chapters are effectively contained within the parameters of the political right—that is, the economic right and the nationalist right. Political observers have well explained how the shift toward liberal economic reforms in the post–Cold War era, and the associated dismantling of the welfare state, sent the political left into a tailspin. This situation forces those with leftist sympathies to choose between neoliberal programs that compromise their ideals and the neo-nationalist politics justified in the interest of the nation's perennially insecure workers, of all classes and education levels. The latter offers community while the former promises economic growth but leaves many people unable to improve or even sustain their social status and material circumstances. Neo-nationalism promises a restoration of direct social connection through the reinvigoration of the national or local community, an inherently exclusive move. If neoliberalism strives to create the conditions for the orderly labor circulation across national boundaries and for tranquility within those boundaries, then it ultimately must rely on the "nation" as a central idiom for that order. This move enables the reification of national groups and specifically immigrant groups. Liberals are then positioned to patronize them, neo-nationalists to identify them as incommensurable, and right-wing extremists to target them as inhuman threats. The latter completes the slip from a discourse of cultural fundamentalism presuming irreconcilable cultural differences to a discourse of *homo sacer* presuming inferior racialized differences.

The function of today's (neo)liberalism is not to undermine nationalism but only to temper its worst excesses by insisting on human rights, on sensible immigrant integration programs, on humane procedures to facilitate labor migration, and on the rule of law rather than state decree. However, neo-nationalism does not logically oppose any of these worthy aims, even if its practitioners dismiss them, but rather argues for a lower immigrant quota, a shorter visa period, greater protection for the domestic workforce, and renewed commitment to cultural identity. It is an oversimplification to argue that liberals welcome immigrants without condition and neo-nationalists reject them without qualification, even if extremists appear at either end of the spectrum. To appreciate this point is not to condone xenophobia and violence against immigrants but rather to recognize that the most successful neo-nationalist politics draw directly on mainstream political assumptions. Furthermore, neoliberals may personally wish for the best for migrants, but the very formation of their policy communities nevertheless segregates them socially and spatially from migrants. Migrants themselves will take advantage of opportunities to highlight the discrepancy between positive intents and negative effects, as their provocations at migration policy conferences show.

3 MAKING THINGS SIMPLE
Forms of Knowledge and Policy Coherence in the "Area of Justice, Freedom and Security"

Normalization is the language of the engineer, and its successful integration as a part of modern institutions marks the moment when this technical language could attain to the status of a common language.

François Ewald 1991a, 149

FROM CHAOS TO ORDER

EU migration policy officials fear what they call "mixed migration flows." Suggesting not simply abnormality but the absence of normality, policy officials use this term to refer to the transnational movements of people whose identities, reasons for migrating, and even migratory routes are indeterminable. "Abnormal" and "normal" (corresponding to "illegal" and "legal" as well as "irregular" and "regular") are definitive and manageable categories in the migration policy cosmology. However, the absence of normality destabilizes that cosmology by robbing it of a standard with which to identify and thus manage the abnormal. To avoid the conceptual destruction that mixed migration flows present, police investigators and border patrol agents routinely struggle to allocate travelers into clear administrative categories. This task presents frequent challenges, for example, as border guards attempt to distinguish between someone who has been smuggled versus someone who has been trafficked. The distinction is critical to determine what role the detained migrant played in the illegal crossing. Similar frustration surrounds the question of whether someone is a "legitimate refugee" or an "economic migrant in disguise." Many high-level border officials complain that the 1951 Geneva Convention on refugees is outdated, as it was designed mainly to accommodate a small handful of individuals fleeing political persecution in the old Soviet bloc. Refugee adjudicators diligently research asylum-seekers' claims about persecution and often find the truth ambiguous. Border control agents worry about fraudulent documents and so rely on biometric data stored in electronic travel documents to catch those who falsely "claim an identity." As a result of this ambiguity, migration officials and policymakers must sort a bewildering array of travelers into a classificatory scheme to facilitate migration management. The chaos must be categorized, organized, and distributed on a curve from normal to abnormal, legal to illegal, desirable to undesirable, and productive to subversive. In short, the ambiguity of travelers' circumstances must be simplified to facilitate migration management.

Harmonizing migration management among the EU member states requires both the image of the EU as a coherent, idiosyncratic space and the material integration of its member states' migration systems. The former process involves the passing of laws and regulations to allow the free circulation of people and commodities within the union. It reaches its most familiar expression in the form of the Schengen Area (described later in this chapter), which the EC would later identify as the "Area of Justice, Freedom and Security" to designate the space that should benefit from managed migration and strengthened police and security capacities. The latter process involves the development of the technical capacity to synthesize unconnected national systems by means of common norms, standards, and generic templates. Different actors can apply these devices to their own contexts according to particular needs. This modus operandi facilitates an apparatus's proliferation through, for example, the integration of information technology systems, the establishment of common technical language for separate policy problems, the maps that present a geographic perspective on public administration, and the creation of common guidelines for disparate policy actors to apply to particular problems. These elements function similarly to Latour's immutable mobiles as they provide a *means* of classifying and explaining the external world that can be rapidly reproduced, disseminated, and further expanded (1990, 26–35). Their integrative power works not simply by tying experts into networks per se but rather by amassing the information they produce and acquire across vast areas of space into a shared, easily accessible, and comprehensible format.

Scholars of language and power have illustrated how language patterns similarly provide an apparatus with its power of convergence. Said (1979, 20) describes the notion of a "strategic formation," which is "a way of analyzing the relationship between texts and the way in which groups of texts, types of texts, even textual genres, acquire mass, density, and referential power among themselves and thereafter culture at large." With regard to policymaking, such formations are often coded in "technostrategic" language (Cohn 1987, 390). This term refers to a manner of observing problems through quantified description, including analytical devices like algorithms, mathematical models, and multivariate analyses. Technostrategic language offers a certain simplicity and adaptability of policy outlooks, which allow policy actors in disparate domains to utilize them in organizing their own policy work. Other analytical parlances might offer Geertz's "models of/for relationships" (1973, 93–94), Gramsci's "hegemony" (1971), or Foucault's "power/knowledge" (1980) as the paradigm through a particular actor's policy interpretation becomes possible. In any case, simplified and ubiquitous templates encourage similar policy problematizations in policy domains as diverse as biometrics, labor circulation, and border security, and across scales from the local to the national and EU levels.

These devices encourage the treatment of people as quantifiable objects rather than living subjects with qualitative experiences. They flatten out history. The effect, in turn, helps to justify policy programs in terms of abstract, simplified narratives and high-scale morality, both of which reduce heterogeneous people with idiosyncratic experiences into legible target populations (Trouillot 2001, 126). Arendt (2006) famously detailed how the work of public administration encourages its bureaucrats to think through empty clichés to simplify the ambiguity they confront in their daily work. As apparatuses simplify complexity into manageable pieces, policymaking is effectively an exercise in (producing) superficiality. To be sure, depth and complexity are its greatest sources of worry.

The integration of this material infrastructure also serves the apparatus's purpose of "normalization," which as mentioned in Chapter 1, involves constant readjustments that bring unfavorable practices in line with favorable practices. Though celebrated in terms of the "good" or the "just," normalization is amoral, utilitarian, and pragmatic. This readjustment is a problem of "biopower" (Foucault 1990), which refers to the modes in which individual behavior is encouraged in a multitude of sites (in schools, hospitals, prisons, and so on) to serve the purpose of societal reproduction (through regional planning, health care programs, economic planning, environmental measures, and the like). Normalization emerges through the nineteenth century in tandem with industrialization and the integration of national and colonial infrastructures. The term itself appears in the policy lexicon in 1928, along with the rise of national and international organizations concerned with establishing norms and standards (Ewald 1991a, 148). Ewald describes normalization not as the production of specific objects that conform to a standard model but rather the "reaching of an understanding with regard to the choice of a model." It is quintessentially about "the production of norms, standards for measurement and comparison, and rules of judgment" (148). Indeed, like rationales of governance so crucial to the fusion of an apparatus (Chapter 1), these models are generic in character but easily adaptable to diverse contexts.

A semantic history of the term "policy" suggests how the rise of expert management foreshadowed the ubiquity of contemporary apparatus. The English word "policy" derives from the French medieval word "police." This older term did not refer narrowly to the protection of society from social deviance, but rather it meant, more broadly, "to organize and regulate the internal order of" society (Wedel et al. 2005, 35; see also *Webster's Third New International Dictionary* 1971, 1754). Thus, in his "theory of police," Foucault illustrates the total attempt at regulation through the example of Delamare's *Compendium*. Delamare argued that police work is administrative work, monitoring eleven elements pertaining to daily life: religion, morals, health, supplies, roads, town buildings, public safety, the liberal arts, trade factories, menservants and labor, and the poor (Foucault 1988, 80). This "police state" regulates everything that forms relations between members of the polis. Indeed, as Foucault notes, Delamare has covered all aspects of social living: the moral quality of life (religion), the preservation of life (health, supplies), the conveniences of life (trade, factories, workers, the poor, public order), and the pleasures of life (theater, literature, entertainment).

While the totalizing aim of the eighteenth-century police state eventually gave way to liberalism, the transition did not necessarily entail the former surrendering to the latter in a zero-sum game. Rather, the shift presented the state with the dilemma of how to make economic freedom both the basis and limit of the state's authority (Foucault 2008, 102). It did not result in the simple collapse of a massive regulatory infrastructure but rather a transition to a new and arguably more sophisticated infrastructure that cultivates individuals instead of making demands on them as preexisting subjects (Rose 1993). Typical of Foucault, "freedom" in this understanding is not a given trait of human nature; rather, it is a quality that liberalism must produce, encourage, and entice into action through mechanisms that simultaneously condition and channel freedom's action. Analytic attention is not given to freedom as an abstraction but rather to actual practices that mobilize a certain kind of self-governing subject who is then likely to describe him or herself as objectively free. The self-governing subject (Rose 1999) is not molded to specific tasks but rather possesses "denotationally indeterminate" skills, which are applicable in diverse situations (Urciuoli 2008, 212; see also Rose 1999). Like shifters, IT standards, and rationales of governance, this individual can be adapted or refitted to varying needs and circumstances.

This chapter first lays out how EU migration officials have come to imagine the union's territory as a clearly demarcated space in need of special protection from a world of chaotic global circulations. This part also provides a sketch of EU-level policy developments that have channeled and encouraged more detailed processes that are collectively giving rise to a common migration management system. The chapter then investigates several examples of tools that standardize knowledge production capabilities, which disparate officials share so that the knowledge systems they operate can integrate into a larger whole without sustained interpersonal contact. These examples all feature devices that function as generic templates, norms, or other modes of reducing complexity into classifiable and manageable policy data.

FUSING POLITICS AND POLICY IN THE
"AREA OF JUSTICE, FREEDOM AND SECURITY"

European Union efforts to harmonize migration management among the member states take place at a moment when wealthy nation-states readily cooperate on security matters as part of their efforts to collectively bolster a liberalized global economy. Harmonization within the EU (and its antecedent European Community) involves a restructuring of the twenty-seven member states' national institutions, national policies, and even national laws on issues ranging from restaurant hygiene standards to border security practices to transportation regulations. The code of law to which member states must conform is the Acquis Communitaire (Community Law), or simply Acquis, which is composed of EU directives, regulations, legal acts, and court decisions dating back as far as the 1950s. Consisting of more than thirty chapters on issues as diverse as statistics, consumer health and protection, intellectual property law, and fisheries, the Acquis has been translated into twenty-two EU languages. The English translation contains a staggering 55,537,910 words (European Commission Joint Research Centre 2009). The Acquis does not simply dictate standards but rather establishes a meta-language, as it were, for the integration of national systems.

A review of EU-level migration developments helps to situate the specific events, processes, and issues that have likewise created the conditions for greater harmonization of migration policy (for institutional analyses see Faist and Ette 2007; Geddes 2000; 2003; Lahav 2008; Messina 2007; Tholen 2005). While western European states had been unwilling to cooperate on immigration matters during most of the Cold War, their attitude changed with the passage of the Single European Act in 1985. This act set up the goal of a union without internal frontiers, which the 1985 signing of the Schengen Agreement and its implementation ten years later ultimately fulfilled. The Schengen Agreement called for the free circulation of goods, finance, and labor within the EU and pushed for the creation of a common market. However, the prospect of eradicating internal EU borders drove the participating states to reinforce external borders, lest undesirable commodities and people from outside circulate unchecked through the entire Schengen Area.

From this point forward, the European Council, the body composed of national ministers that establishes the EU's political priorities, began empowering the European Commission (EC), the EU's administrative arm, with a proactive role in harmonizing migration management among the member states. The 1992 Treaty of the European Union (TEU; also called the Maastricht Treaty) placed immigration along with criminal justice, judicial cooperation, law enforcement, and asylum under the third of the EU's three legal pillars. Each pillar contains a different set of common issues and is defined by a different legal decision-making process between the EC, the European Parliament, and the member states. Individual member states and the EC can initiate legislation on third-pillar issues, but voting requires unanimous support from the European Council in order to pass a directive or regulation. EU law is difficult to achieve in this scenario. The 1997 Treaty of Amsterdam transposed the Schengen Agreement into EU law applicable to all fifteen EU countries at the time (except for the UK, Ireland, and Denmark). By 2010, twenty-five of the twenty-seven member states would incorporate it into national legislation, with Romania and Bulgaria to follow. This treaty also moved matters of immigration and asylum from Pillar III to Pillar I, which broadened the migration policy umbrella to encompass the whole issue of free movement along with police and judicial matters. Moreover, Pillar I allows only the EC to submit legislative proposals to the European Council and the European Parliament. These proposals require only a qualified majority from the European Council to be adopted. In other words, to expedite the decision-making process, the EC can initiate EU-wide legislation, which could be transposed into member states' national legislation with majority (not unanimous) agreement at the European Council. Legislation no longer needs to emerge out of laborious negotiations among all EU member states.

As the EC gained strength in migration matters, the European Council began creating a series of five-year plans consisting of general guidelines for the harmonization of a common EU migration management system. Again, these documents emphasized not specific actions that member states should take but rather the conditions through which member states would be politically and logistically able to move toward such a system. The 1999 European Council summit in Tampere, Finland, required the EC to make comprehensive proposals on immigration and asylum with four priority areas: immigrant integration and fair treatment of third-country nationals (that is, anyone who is not a citizen of an EU member state); development of a common asylum regime; management of migration flows; and the development of partnerships with non-EU immigrant-sending countries. All member states could at least agree on the common value of these agenda items. The 2002 Seville Council resulted in much greater cooperation on strengthening border control. It called for more joint operations at airports and seaports, for an intergovernmental coordinating unit composed of heads of national border control agencies, and for a review of visa requirements with an eye toward harmonization. Seville also laid the cornerstone for Frontex, which became the EU agency responsible for the management of the external borders. Since the creation of the Schengen Area, external border control has been the easiest domain for member state cooperation. The next major policy step toward harmonization took place in January 2003 when the EU went live with the EURODAC system, which contains digitalized fingerprints of asylum-seekers and individuals caught illegally entering union territory (Chapter 5).

The Dublin Convention, signed in 1990 and entering into force in 1997, established common criteria for determining which member state should adjudicate an asylum claim (usually the one in which the claimant first landed). Furthermore, it declared that once an asylum decision is reached, all other member states must respect it. This measure greatly reduced what EU officials call "asylum shopping," whereby asylum-seekers apply in different EU countries until they get a favorable decision. The convention no doubt helped to reduce the number of asylum applications from 670,000 in 1992 for the EU-15 to 192,000 for the EU-27 (Juchno 2007). Among other effects, the Schengen and Dublin agreements consolidated the policy ideal of a seamless European space and transformed it into a practical (if imperfect) reality. These steps toward common migration management also meant that migrants themselves were now dealing with the combined forces of the EU member states rather than any one of them alone. If playing one state off another were ever a migrant's viable option, then it had now become much harder.

The 2004 Hague Programme, succeeding Tampere, introduced the monumental phrase "an area of justice, freedom and security" into the EU migration policy lexicon. This epithet, matched with an equally robust commitment to border management, edified a policy vision of the EU as a morally elevated space composed of decent individuals in need of protection from the threats of transnational criminal and terrorist networks. In a 2005 speech delivered at the Bundestag, then European commissioner for justice, freedom and security Franco Frattini described the rise of these three ideals on the EU agenda as an "explosion . . . due to the fact that reality has imposed itself and showed the need for common policies on a number of key areas, areas very close to the daily life of every citizen." Arguing for enhanced security precautions to protect honest individuals, he identified these areas as border control; policies on visas, asylum, and immigration; cooperation to fight terrorism and organized crime; and enhancing human rights so that "citizens and business are not discouraged by cross-border obstacles when seeking to exercise their rights" (Frattini 2005). The Hague Programme likewise highlighted ten priority points necessary to transform EU territory from a collection of nation-states into a synergistic area of justice, freedom, and security, and that properly manages migration: privacy and security, fundamental rights, fighting transnational crime and terrorism, and the many dimensions of migration management such as borders, visas, asylum, integration, and illegal migration (European Commission 2005). Migration management thus expanded from the simple matter of issuing visas and stamping passports at a national level to a full-scale monitoring of transnational population movements along the union's entire external border. It mushroomed from isolated bureaucratic procedures into a multinational apparatus.

The conflation of the European Council's political agenda with the EC's policy agenda is perhaps best expressed in the EC's full adoption of the "Directorate-General for Justice, Freedom and Security," which is now responsible for harmonizing EU migration policy among the twenty-seven member states. (This directorate-general, which is analogous to a national interior ministry, was divided into two directorate-generals on July 1, 2010: the Directorate-Generals for Home Affairs and for Justice.) The EC's rise in power has not given its technocrats the authority to dictate migration policy, but rather it allows them to consolidate and standardize a migration policy paradigm that precipitates out of disparate and ongoing policy practices across the union in many different locales. Recall that the legislation it initiates is subject to compromise and approval by the European Council and European Parliament, both of which must balance countless demands from their own constituents. However, once the legislation is finalized, the funding requests from international organizations, NGOs, and state agencies are evaluated in its terms, thus shaping future migration policy directions across the EU. One project officer from a prominent international organization explained that "the EU is a huge source of funding. So anything [we do] has that in mind. But, we are a good vehicle to communicate priorities of smaller states back to Brussels. . . . They have needs that cannot be communicated officially." Her colleague explained how those priorities ricochet back in a more rigid form to non-EU states within the union's sphere of influence:

> Brussels is key. Brussels has written the music and we [the IGO] play the music. He who pays the piper picks the tune. . . . We always meet the EC delegation in the field [as when working with non-EU states in Africa and Asia]. It never goes against EU guidelines. Not in the colonial sense, but because they are effective. [Third countries] can never really go against it.

Policy rationales are sedimented in Brussels and boomeranged back out to standardize practice among actors working in local, national, and international policy settings. This phenomenon of exporting standards from the center to the periphery is not particular to migration management in the EU. Through the example of the production of a staff report, Harper (1998, 45) shows how loan programs from the IMF begin with an apparent diversity of perspectives that ultimately get whittled down because the prediction of possible outcomes is built on IMF assumptions of desirability/undesirability. Martha Feldman (1989) illustrates the same point with the example of policy consolidation in the US Department of Energy.

A SHARED GLOSSARY AND A SHARED OUTLOOK

The 2001 Laeken meeting of the European Council spotlighted the need for a harmonized system for exchanging migration policy knowledge among the relevant EU agencies. By 2003, the European Migration Network (EMN) started as a pilot project for this purpose. The Hague Programme went a step further and called for a common analytical capability for migration phenomena. The Stockholm Programme, running from 2010 to 2014, calls for "further development of the European Migration Network with a view to better informing policy choices, which also takes account of recent developments" (European Commission 2010, 52). It now works under the Immigration and Integration unit of the Directorate-General for Home Affairs.

The work of the EMN illustrates the institutionalization of a common framework of knowledge production that need not be centrally imposed on disparate policy actors since it is crystallized out of existing practices. An EC Desk Officer, a former physicist, coordinates the EMN, which is composed of representative officials from each participating member state with their various agencies designated as the "national contact points" (NCPs). They meet bimonthly in Brussels in an unappealing meeting room ringed with translator booths. They discuss how to organize comparative research projects on such topics as return migration, conditions of entry for third-country highly skilled workers, reception capacities for asylum applicants, or managed labor migration in the health sector. They decide which studies would be most useful across the EU and which member states should conduct them, and then they return home to commission the studies to researchers in local universities and think tanks. Communication at EMN meetings transpires through rigorously controlled procedures. The desk officer's supervisor chairs the meetings. He calls on delegates by their nationality, not their own names, to speak: "Yes, Italy, do you have something to add?" or "Sweden, please summarize your response to the draft." Delegates wishing to add something to this discussion raise their hands and wait to speak until called upon, again by their nationality: "Belgium, do you wish to ask a question?" The research that EMN coordinates creates a reservoir of common knowledge from which officials across the EU can draw when making common migration policy decisions, or at least national policy decisions through a shared EU optic.

Once the network was initiated, the problem immediately arose that each member state applies different shades of meaning to different migration terms, and those meanings often get lost in translation from, say, Portuguese to Lithuanian via German. The EMN created the online *Asylum and Migration Glossary: A Tool for Better Comparability* to mitigate this problem, a task they assigned to a Glossary and Thesaurus Working Group composed of a subset of EMN representatives. This group met every six to eight weeks for four years to sort out the raft of terminology that appears in migration policy discussions. The glossary provides "common definitions and understandings of terms in the field of asylum and migration which are then used, for example, in the formulation of queries and undertaking of studies according to common specifications by the EMN NCPs" (European Migration Network 2010, 5). The glossary will also support the development of the EMN thesaurus and facilitate document searches on the EMN's Information Exchange System, which is an EU-wide clearinghouse for national migration policy documents. The EMN described the problem of heterogeneity that they confront:

> As the EMN is shaped through both a multinational environment and the multidisciplinary background of the complex field of migration and asylum, definitional and interpretative differences of certain terms are encountered, depending on various linguistic contexts and different approaches (politics, law, sociology) in which the terms are used. Because of the lack of universally accepted definitions, different groups of interest and bodies (e.g., governments, police and border authorities, governmental and non-governmental organizations) tend to use their own definitions, according to their perspective. To further complicate matters, there are not only within the same Member State different approaches followed, but also the usage of migration terms varies between Member States. (5)

The Glossary and Thesaurus Working Group prioritized its definitions to suit a hierarchy of policy needs, beginning with words and phrases that facilitate the harmonization of migration-related law and policy among member states (5–6). Top priority was thus given to key terms in EU directives, regulations, and decisions and then to terms in EC communications, as all member states are obliged to honor them. Second priority was given to terms used by various EU agencies such as Eurostat, Frontex, the Fundamental Rights Agency, EUROJUST, and EUROPOL, as these facilitate intergovernmental cooperation. Third priority was given to those in European and international conventions, treaties, and protocols on, for example, smuggling and trafficking. Finally, the glossary includes terms from other glossaries, written by the International Labour Organization (ILO), IOM, Organisation for Economic Co-operation and Development (OECD), and UNHCR. The group's initial task was to translate the relevant legal definitions from the Acquis. These definitions mostly pertained to asylum, refugees, illegal migration, and return. Negative sanctions against migrants thus dominate EU law, though the EMN has future plans to add migration terms pertaining to integration and the economy (6).

Of course, not all English or French terms have an exact analogue in other European languages. The group's solution was to focus on terms already present in EU-level policy, or as explained in the glossary, "one consideration in the discussion and development of terms was for them to be of practical use at EU level, meaning that whilst the definition of the term might not reflect exactly that at the national level, nevertheless it was sufficient to give at least the same broad meaning" (European Migration Network 2010, 5). The appearance of the word "development" in this passage is crucial because the glossary does not merely organize current terminology in use across the union. Rather, it actively shapes language by standardizing terminology (and thus narrowing its existing range of meanings) for the sake of unifying migration policy outlooks among officials in the twenty-seven member states. The adjective "broad" to describe meaning is deceptive, as it effectively means "practical" from the standpoint of EU cooperation. If national meanings are not practical (or in other words, if they are idiosyncratic), then they are more likely to fall out of usage altogether.

The hyperlinks to the sources of the English definitions further suggest the impracticality of exclusively national terms. Many terms derive from usages in the documents of the EU and other international organizations. The online version of the glossary allows the reader to connect instantly to, for example, the origin of the term "resident document," which is in Council Regulation (EC) 343/2003 (European Migration Network, 231); or the origin of "Country of Transit," which is in the IOM *Glossary on Migration*. Thus, the reader can see how the entire range of migration policy vocabulary is sewn into a myriad of other legal and policy documents, which themselves draw on each other for their terminologies and implicit epistemologies. Per Said's (1979, 20) strategic formation, the mere self-referentiality in this sea of documents establishes a hegemonic discourse of migration that enables a migration policy language. As Ewald (1991a, 154) puts it, this "rigorous principle of self-referentiality . . . [provides] . . . no recourse to any kind of external reference point." Therefore, a standpoint from which to critique it is difficult to find. The glossary also helps to import certain terms into national lexicons that did not exist there previously. The official representing Estonia's NCP explained that

> Asylum terms were difficult because Estonia has very little experience in the asylum field, for example words like "refugee in orbit," "refugee in transit," "asylum shopping." For "refugee in orbit" and "refugee in transit" we didn't find any Estonian equivalents. These terms are used (if used) in English or by explaining their [literal] meaning. For "asylum shopping" our language experts came up with a new Estonian equivalent, "*varjupaigaostlemine*." We tried to use as much as possible Estonian words, even though in spoken language we use "shopping."

Creating an apparatus, however, involves not only the standardization of a common policy outlook, which the glossary exemplifies, but also ad hoc, informal communication channels that policy actors can mobilize. Regarding the latter, an official from one east European national contact point explained:

> In my opinion it is good that we have different NCPs in EMN, so for example in asylum matters we can consult with IOM Austria [the Austrian NCP] . . . to improve [our country's] migration statistics. We already had meetings with Statistics Sweden [Swedish NCP] . . . about [the] return of Soviet-era migrants. We can exchange experience with [the] Latvian NCP, etc.

These networks, which often form on an ad hoc basis, rely on multiple forms of instant communication such as e-mail, tweets, and text messaging, which allow technocrats to move more nimbly (and for the same purposes) than the bureaucracies they serve. When acting on their own impulses rather than their bosses' demands, these disparate policy actors create a sense of organic, if short-lived, community aimed at a higher purpose in line with the apparatus itself. (They exemplify the concept of "nonce bureaucrat" described further in Chapter 4.) Divided into national agencies, then, this approach to harmonization allows policy actors to integrate national systems of border patrolling, biometric surveillance, asylum claims processing, and so on much more efficiently than would a central order emanating from Brussels. Centralized command fails to account for the nuanced differences found at the national and local levels that obstruct integration.

Still, informal networks might need coaxing along so that people feel comfortable with each other outside formalized professional venues. To that end, the EMN desk officer always organizes evening dinners at restaurants in the Brussels old town for the NCPs, so as to build community sentiment among them. After a lengthy two-day meeting the EMN organized a party, which the author was privileged to attend, where the national representatives shared their country's leading liqueur. Such events aim to establish continuity within a policy network that would be precluded within mediated communication channels. However, we should remain cautious about the emancipatory or transformative potential of the proverbial network (Riles 2000, 173–74). The informal networking requires a standard policy understanding, outlook, and language as well as some formalized occasions for face-to-face meetings, all of which helps to coordinate the activities of an otherwise unconnected set of experts.

THE I-MAP

This process of standardizing modes of knowledge pertains to visual representation as well as written language. At EMPO, a rising migration policy star with postgraduate education in law and business crime manages a small, industrious, and young team to develop an online, interactive map as part of his responsibilities at the Mediterranean Managed Migration Project (3MP). This I-Map, as it is called, works as an online clearinghouse of migration information about Europe, the Middle East, and North Africa. The program manager explained that the I-Map

> provides you with the latest figures of apprehension, smuggling networks, etc. It can provide briefing notes. If countries use the I-Map for policy positions, then this helps in creating agreements between countries. It will probably bring the positions of the countries much closer. . . . It's a tool at the service of states. We are here to sell the service.

The notion of service features prominently in the migration apparatus as it allows for a certain adaptability in the larger flow of events. Those selling the service do not see themselves imposing a way of knowing but only coordinating it among unconnected policy actors. The program manager's colleague noted that "[Service providing] is clearly our role. We have no choice. We are embedded in certain forces. Migration is too complex to have a clear-cut point of view. Organizations that have a clear-cut policy will fail. A service provider is a communicator." (His service orientation matches that of the chair of the European Biometrics Group described in Chapter 5.) The I-Map grew out of 3MP discussions that facilitate dialogue between European and Arabic nation-states on migration management, mostly as it pertains to security matters. It is intended to expedite communication, the patterns and priorities of which are buried in its deeper rationales. EUROPOL and Frontex are cosponsors of the dialogue along with the UNHCR. Furthermore, INTERPOL, the United Nations Office on Drugs and Crime (UNODC), and the Odysseus Academic Network (an EU-funded academic consortium focusing on policy-relevant current events) specifically participate on the I-Map to check the accuracy of uploaded information.

The program manager, a French master's graduate in international relations from a prestigious European university, laboriously designed the visual interface. Another project officer, who was completing a doctorate in migration studies, drafted questionnaires to be sent to thirty-seven European and

Arabic partner states and international organizations to receive input for developing common migration policy guidelines. Representatives in the corresponding offices are given restricted access to upload information about the migration situation in their own countries and to retrieve such information about other countries. The EC as well as the governments of Cyprus, Switzerland, France, Italy, the Netherlands, Malta, and Sweden fund the I-Map's production. It is designed for analysts, law enforcement officers, border officials, and decision makers.

The restricted version of the I-Map features a wide range of information including migration statistics for participating member states, detention policies, migration-related laws, migration-related development programs, border security policies, airport information, and regional and local migration-related information. The publicly accessible version of I-Map geographically covers countries from North, West, and East Africa, the Middle East, and the EU, and plans are in place to provide data for Eurasia and southeast Europe as well. It portrays the oceans in deep blue and the continents in green with individual countries in black outline. The navigation bar allows the viewer to move in the four cardinal directions. As the viewer zooms in, features such as cities and towns appear. Hover the mouse on top of them and a caption full of information appears, noting, for example, that the distance from Accra to the Canary Islands is over 4,000 kilometers by sea and 3,000 if first traveling directly over land. Scroll over the lines illuminating clandestine migration routes and the entire group of associated routes flashes in bright gold. The I-Map identifies groups such as the Central Mediterranean Route, West African Route, East Mediterranean Route, and so on. Individual routes are coded according to their mode of travel: heavy black lines for major land routes, black lines for major connecting land routes, dashed black lines for minor connecting land routes, white for sea routes, dotted white for maritime routes, dashed white for minor maritime routes, dotted yellow for ferry routes, and dashed yellow lines for major air routes.

The I-Map also features four zones to show how route groups converge at certain entry points into the EU: West Africa routes to the Canary Islands; West Mediterranean routes, including points from Morocco and Algeria to the Spanish mainland and Ceuta and Melilla; Central Mediterranean routes from Libya to Italy and Malta; and East Mediterranean routes from points in the Middle East to the EU through Turkey and southeastern Europe. The viewer enjoys a god's-eye view of the African land mass and the expanses of the Mediterranean

Sea and a sense of mastery over clandestine movements. The people and the nation-states they traverse are knowable, understandable, and thus manageable at least in conceptual terms. They are simplified and neatly packaged in easy-to-understand graphic form with bite-size pieces of essential information about where migrants are going, how far they travel, the methods they use to get there, immigration and border policies of the countries they traverse, and so on. One border official's joke seemed apposite when he referred to the I-Map as the "crystal ball."

At a summit meeting of the 3MP participants, the I-Map programme manager gave a spirited presentation of the I-Map when it was still in its early phases. He spoke to the delegates, who speak English, French, and/or Arabic to varying degrees of fluency, seated around a large, open square table with small national flags of each of their countries stationed neatly by their right hands. Four translators tucked away in booths in a corner of the room interpreted his remarks into Arabic, French, and English. He emphasized the need for information exchange in all high-level processes as the path to common understanding and as a basis for cooperation. He then explained that the I-Map had been advancing in three phases beginning with its graphic development followed by the uploading of initial content and the support of financial contributions from "end users" (participating states). He explained that future information-gathering activities could draw from field missions to strategic migration points, information-gathering meetings, and expedited communication among partner states. He then showed the I-Map on a large video screen to the delegates, who expressed considerable interest, particularly those located on the EU's southern external border. One of the delegates enthusiastically expressed to his colleagues that the I-Map "will provide a platform for bringing us together . . . beyond the technological aspects." One national delegate was particularly candid in explaining her country's interests in its applications for intelligence analysis. Another west European delegate asked how partner states could use it while avoiding a negative police-state image and promoting legal migration. To this point, the EMPO director-general remarked defensively:

> [Our position] is absolutely clear. We are engaged in visualizing the information for those who use this I-Map. We want to be close to the user side. This is the way to make sure the information is useful. . . . I think it's very much in its development phase for Working Group I [focusing on security]. We all recognize that Working Group II [focusing on economic development] is important. It's

for us absolutely clear that we should accommodate this need for visualization. . . . It would be an excellent occasion to keep a balanced approach, not only on migration management, its security, but with other parts of migration management [development]. It would be a balanced approach, which is in the interest of all participating states. We welcome the invitation from our . . . colleagues to learn more.

The director-general's remarks reflect the replacement of verbal with visual communication and the subordination of economy to security.

Tools like the I-Map encourage officials, who rarely engage each other directly, to literally see the world of migration through the same visual representations, the same types of factoids, and the same overall lens. This standardization requires little face-to-face contact because the common outlook required to sustain this policy community is maintained online in the form of devices like the I-Map.

HARMONIZING POLICY GUIDELINES

While the above example shows the decentralized character of standardizing discussions in a singular migration policy domain (border control), the following example shows more fully the convergence of different domains through language standardization and meeting rituals. The I-Map grew out of 3MP, which develops nonbinding common migration management guidelines between governments from North African countries (the Arab partner states, or APS) and European countries (the European partner states, or EPS). It began as a trust-building exercise in 2002 between the two sets of partner states to help identify common priorities for migration management. One European 3MP official explained: "You need to show you are reliable, that you are listening to their concerns. . . . With Arabs, they need to know where you are from. The personal side is important. They need to trust you. EMPO was not known in the Mediterranean, but communication is now set." Though a pattern of communication is established, it may not be on the terms that Arab partner states prefer. They expressed their priority for a cooperative relationship in the concluding report of a May 2004 meeting (European Migration Policy Organization 2004): "The suffering of the countries on the southern and eastern shores of the Mediterranean from the illegal migration as transit countries and as countries of temporary illegal residence represents the same suffering as that of the European States as countries of destination."

This thinly veiled effort to equate the APS' problems of illegal migration with those of the EPS did not succeed. The two priorities that emerged in the project's early stages were, predictably, the strengthening of measures to fight illegal migration (delegated to Working Group I) and long-term efforts to tackle the migration problem at its roots through economic development (delegated to Working Group II). To the chagrin of APS delegates, 3MP ended up strongly favoring the former over the latter. APS frame trans-Mediterranean migration primarily as an economic issue, while the EPS frame it as a security issue. Animosity pervaded early meetings, with APS charges of colonialism against the European partner states. APS delegates often argued that "We are simply solving Europe's migration problem for them." Nevertheless, a retired, veteran UNHCR official from Lebanon played an instrumental role in convincing many APS delegates to stick with the project, to make their contributions where they could, and to persuade EPS delegates to at least agree to return to outstanding APS concerns at a later date. From that point, APS officials began bringing initiatives agreeable to their EPS counterparts, and one APS official was even rumoured to have been demoted by his government for baldly asserting at a 2007 meeting that "the position of European countries is to forget why people migrate: economic. . . . It is a form of colonialism and looting of Africa's richness." In this newly standardized dialogue EPS delegates described the more cooperative among their APS counterparts as "pragmatic." Working Group I could now focus on its four priority areas: reception and detention of illegal immigrants; return and readmission of illegal immigrants; antitrafficking and antismuggling; and border management. A potentially undermining position fell away, allowing the 3MP to continue on common (but not necessarily equal) security-conscious ground.

Hidden factors in the structural relationship between the EPS and APS also evoke the latter's acquiescence. Since most EPS partners are also EU member states, they know that the EC negotiates "mobility partnerships" with "third countries" along its southern maritime border and eastern land border (see Chapter 6). These deals make development aid and more favorable immigration quotas contingent on the third country's agreement to strengthen its border control practices (often with EU support) and to accept the illegal migrants held in EU member states' detention facilities. As one IGO official explained, "The EU approach to border management doesn't apply to [places like] Libya, Kenya, or Ethiopia; thousands of kilometers of borders, people, tribes, pastoral people move between countries all the time." The 3MP team can adopt a softer tone and ultimately expect APS cooperation in developing common migration management guidelines because they know that the EC exerts great leverage to gain third-country compliance on these measures. As a result, the EU's structural advantage over the APS does not need to be called attention to in 3MP discussions.

Among other tasks, the EMPO secretariat collates the preferences and priorities of participating states as these pertain to the 3MP's four priority areas in order to develop common migration policy guidelines. This involves much electronic communication with representatives in the thirty-three states participating in the project. The 3MP staff, in consultation with their Frontex and EUROPOL liaisons, devise discussion points and guiding questions to format the project's two- or three-day meetings. The project officer handles the laborious task of assembling the varied input from participating states into written form. The program manager strategizes with contacts in the participating states on how to develop converging policy positions between the APS and EPS. An ordinary working day stretches from 9:00 A.M. to 6:30 P.M. Several staff talked of staying until 10:00 P.M. during peak times, while a few even worked past the midnight hour.

The EMPO staff's work routines are fairly uneventful, though the demands on their time are high: revise this draft of a concluding statement; contact that official to clarify his comment on x; see which direction a more senior staff member wants to take on a particular item of discussion. Much of this occurs in front of a computer terminal. Yet the written word is vital in harmonizing a common policy outlook among numerous nation-states. For example, one post-meeting questionnaire asked: "What national, regional and/or international legislations best address smuggling and trafficking and in which way?"; "Have previous investigation [sic] failed or yielded fewer results because of the lack of joint initiatives?"; "How did your country learn from these failures?"; "How would you describe the efficiency of 'minimum standards' in the actual 'on the ground' management of detention centres?"; "How do you efficiently organize different migrant groups into different centres?"; or "How do you implement social care for vulnerable groups in (a) reception centres and (b) detention centres?" Though delegates routinely describe these questions as technical matters, they limit the range of discussion and standardize the type of knowledge produced, thus institutionalizing the issue's political parameters.

In 2007 and 2008, 3MP held five meetings of the full delegation of EPS, APS, and the other contributing agencies, which were dedicated to the four priority areas, plus a concluding meeting. The locations of such meetings rotate according to the conference theme. For example, the meeting on combating human trafficking and smuggling took place in EUROPOL Headquarters in The Hague. Each meeting is cochaired by delegates from one European and one Arab partner state. The cochairs routinely thank the hosts "for making it possible to bring us together here in [city name]." Particular sessions feature a preselected delegate presenting on how his or her own government deals with, for example, the reception and detention of illegal immigrants. The subsequent discussion period occasionally draws questions from other delegates interested in the comparison with their own government's practices. Hosts, chairs, and delegates thank one another for stimulating interventions.

During the 3MP meetings, the project officer endures three grueling days of taking notes and preparing drafts of the meeting's concluding statement. Much of her work occurs in the dead of night. I arrived one morning at 6:30 for breakfast at the meeting hotel only to find her exiting the dining room to catch two hours of sleep before things began. At the intense last session, the cochairs proceed through the typically three-page draft one line at a time while the delegates announce their suggestions for alternative phrasing. The project officer inputs many of the changes on the spot: one delegate requests the deletion of the word "official" as an adjective describing the meeting's summary points; two others debate whether "informal" should be used to describe the project; another delegate requests that "fighting human trafficking" be included. These tedious and dry discussions result in a set of conclusions that APS and EPS officials find mutually agreeable.

At the end of The Hague meeting, the current hosts handed over a brown teddy bear wearing a EUROPOL T-shirt to the hosts of the next meeting. The EUROPOL liaison explained that ever since an April 2006 meeting delegates have passed the teddy bear on from one host to the next so as to establish a tangible connection among the delegates. The host and cochairs of the next meeting will likely announce that they are "looking forward to working with our partners from [country name] and to having a productive meeting." The next several weeks will find the EMPO team busily finalizing the meeting's conclusions, then e-mailing or faxing them back to the participating states for approval. The process moves slowly since the delegates will show them to their superiors, who themselves are inundated with work. To solicit further feedback the team has also created a secure website on which it posts questionnaires about the meetings' substantive discussions, technical format, and logistical arrangements. The meeting's final recommendations are translated into English, French, and Arabic. While there is still no legal requirement to adopt the migration management guidelines that all partners have approved, the work of the 3MP illustrates how a framework of understanding emerges between EPS and APS with which to define migration as a security problem and solve it accordingly.

The work of 3MP staff shows how banal office routines help to generate a common policy outlook. This convergence is not observable in the staff's mundane practices per se, which largely amount to drafting documents at computers, communicating through e-mail, and attending meetings. Rather, it lies in the agreed-upon set of lenses through which they collectively look, so to speak, at the migration situation "on the ground." This perspective, in turn, delimits the range of acceptable policy options for questions such as: Who is allowed to enter a country and on what conditions? Which measures should be deployed to thwart illegal migratory flows? and, How can the migrant's potential be channelled into productive economic activity? Convergence involves learning how notions of "public order"—motivated by an implicit notion of the "crisis" of mixed migration flows—delimit the range of acceptable interpretations of social reality as a particular policy problem; for example, What is the risk posed by the EU's aging workforce? What is threatening about uncontrolled migration? and What are the causes of illegal migratory flows?

The meetings ossify a communication pattern: radical views are marginalized; processes get institutionalized; and rituals take on affective powers. The numerous discussions, the production of draft guidelines, and the subsequent meetings replete with their routinized opening and closing statements have the effect of framing key migration issues. A reduced vocabulary and a stock-in-trade phraseology of "problem" and "solution" normalize power-knowledge practices commanded by an array of technocrats from governments and international organizations. The face-to-face rituals—from meeting protocols and procedures to the exchanging of the teddy bear—help to standardize communication, which continues with much greater force through e-mail, faxes, websites, and other forms of mediated communication.

THE WORK OF KNOWLEDGE

Knowledge practices expedite public administration by simplifying the enormous complexity that the contingencies of the wider world inevitably deliver. The techniques of simplification can then be applied to new migration problems as they arise and even new policy domains, allowing new policy players to reproduce and proliferate the apparatus. It is important to recognize that knowledge practices do not apply only to writing practices or formal mathematical analyses (as described in Chapter 4) but to visual representations that condition how a policy official casually looks at a map. Such knowledge practices become ubiquitous as they are unbound by local constraints or particular social networks and instantly available to anyone with an Internet connection. They circulate virtually and can be applied to any particular location in which policy officials converge or happen to be doing their work. As such, they can standardize and integrate frameworks of meaning that are not tied to place but rather extend virtually across space. These templates are tools for creating, understanding, regulating, and normalizing a world "out there." However, their effects are not merely conceptual as they enable legal codes, public opinions, and a material infrastructure that collectively channel and encourage cross-border human movements in particular ways. The next chapter links the practice of risk assessment to the wave of external border control practices that have unfolded over the last several years.

4 BORDER CONTROL
The New Meaning of Containment

*We [the USA] have 50 percent of the world's wealth but only 6.3 percent of
its population. In this situation, our real job in the coming period . . . is to
maintain this position of disparity. To do so, we have to dispense with all
sentimentality . . . we should cease thinking about human rights, the raising of
living standards and democratisation.*

George Kennan cited in Pilger 2002, 98

THE GLOBAL IN LOCAL MIGRATION DECISIONS

George Kennan, the American diplomat who designed the Cold War containment
strategy, penned these words in 1948. Slavoj Žižek argues that Kennan's candid
remark reflects a "simple awareness that the present model of late capitalist prosperity *cannot be universalized*" (2002, 149, italics original). In the post–Cold War
era, the containment strategy shifts from its original purpose of deterring Soviet-
inspired revolutionary movements in Europe (and elsewhere) to deterring the
movement of migrants into Europe (and elsewhere). Structural economics plays
a prominent role in the new "problem" of containment. The *Financial Times* reports that today the richest 2 percent of the world's population own 50 percent
of the world's wealth, while the poorest 50 percent of the world's population own
less than 2 percent of the world's wealth (Giles 2006, 8). This degree of difference exceeds that in Kennan's Cold War days, but his remark distills the logic
behind contemporary border control practices with respect to the North's global
position of disparity: use negative measures to contain the threat of unwanted
migration that structural economic inequality generates rather than rectify that
inequality. However, unlike the Cold War era, security as a spatial problem is not
a matter of maintaining highly charged borders between antagonistic blocs of
space. Rather, it is about expanding the uniform space of neoliberal capitalism to
expedite the flow of commodities and finance, on the one hand, while condition-
ing the circulation of peoples within that space, on the other.

This chapter focuses on EU efforts to harmonize border control practices
in order to keep unwanted migrants in the global South. These practices attempt to manage migration as a mass phenomenon while biometric informa-

tion systems regulate travelers as hyperindividualized entities (Chapter 5). This chapter describes a wide range of Frontex-led initiatives that integrate national infrastructures for the sake of generating a pervasive surveillance capacity with enormous geographic scope. Some examples include the merging of research and analytical practices among member states, remote maritime monitoring systems, coordinated sea patrols to push back illegal migrants, and rapid response teams to stop acute breaches at the external border. This integration also allows (and requires) dispersed officials to communicate quickly, informally, and outside established bureaucratic channels as shown in other migration policy domains as well. The chapter concludes by exploring how the EU's emerging border control apparatus interfaces with migrants, how migrants experience it, and how government officials, border control experts, and industry executives rationalize it.

This chapter also explains how the particular devices that fuse an apparatus together apply to the policy domain of external border control. Risk assessment and the identification of "crisis" play a critical role in justifying the integration of national systems as a positive humanitarian effort as opposed to a negative police effort. However, the tight integration of material systems, which establishes a dense, tangible network between EU member states, succeeds and even depends on indirect, ephemeral, and informal connections between policy officials. This arrangement needs a central EU agency only to coordinate (not direct) communication among member states so that coherence is achieved through the usage of shared policy outlooks. The role of the center here is to help crystallize that outlook and to provide logistical assistance for joint efforts at the national and local levels. The chapter focuses mainly on the laboriously named European Agency for the Management of Operational Cooperation at the External Borders of the Member States of the European Union. In French this agency's name is simplified to Frontières extérieures and is commonly known as Frontex. Žižek notes the "ominous decision of the European Union [which] passed almost unnoticed: the plan to establish an all-European border police force to secure the isolation of the Union territory and thus prevent the influx of immigrants" (2002, 149). He argues that this development takes racism to an even more brutal form of reasoning that is based neither on naturalism (the West as the best) nor culturalism (the West must also preserve its cultural identity) but rather on "unabashed economic egotism" in which the fundamental divide is between those in the sphere of prosperity and those excluded from it (149).

In that context, the local decision to undertake a clandestine border crossing is invariably bound up with global capitalism. In Senegal, for example, the fishing industry suffered a devastating blow as a result of seventeen agreements with the EU. These agreements gave the EU the right to fish in Senegalese waters while setting tight quotas on Senegalese exports back to its markets. The 2002–2006 agreement guaranteed Senegal $15 million in annual compensation for the loss, but negotiations for the next agreement failed over protests that the local industry incurred far too much damage. The resulting economic difficulties contributed to an increase in attempted illegal entries into the EU (Ndiaye 2007, 9). The fisherman-turned-migrant now confronts a harmonized EU border security apparatus that props up the global imbalances triggering his journey in the first place. In the following synopsis selections from a documentary released by Journeyman Pictures (*Spain—Out of Africa* 2007) show the competing moral economies between West African illegal migrants and EU and Spanish immigration policy:

The journey that dozens of African migrants undertook lasted six days and covered 1,400 kilometers in the open Atlantic Ocean. One Red Cross worker estimates that 40 percent of the *cayucos* (long narrow boats) are lost during such an attempt. When the ship is brought to dock, the migrants are taken off by aid workers wearing facemasks and synthetic gloves while the boat itself is emptied of its contents and then destroyed. In a tent, the migrants are given food and drink. Thierry, a Red Cross medic, establishes rapport by letting himself fall backwards into the crowd of seated men so that they put up their arms to stop his crash onto the ground. The crowd responds enthusiastically to it, but more than building relations, he is checking the migrants' strength after the arduous journey. The medic then pulls one up by the arm and helps him out of the tent to a makeshift clinic. All migrants are being checked for dehydration, sunburn, sickness, and wounds. Meanwhile, other aid workers identify those under eighteen and place tape around their upper arms with their birthdates written on it. They will automatically become wards of the state and cannot be sent back home against their will. The head of the Red Cross emergency response team, who has unloaded two hundred *cayucos*, says "They've spent several days on the high seas in cold temperatures, rough seas, darkness and silence, and when they land they get the feeling that they've made it, that it's over. It's very stressful."

The next stage of their journey ends in a detention center where they are interviewed and their cases processed. In Spain, the authorities can hold them for up to forty days. If within that time, their nationality is established, they can be returned to their home countries. If not, they are released into the host country. Most migrants, therefore, do not bring documentation with them lest that be used to facilitate their return. The narrator explains that while it is easy to see the migrants arrive, seeing what happens to them next is much more difficult. He was not able to approach the police station where they were taken or the makeshift tents next to it where 1,500 are waiting for their interviews. After three days they are taken to detention camps out of public view and often in buildings originally constructed for other purposes, such as an abandoned restaurant.

The Harbor Master explains that many people on the Canary Islands are worried that their small territory cannot absorb all these migrants—twenty-five thousand have arrived this year already. He well understands the economic situation causing the migrants to take the dangerous trip by the tens of thousands. "For the last two years, Senegal has been in a serious economic crisis," he explains. "They used to have a strong, reasonably well managed fishing industry, but prices have dropped drastically and the whole fishing sector along the coast of Senegal was thrown into serious crisis."

Back in Senegal, the narrator finds a local fisherman, Pape, to explain how the illegal business of transporting migrants works. Pape says that it is simple. He must only wait until he has the names of enough people to fill his fishing boat. When the number is high enough for the trip to be profitable, he arranges a departure time and place. The Senegalese coast now attracts migrants from West and Central Africa, many of whom have never seen the ocean. Pape explains, "those who come from the bush. . . . Many lost their lives at sea. On the whole, those who died were people . . . who took a boat for the first time."

The story of Okale Saha illustrates how such a migration decision is much more than an economic matter. Okale, a young Senegalese man, vows to enter the EU again after Spain returned him from the Canary Islands. From him, we learn the psychological damage and the social cost caused by his inability to reach Europe and enhance his family's living standard through remittances. One week after being returned from the Canary Islands, he says,

> I've missed my big chance. I'm ashamed to face my family. I can't even tell you how bad I feel. I feel shame. . . . In front of my family, my father. My father is an old man. My mother is a very brave woman, very courageous. They sold everything to help the family. That's why I wanted to go to Spain. Here in Senegal, young people have no future. . . . There's no work for the young. That's why.

One local, older fisherman laments, "We've lost more than two hundred in our village. It's because life in the village is very hard." His own brother died on a boat trying to reach the Canary Islands; the body was simply dumped into the ocean. The high death rate of Senegalese is a mainstream theme of public culture represented in murals and hip-hop music that dramatize the economic degradation, personal despair, and the effects of the life-risking journey on migrants and their families. One women's association based in a single Senegalese fishing village consists of 375 members who have all lost a husband or son on the illegal migratory journey. Lured to Europe with wages fifty times greater than those in Senegal, they fatally decided to take the risk. The women have banded together to make up for the lost household labor by producing and selling couscous.

The documentary concludes by shifting the scene from fishing boats on the beach to an IOM office in Senegal. Laurent de Boeck, IOM's spokesman for West and Central Africa, is given the final statement: "If the word spreads all Western Africa or Central Africa . . . that they can all go to Spain . . . Canary Islands . . . or whatever, you may empty Africa easily. So, that's dangerous. So, you also have to think about emptying a country of its youth, which should be the future of a country."

This documentary captures well the ambivalent position of these African migrants in the European imagination. They are a faceless mass to be repelled, even if one personally sympathizes with them. People are worried, the harbor master explains, that they cannot absorb so many alien people on a collection of tiny islands. Thierry, the Red Cross medic, means well as he tries to establish rapport with the recent arrivals, yet he ultimately supports their likely return to poverty. European officials' structural location in the global economy diminishes any effort they might make to establish direct, personal connections with the migrants. The apparatus imposes the indirect conditions of engagement mediated through laws, medical tests, identification checks, and policy prescriptions that help to process migrants as faceless cases. The IOM official, to whom the documentary gives the final word, synopsizes the European voice by reconciling neoliberal and neo-nationalist agendas. He speaks with a blend of humanitarian concern about formerly colonized people and—the familiar paranoia about masses of dark-skinned people being emptied into Europe. He deploys this neo-nationalist nightmare scenario, which might prompt neo-liberals to respond with a greater commitment to development so that African youth remain to build their countries' futures. Otherwise, attempts to illegally enter the EU will continue to be managed through enhanced and integrated border security practices.

To justify the apparatus in humanitarian terms, EU officials speak fluently in the language of human rights with regular references to fair treatment, due process, and personal dignity. Emphasizing the isolated individual allows the structural inequality behind the matter to remain obscure. This move succeeds only if EU officials treat migration as an *objective* threat or a problem that arrives on their shores independent of any systemic political and economic relations between the EU and the wider world. This radical separation of the threat and the threatened allows for the security apparatus to present itself as being called into existence for the sake of selfless acts of mercy and good (Hardt and Negri 2000, 15). Those acts may protect EU citizens from the migrant's unwanted arrival, or protect illegal migrants themselves from their perilous journeys. Regarding the latter, one Frontex official suggested that there is a need for European intervention in the open seas to protect migrants from dangerous smugglers. He explained that "some people are thrown overboard because others think they are witches and do voodoo. The more we can get people back to shore, the more lives we save, the better. . . . The smugglers can be murderers." While lives may be saved, these border practices have the effect of restricting the circulation of bodies and sustaining a gross imbalance of power that, according to George Kennan's logic, should not be rectified if that imbalance is to remain in one's favor. Border control, then, becomes a major security practice because an increase in redundant labor from the South, it is feared, would jeopardize the EU's internal social-cum-national order.

MASTERING SPACE AND THE REPURPOSING
OF SURVEILLANCE INFRASTRUCTURES

EMPO, and specifically its 3MP initiative, illustrates how migration policy convergence is achieved in the form of text. Common border control, of course, also requires convergence of a material infrastructure to detect and deter unwanted crossings. This process involves the repurposing of existing military infrastructures, among others, to focus surveillance on the circulation of human-objects in the EU's extraterritorial space. Frontex is the EU agency responsible for this task. At the December 2001 meeting in Laeken, the European Council sounded the alarm about acute legal and humanitarian situations and concluded that the member states should "manage better the Union's external border controls so as to combat more effectively terrorism, illegal immigration and human trafficking." It also for the first time called for:

> The most wide-ranging definition of "security of external borders," with the exception of military defence. It thus calls on Member States also to take into consideration at external borders the magnitude of crime, terrorism, crimes against children, arms trafficking, corruption and fraud in accordance with Article 29 of the European Union Treaty. (SCADPlus 2004)

To sharpen border control measures in light of this broadly defined security threat, the council at Laeken called for "an 'External Border Practitioners' Common Unit' [that] will be responsible for carrying out risk analysis, coordinating operation projects on the ground and devising a common strategy for coordinating national policies. In addition, a power of inspection can be conferred on it in crisis situations" (SCADPlus 2004). Frontex takes up these tasks not by building a border control infrastructure from scratch but rather by drawing on a plethora of existing systems whose adaptation and mutual integration achieve the result much more easily. These agencies include EUROPOL, the European Union Satellite Centre (EUSC), the European Defence Agency (EDA), the European Maritime Safety Agency (EMSA), the European Space Agency (ESA), and the European Centre for Disease Control (ECDC). These diverse agencies' collective input signifies an effort of total surveillance of the external border, the member states' territorial waters, the open seas, the territorial waters of migrant departure countries, and the biological health of any migrants apprehended on their journey. Though Frontex focuses on illegal migrant border crossings, the full suite of organizations guards against the unwanted entries of commodities, animals, and plant material (Frontex 2009, 8).

No specific master plan exists to coordinate the activities of Frontex and its affiliates. Rather, various strategies are drawn up to guide individual cooperative ventures with the relevant government, agency, or organization. Frontex calls this strategy the "'network' approach" (16). The overall guidelines are found in what the EU now calls "integrated border management" (IBM), which was first outlined during the 2006 Finnish EU presidency at the Justice and Home Affairs (JHA) ministerial meeting. In December of the same year, the JHA council identified IBM's five areas of emphasis, from which more specific cooperative practices are drawn: (1) border control; (2) fighting cross-border crime; (3) the four-tier/filter access control model (which involves cooperation with non-EU countries of migrant transit and origin); (4) interagency cooperation on border management; and (5) coordination at national and trans-national levels. The IBM concept is coupled with the EU's global approach to migration, which outlines a multidimensional approach to eliminate the economic causes of migration, to manage legal migration in the most orderly way possible, and to strengthen the union's external border. Border control and biometric measures top the list of priorities in this otherwise comprehensive view of the migration "problem." The network approach involves a curious mix of ever-tightening connections between nation-based material infrastructures and looser, fluid, and ephemeral links between actual policy officials.

The Arrival of the Unexpected

Frontex confronts the issue of global circulation and the insecurity it introduces when foreign elements enter into bounded, sovereign space. *Security* is a more complicated challenge than stabilizing internal social order through *discipline*. Disciplinary power, as Foucault (2007) reasons, works through a negative feedback mechanism to create homeostasis in a closed territory: the deviant is detained, quarantined, or restricted, and the requisite spatial control allows for medicalized, moralized, or legalized social technologies to induce the individual to internalize passive and productive norms. For Foucault, *security* confronts the unpredictable arrival of foreign elements onto sovereign territory, and so the spatial dimension of security is, unlike disciplinary power, open-ended (2007, 20). Security amounts to the management of indefinite series of mobile elements, be they carts, travelers, thieves, disease, tourists, migrants, and so on. Again, the subject of movement is reduced to an object of analysis. Given the fluid quality to the problem of security, analyses based on probabilities calculate the likelihood of an illegal entry actually occurring, and thus inform decisions as to the resources needed to minimize that potential security threat. If statistics is the science deployed to regulate the state's internal elements, then probability is the science with which the state tries to manage the arrival of unpredictable elements into the state's territory. Foucault illustrates the problem of security through the example of the eighteenth-century town at a time when mercantilism gave way to free trade. Towns opened their walls to trade routes to prompt economic growth but made themselves vulnerable to a whole host of undesirable objects. Foreshadowing the concern over undesirable circulations in the Schengen Area, city planners understood their new challenge in an open economy:

> And finally, an important problem for towns in the eighteenth century was allowing for surveillance, since the suppression of city walls made necessary by

economic development meant that one could no longer close towns in the evening or closely supervise daily comings and goings, so that the insecurity of the towns was increased by the influx of the floating population of beggars, vagrants, delinquents, criminals, thieves, murderers, and so on, who might come, as everyone knows from the country. . . . In other words, it was a matter of organizing circulation, eliminating its dangerous elements, making a division between good and bad circulation, and maximizing good circulation by diminishing the bad. (Foucault 2007, 18)

To plan for "good" rather than "bad" circulation (wanted versus unwanted in contemporary parlance) the state must try to designate the milieu in which circulation occurs. The milieu is much more than the "context," which implies an objective reality external to the sovereign state and the flows it encounters. Foucault defines the milieu as "what is needed to account for action at a distance of one body on another. The milieu is, therefore, the medium of an action and the element in which it circulates" (2007, 20–21). The medium refers to natural elements such as hills, rivers, and marshes and social elements such as housing, population concentrations, and urban layout. Defining the social character of the milieu is a policy practice made sensible through the dominant rationales of governance available to the policymaker—for a hill might be an asset or a liability depending on how the milieu is constructed. Therefore, the problems which the policymaker comes to identify in the milieu are inseparable from that individual's very act of identifying the milieu. The ensuing apparatus can evolve and adapt to changing circumstances, because security practices "try to plan a milieu in terms of events or series of events or possible elements, of series that will have to be regulated within a *multivalent* and *transformable* framework" (Foucault 2007, 20, emphasis added). In constructing the milieu—or field of policy intervention—migration officials mutually define the "order" and "crisis" with respect to border crossings (cf. Bauman 1991, 7; Butler 1990, 145; Feldman 2005c). They externalize "crisis" as an objective threat to the EU or to the migrants themselves, rather than locate the crisis in a system of relations to which they themselves belong.

Military in Form

Integrated border management requires a massive infrastructure to achieve its stated goals. Much of that infrastructure involves the retooling and integration of existing national security structures. The resulting expansion of border control capacity opens the EU to the charge that Frontex is simply building

"Fortress Europe," and not just from left-wing activists. One official who works in his own country's federal police said to me, "I think they are part of Fortress Europe. It's already in their name: Frontex, like frontier. It's a military term. I think of the joint operations in the Aegean Sea with their patrol boats" (Feldman, 2011). When I asked one veteran official working on refugee matters if Frontex was building "Fortress Europe," as many of its critics assert, he reasoned that "it's difficult to come to any other conclusion. There's something very authoritative about their name." He drew on an inverse comparison with China's emigration policy to illustrate the restrictive intention implied in the term "migration management":

> Something quite interesting: I went to China. We went to a detention facility for snakeheads [human smugglers] and people trying to leave illegally. A nice facility, but no one was there. They said that "our deterrence policy is so good" that we don't need to detain anyone. It was a Potemkin village. It had a sign that said "Strict Migration Management." That's what it's all about [everywhere including Europe].

Whether the aim is to prevent emigration or immigration, this official sees any state's effort to create an orderly migration process as an effort to slow it down and select desirable migrants as needed for particular purposes. As China enjoys empty emigrant detention facilities, the EU would surely embrace empty immigrant detention facilities, which is a main reason it is strengthening external border control.

In contrast, Frontex officials accept that their mission is military in form, but they stress their commitment to the liberal virtues of humanitarianism and legalism in all their practices, including their relations with third countries of dubious reputations. One official explained:

> We can't just isolate countries that violate human rights. We try to bring them into the fold and encourage them to modernize. Sometimes that improves things more than just ignoring them. It also means that we are not building a Fortress Europe. We are not building walls. We are establishing connections with transit countries.

Forging these connections is the larger ambition of the EU's European Neighbourhood Policy (ENP), which exists to "export the Acquis" to buffering countries so as to mold them in the EU's image (Kuus, in press 2011). It works by pushing agreements with third countries that will adopt EU standards on, in this case, migration management in exchange for more favorable terms on other issues under negotiation. In 2008 Frontex's management board mandated the director, Ilkka Laitinen, to negotiate arrangements in this way with Albania, Bosnia and Herzegovina, Montenegro, and Serbia as well as Croatia, Georgia, and Moldova (Frontex 2009, 17).

To push back harder against the Fortress Europe label, Frontex officials quickly make a distinction between today's border guards and military personnel who have filled that role in years past. These officials caricature the military border guard as a slow-witted throwback in order to present Frontex as a progressive, humanitarian organization. Overlooking Warsaw from Frontex Headquarters high up in a new skyscraper, one official mentioned, "A few years ago, it was usual to have conscripts. We got rid of this and put in professional border guards and officials. No military. It is not feasible that someone with a gun for twenty years would do it [work at a border crossing post]." His colleague stressed a technocratic dimension of border control work that the military was unfit to handle: "All border guards must comply with the Schengen Code. You need people who know the regulations, who know how to read documents. We want to make it easier for bona fide travelers to come in. This needs something other than a gun." However, fully recognizing the sheer scope and scale of securing the EU's external borders, the official explained the logistical task as follows: "We have a command and control center [for our operation]. This is where it looks like the military. . . . You need great coordination, but this is the only way it is like the military." "The equipment is the same, but the people are different. We are not soldiers," added his colleague. This phrase—"The equipment is the same, but the people are different"—presents the homologous logic between neoliberals and neo-nationalists described in Chapter 2. While the particular actors and events change in the play, the structure of the script of border control remains constant: if European nationalists used to guard borders to repel invading state armies, now European liberals guard borders to repel unwanted migrants.

The post–Cold War redeployment of things military to things managerial is further illustrated in the March 2006 testimony of Frontex executive director Ilkka Laitinen given to the UK House of Lords' Select Committee on the European Union (United Kingdom Parliament 2006). The committee was hearing testimonies from EC officials to determine how the UK's participation in common EU rules on detaining illegal immigrants might affect common border management practices. Lord Wright of Richmond, the committee chairman, eagerly greeted Laitinen, a brigadier general in the Finnish Border Patrol, because of his experience in managing its border with Russia:

> It is our great pleasure to welcome you as the first Director of Frontex. This is the first time our committee has had a meeting with Frontex. It is a particular pleasure to welcome, if I may say so, a Finnish Director of Frontex, although I know you regard yourself as an international and not as a Finn because I am told, and I have frequently been told, that Finland has a very high reputation indeed in the management of its external borders and, if I may say so, on historical terms you have had plenty of reason to do so.

Lord Richmond was no doubt referring to Finland's delicate border relations with the Soviet Union beginning with the 1940–41 Winter War and extending throughout the Cold War. His insinuation that the skills necessary to forestall a Soviet military invasion are directly transferable to the task of precluding an "invasion" of migrants reflects a common militarized metaphor for border control. Moreover, Lord Richmond's description of Laitinen as "international" reinforced the expectation that the new Frontex director place common EU needs ahead of Finland's own national needs, as is expected of any EC or EU agency official.

The militarized precedent for border control appears directly in the discussions on creating a common maritime border control service. Laitinen explained to the committee:

> Vice-President Frattini—he did it twice—called on Frontex to launch a feasibility study on creating a network of coastguards in the Mediterranean Area. . . . There are good references for systems like that. One has been in place in the Baltic Sea region since 1997. . . . It is a regional concept where all the coastal countries co-operate. There is a similar system in the Northern Pacific and the Black Sea regions. We do not have to reinvent the wheel [as we try] to adapt these systems to the Mediterranean area. (United Kingdom Parliament 2006, Q610)

The study Laitinen mentioned became the Mediterranean Coast Patrols Network (MEDSEA) study. The Baltic example grew out of joint operations between NATO and the republics of Estonia, Latvia, and Lithuania prior to their accession to the alliance. These operations were incorporated into the Baltic Sea Region Border Control Cooperation, with which Frontex continues its involvement (Carrera 2007, 19).

Harmonizing Risk Analysis

Frontex divides the analysis of the risk of illegal border crossings into two sectors: one supporting long-term planning and the other supporting short-term operations. The latter begins with an analysis of where a migration "threat" is most likely to occur—West Africa to the Canary Islands, Turkey onto the Greek islands, Ukraine into Poland—before designing the operation's planning, implementation, and evaluation phases. Those working in long-term analysis, as one Frontex risk analyst explained, "look at borders, methodological research, statistical analysis, Geographic Information Systems to determine trends, patterns, etc. so the Commission and Council can make policy decisions." Risk analysis determines the probability of an illegal border crossing. It should provide "actionable" information, which includes the legal conditions for any particular operations. The head of the sector for long-term planning holds a doctorate in social science and has a background in law enforcement. The sector for analysis supporting short-term operations utilizes long-term analysis of known illegal migration destinations in its specific assessments of which and how operations should be undertaken: "How to do it during the day or evening? What specialists are needed? Biometrics, technical experts, and technical equipment?" He continued, "We put all relevant information into a template and we are expanding into more statistical analyses to increase our knowledge with multivariate analyses." The Frontex Situation Centre was established in 2008 to augment this work on short-term operations (Frontex 2009, 18). Frontex is building a third sector to provide advanced geospatial analysis and photographic analysis.

Risk analysis in both sectors examines, among other factors, the routes, modi operandi, patterns of irregular movements, conditions of countries of transit, statistics of irregular flows, and so on (Carrera 2007, 14). However, if Frontex's task is to integrate the border control capabilities of EU member states, then harmonization of problem definition and problem analysis is essential. The relevant national ministries and agencies with which Frontex liaises must speak the same analytical language for harmonization to succeed. The conclusion of the 2002 Seville meeting of the European Council mandated the Common Integrated Risk Analysis Model (CIRAM) to attain "systematic evaluation of border control" (citied in Carrera 2007, 15). The Strategic Committee on Immigration, Frontiers, and Asylum with support of the head of national border control services took up the task. Finland hosted the project, which led to the 2003 creation of the Risk Analysis Centre that later became the Risk Analysis Unit (RAU). CIRAM utilizes six categories of analysis: (1) illegal border crossing points; (2) refusal of entry; (3) false documents; (4) facilitators of illegal migration; (5) illegal overstayers; and (6) "abuse" of asylum claims. These are further divided into threat assessments at air, sea, and land borders, all of which account for the findings in national-level risk assessments. Analysts acquire data: from questionnaires sent to member states about their challenges with illegal border crossing, from relevant EU institutions, from publicly available documents, and from EU member states' immigration liaison officers posted in third countries known to be transit or source countries of illegal migration. The European Council approved a regulation mandating the immigration liaison officers to collect information about illegal migration for "use either at the operational level, or at a strategic level, or both" (cited in Carrera 2007, 17). Critical information on illegal border crossing is uploaded and shared among Frontex and member states on the web-based Information and Coordination Network, or ICONet (17). To further facilitate communication and create more institutional memory, Frontex has now commissioned "Frontex intelligence support officers," or FISOs, who are stationed in national agencies of member states where border crossing threats are most likely, such as Italy, Spain, and Greece (Frontex 2009, 29–31). FISOs face the daunting challenge of amalgamating twenty-seven national reports on border management, numerous reports from international organizations, and a wide range of open-source reports from think tanks, research institutes, universities, and so on.

Member states agreed in 2007 to create EU-wide analytical standards to simplify the work of the RAU. That particular endeavor involves the establishment of a "transparent and clear methodology for Frontex risk analysis and to set the standards (benchmark) for Member States' analytical activities to create preconditions for efficient information exchange and cooperation in the field of border security" (Frontex 2006c). Frontex is also planning a glossary of border control terminology and possibly analytical guidelines for common terminology and methodology (ibid.). These measures aim to mitigate Frontex's twofold analytical problem. On the one hand, the RAU must merge together different types of analysis ranging from content and semantic analysis of countless confidential and open-source documents, to large-scale statistical analysis, to qualitative legal analysis that includes interviews with detained migrants. On the other, it must account for the different definitions that each report gives to its analytical categories.

The RAU also helps Frontex look into the future. One analyst explained that most current analyses draw on past data, "but we need to predict what might happen. We have new colleagues coming from Eurostat and the EUSC. They have statistical and analytical skills to try to lay out future scenarios. We also use law enforcement for hidden migration. We need indicators to catch them." Updated monthly, RAU allows the analyst to "see who has tried to enter and how many and what category [so we can] put pressure on a particular border stop." Ultimately, the purpose of risk analysis is to determine the chances of a breach of the EU's external border. As Frontex defines the milieu, so it aims to control it in order to minimize the unpredictable, unwanted circulation of migrants. One Frontex analyst explained the basic concepts at work:

> "Threat" as we define it is a combination of intention and capability. We look at criminals and who could generate an action that is harmful. This capability depends upon knowledge and the resources that are available. "Risk"—we add our own vulnerability to the threat. Are our borders secure enough? Do we have the boats, manpower, etc.? Risk and threat are put together. "Intention" is the willingness of the person/group to do harm. The "pre-frontier" picture: if they are gathered in a part of the city somehow, then you can evaluate the situation.

The prefrontier picture refers to the geographic space beyond the frontier, roughly identified as the space visible with advanced technology stationed on or near the EU's external border. From that vantage point, one sees the frontier, which is often the open sea. In the context of the Mediterranean Sea, the "prefrontier picture" specifically refers to the North African coast and further inland. It is painted with a combination of satellite imagery and intelligence from the member states, which includes interviews of migrants conducted by border guards. If the analysts suspect a possible breach, then they notify higher officials that an operation might be necessary. Nevertheless, risk analysis is a principle of objectification (Ewald 1991a, 142), as it converts the potential migrant to an irreducible unit to be managed through border protection. It ascribes a status on the traveler that is meaningful within the cosmology of the interstate system and regulates that individual accordingly. The shift from statistical analysis to that of risk and probability analysis signifies the data. If statistics describes the mere appearance of data, which ostensibly speaks for itself and highlights the norm, risk and probability analysis must specify the element that might threaten the norm, an analysis based on circular reasoning: given the normality of the territorial nation-state, nonnationals are aliens whose illegal entry would threaten that norm. These analyses generate for the migration apparatus the very threat to which it attributes an objective existence (143–44).

Border Surveillance and Patrol

Surveillance beyond the external border should clarify the "limes." This term derives from the ancient Roman concept of a border loosely marked by amorphous natural features like a marsh, bog, or forest and then further demarcated by a stone fortification. Such fortifications were built to repel invasions of German barbarians and other threatening tribes. In today's EU, LIMES is an acronym standing for "Land and Sea Integrated Monitoring for European Security," which is a four-year EU project (2006–2010) built to intensify and identify destabilizing events with the aid of satellites and land-, air-, and sea-based surveillance equipment. The significance of LIMES lies not only in the cooperation it engenders among members states but in the systematic separation of the EU's external border and the space of surveillance and control over the movement of mobile subjects located far beyond it. "Borders may be found anywhere" as Guild aptly notes (2003, 103; see also 2005; Vaughan-Williams 2008). Thirteen EU member states and over a dozen EU and international agencies and organizations including Frontex are classified as "institutional users" of its analytical "products." LIMES utilizes satellite surveillance provided by the European Maritime Security Services (MARISS), which as it boasts, can spot "infrastructure and changes related to illegal trafficking such as boat building facilities, new mustering and embarkation facilities, storage facilities or the build up of people in sensitive areas close to the coast or to national borders" (MARISS 2007, 3). Satellites can identify population concentrations at any given location. Reflecting the dual coding of travelers as either agents of threat or objects of sympathy, its capabilities can be deployed either for dealing with humanitarian crises such as natural disasters or for policing purposes such as identifying contraband on cargo ships and spotting illegal border crossings in remote areas. Testifying to the migrant's ambivalent significance to the apparatus, this capability allows for the distribution of food and medical supplies, on the one hand, while it prevents the departure of would-be illegal migrants seeking sustaining income in the EU, on the other. The degree of sympathy is a function of the migrant's distance from EU territory.

Frontex is also pursuing a major border surveillance network to track migration flows, as described in the BORTEC feasibility study (known in full as the study of the technical surveillance of Southern maritime borders of European Union). The European Council ordered this study from Frontex in December 2005 to assess the prospects of creating a common European border surveillance system, which became known as the EUROSUR (for European

Border Surveillance System) in 2008. The council reasoned that the study was particularly important after the unpredicted exodus of Lebanese into Cyprus (a new EU member state) during the 2006 Israeli invasion. As a Frontex public relations officer explained, this system would provide "coverage not only of the maritime borders but all the Mediterranean Sea and part of the Atlantic Ocean, providing real time information on maritime activities" (Frontex 2006a, 4). The Black Sea was incorporated into the plan after Romania and Bulgaria joined the EU in 2007. Frontex plays a catalyzing role in integrating national surveillance systems for EUROSUR. It envisions this goal as follows:

> The European Surveillance System requires the detection of all targets early to enable the identification of emergencies to give adequate help and intercept the targets before they are able to hide or disappear at sea or on land. In order to have a sufficient structure, it is necessary to establish a control and surveillance concept which has to cover the surveillance activities, the handling and assessment of the collected information and the operational intervention by aerial, land and naval means. (4)

The BORTEC report's semantics illustrate the objectification of people in large-scale population regulation. The words "migrant," "immigrant," "trafficker," and "smuggler" do not appear in the nineteen-page unclassified version. It makes no reference to actual types of individuals involved in the migration process, to say nothing of individual personalities. The most specific identifier in the text is the word "targets," which appears forty-three times and is used to describe those whom the surveillance system is meant to detect. The word "immigration" appears only five times, in the foreword, background, concluding, and recommendation sections. It does not appear in the bulk of the report covering the technical, legal, and operational aspects of the surveillance system. In the five instances when "immigration" appears, it is modified by the adjective "illegal." In four of the instances, the sentence in which it appears couples the priority of "tackling" illegal immigration with that of "saving lives" in the sea, but again this humanitarian gesture is greatest when the migrant is farthest away from EU territory.

The surveillance measures outlined in the BORTEC report require, first, the subdividing of sea space into defined areas, and second, the monitoring of all movement through the grid. Establishing grid coordinates is not such a straightforward task: "Whereas the location of land borders is well defined, the exact location of Member States' maritime borders is not. Therefore, surveillance of the maritime border is not surveillance of movements across a *line* but across an *area* which has its inner boundary at the coast" (Frontex 2006a, 4, emphasis added). The sea is divided into three areas for operational purposes (as opposed to purposes of international law) including the coastal waters of EU member states' territories, the open sea, and the coastal waters of third countries. EU coastal waters are defined as "maritime areas of mainland and islands which can have adequate surveillance by land-based infrastructure. The extent of the Coastal Waters is not a distance fixed in nautical miles, but depends on the surveillance system capabilities to detect targets." The open sea lies beyond coastal waters as "the sea out of range of adequate coverage by land based sensors" (8). The report also explains that the surveillance of departure countries' coastal waters must occur cooperatively with those countries in order to legally and usefully "deal with immigrants at sea" (6).

The tasks of detecting and identifying "targets" are divided according to the target's spatial location in EU coastal waters, the open sea, or the coastal waters abroad. Radar (whether land-based, airborne, or satellite-based) is the first method of detection, followed by identification through the Vessel Monitoring System, Automatic Identification System, and Long Range Identification and Tracking System. Failing these measures, daytime visual cameras or nighttime infrared cameras can help to detect and identify unrecognized targets. Assistance can even come from operators with intimate knowledge of local boating patterns who can recognize, for example, fishing or recreational vessels by how they move across the sea. When vessels remain unidentified or do not reply to requests for contact, then patrol boats or aircraft are sent "to make the final decision to identify the target as a threat, necessitating interception, or not" (Frontex 2006a, 12). Member states' national coordination centers along with Frontex arrange for the common surveillance of the open sea, which is an area outside the sovereignty of any EU member state. Frontex lists the priorities for open seas surveillance as early warning, identification of new trends and threats, detection, identification, and if needed, interception of targets and saving lives (16).

Creating EUROSUR does not require the wholesale installation of a new infrastructure but rather the integration of existing surveillance systems that until now may not have served security purposes. The new creation is what the EC calls a "system of systems" (Europa 2008a). (The same retooling and integration of surveillance systems is central to the rapid growth of the biometric information technology systems described in Chapter 5.) Frontex suggests, for example, drawing on fisheries control, maritime traffic control, and border surveillance, which between them offer a range of tools including vessel monitoring systems, patrol vessels, radio, automated identification systems, coastal radar, and infrared cameras. These "sensors" used in coastal waters are linked into reporting systems. Member states will establish "operational centers" that "have access to all information coming from sensors, platforms, reporting and communication systems, enabling the interconnection of all elements of the surveillance system, particularly the integration of data from [fisheries, maritime traffic, and border controls] and intelligence concerning activities at sea" (9–10). They will function as the local centers for handling routine surveillance in defined sectors of the national coastal waters, with each consisting of one or more sensor stations. These operational centers will work one level below the "national coordination center," which liaises with the EU level. Frontex will facilitate communication among the national coordination centers to complete the "system of systems."

EUROSUR draws on a vast inventory of hardware. Fixed wing airplanes, which can cover greater surface areas, complement seagoing vessels, which are slower and have short sensor range because of their lower height. Helicopters are also used to extend the coverage of a vessel. Satellites extend the aircraft's field of view and serve as "early warning" devices, and remote sensing provides images of vessels in nearly real time (less than an hour). This information can be used to direct aircraft "to zones which appear to have abnormal vessel activity" (Europa 2008a, 17). Frontex is also exploring the possible role of unmanned aerial vehicles (UAVs), commonly known as drones, largely through the efforts of Erik Berglund, director of capacity building. Berglund, educated at the Royal Institute of Technology in Stockholm and the US Naval Postgraduate School, argues that UAVs offer the benefit of twenty-four-hour surveillance missions. This capability would prove particularly useful in difficult weather conditions and in covering a multitude of topographies in a single mission, ranging from forested land areas to the rocky crags of the Greek islands to the open expanses of the Atlantic Ocean, Mediterranean Sea, and Black Sea. Given their long-range capabilities, UAVs offer economies of scale thus keeping down costs of border surveillance over the long run. Supporters of UAVs point to their successful deployment along the American and Israeli borders. They envision deploying small unmanned aerial vehicles to assist in surveillance of coastal waters, and large ones for higher altitude missions further out to sea (Berglund n.d.). This equipment, in concert with the network of "operational control centers" and national control centers, would vastly improve EU maritime surveillance capabilities, which currently cover only "certain flat or coastal areas and those areas in which operations are carried out" (Europa 2008a).

The coastal waters of third countries, mostly African or Middle Eastern countries, are monitored through partnerships with the EU or through satellite imagery combined with intelligence reports. The former involves creating legal and diplomatic arrangements with third countries, which for example occurred in the Hera II operation (see below) designed to repel an exodus of migrants from Africa's west coast to Spain's Canary Islands. Spain, Italy, Portugal, and Finland provided navy vessels and military aircraft to patrol the coasts of Senegal, Mauritania, and Guinea. This mission pushed *cayucos*, or fishing boats, carrying over 3,500 migrants back to the shores of Senegal, Mauritania, and Cape Verde (Frontex 2006d). The governments of these countries agreed to process the identification and return of the migrants with the assistance of EU experts.

BORTEC outlines the plans for a networked surveillance system for the EU's southern maritime border and the open Mediterranean Sea. The MEDSEA study investigated how those same spaces would be patrolled and controlled with third-country cooperation. Claims of objective threats and humanitarian crises justify the deployment of border patrol regimes that extend coverage onto the shores of North Africa:

> According to risk analysis carried out, the EU southern maritime borders remain the area mostly affected by illegal immigration. When third countries are unable to satisfy the expectation of their people, the situation becomes an incentive to leave for the EU Member States offering an advantage over the source country.
>
> Criminal networks involved in the phenomenon are well organized and flexible, finding continuously new ways of actions, new routes and means, depending on the measures that law enforcement authorities undertake to face the challenges. As soon as effective tackling measures are adopted, the phenomenon of the "displacement effects" occurs immediately. The initiative to establish the Mediterranean Coastal Patrols Network is to set up a flexible tool to face these continuously changes [sic] of phenomenon. Cooperation with third countries of origin and transit is essential on the one hand to help third countries to fulfill the expectation of their people and on the other hand to receive early warnings about new trends. Real time intelligence allows the EU Member States to anticipate new modi operandi. Even though a coastal patrols network is able to handle the surveillance and control of the EU southern maritime borders the

patrolling network will not itself solve the problem of illegal immigration. An EU approach towards third countries is important to promote their efforts to avoid illegal immigrants' departing. The surveillance and patrolling network has to cover not only the coastal area, but also the high seas and the territorial waters of neighbouring countries. Therefore agreements with third countries are essential. The Mediterranean Coastal Patrols Network needs common application of the international law of the sea as well as common legal framework [sic] at EU level in order to agree on operational procedures. (Frontex 2006b, 9)

The passage renders the EU a passive player that responds only to the events that history throws at it. Southern countries are derelict in their duty of satisfying the demands of their people. Clever criminal networks evade the border controls of any individual member state trying to defend its territorial integrity on its own. The added value in pooling member states' intelligence is to somehow find those needles in the haystack that are too small to be detected and intercepted through a singular national surveillance or patrol agency. An integrated monitoring system enhances the policing capability of any individual state "to discover those vessels and small boats which are not obliged to or avoid to [sic], transmit information" (10). A range of border services such as coast guards, police forces, customs, naval forces, search and rescue outfits, fishing inspection, and maritime and port authorities either gather data from coastal radar or receive data from reports transmitted by the crews of incoming vessels. The desired information includes destination, positions, cargoes, and activities. If vessels are docking at a member state's port, then they have to submit lists of crew and passengers for border control (9–10). The plan then is to integrate the various national patrolling agencies into a network of southern EU agencies with Frontex serving as the interface among national coordination centers. It is a daunting organizational challenge but one with great support, as fifty different authorities under thirty different ministries are involved. Frontex has announced that it is prepared to begin work on creating an intranet communication system for what is to be called the Mediterranean Coastal Patrols Network, along with common standards for operational equipment and common evaluation systems (22).

Operations

Frontex estimates that 175,000 detected illegal border crossings into the EU occurred in 2008 (Frontex 2009, 12–13). This figure is 20 percent higher than in

2007. Slightly more than half of these occurred at sea borders, which signified a 69 percent increase. Fifty percent of the EU total occurred at the Greek sea border with Turkey and Greek land border with Albania. The number of detected attempts at the Greek sea border doubled to 29,100 between 2007 and 2008, mainly at the islands of Lesvos, Chios, Samos, Patos, Leros, and Kos, all near the Turkish border. The Greek-Albanian land border accounted for the largest number of detected illegal land border crossings at 38,600, though this signified a 10 percent decrease from 2007. Attempts on the Italian sea border accounted for 41 percent of the total (or 37,000 people), with over 31,000 of the attempts at the Mediterranean island of Lampedusa near the Libyan coast. This 2008 figure doubles that of 2007, an increase attributable to Operation Hera, which pushed migrants through Libya after it nearly shut down the route from West Africa to Spain's Canary Islands. Similarly, the number of detections at Malta increased from 1,700 to 2,800. Detections along the EU's eastern external border, including Finland, Estonia, Latvia, Lithuania, Poland, Slovakia, Hungary, and Romania, reached 6,200, with over half of them at the Polish border alone. By October 2010, Frontex announced a decline in the number of illegal migrants seeking to enter the EU. However, attempts by Afghanis on the Greek-Turkey land border increased sixfold by the second quarter of that year, and 90 percent of all detected attempts to enter the EU occurred somewhere on a Greek land border, half of those by Albanians. These developments indicate a shift away from the Greek sea borders. Greece reported 45,000 illegal crossings during the first half of 2010 (BBC 2010).

While the number of undetected migrants can never be precisely determined, the number of intercepted migrants is large and growing. Since its inception in 2005, Frontex has coordinated joint operations among the member states aimed at slowing down or repelling illegal border crossings, particularly along the southern maritime border. For example, to protect Spain's southern coast, Frontex ran Operation Minerva, patrolling from Algeciras to Almería and from Ceuta to Melilla, the coastal enclaves adjacent to Morocco. Running from mid-August to mid-September 2007, Minerva involved thirteen member states, two coastal patrol vessels, two dog teams, and seventeen experts (with unidentified specialties). It "intercepted" 1,260 illegal migrants, "diverted" 1,105, and discovered 765 falsified documents. Operation Nautilus, running in the early summer of 2007, halted flows from Libya and Tunisia to Malta and the Italian islands of Lampedusa, Panteleria, and Sicily. It intercepted 3,173 migrants while drawing on the resources of nine EU member states. Operation Poseidon was initiated to support national efforts to halt flows through the southeast Mediterranean and Aegean Seas. It was carried out in intermittent phases in 2006 and 2007 and involved experts from sixteen member states. At least 2,253 people were either apprehended or returned to a sending or transit country, and seventeen smugglers or facilitators were also apprehended. Operation Niris blocked Indian and Chinese illegal movements into Estonia, Latvia, Lithuania, and other Baltic Sea countries. Officials in this operation interviewed 579 travelers of Chinese or Indian origin with fifteen refused entries. Operation Amazon confronted illegal flows destined for Spain and Portugal through European airports and resulted in 3,170 refused entries, largely of travelers from Bolivia, Brazil, and Paraguay.

Consistent with running an outfit that is military in form (but not content), operations are given names that resemble US military ventures in distant lands. However, a coordination officer in the operations unit explained that names for operations are also common in law enforcement. "This is very normal," he reflected. "It's politically correct to use European culture. We borrowed once from Northern mythology." At times the name refers to the target: "If the operation is defined by snakeheads [human smugglers], then we picked Hydra. If you cut off the head, then others appear." One of his colleagues added, "Sea operations go to Nautilus; air operations to Zarathustra."

A closer look at Operation Hera, designed to forestall illegal entries into Spain's Canary Islands, illustrates Frontex's role in organizing the joint patrolling of the EU's external border. On May 24, 2006, the Spanish government requested assistance from Frontex through Article 8 of Council Regulation 2007/2004 (Carrera 2007, 20). The number of illegal migrants arriving at the Canary Islands increased considerably to 31,000 in 2006, in contrast to 4,751 in 2005 and 8,519 in 2004 (Frontex 2007a). The increase is partly attributable to Spain's deployment of a high-tech surveillance system monitoring the seventy-one-mile shoreline along the Straight of Gibraltar, which diverted migratory routes across the ocean to the islands rather than to the mainland (Leidel 2007). Hera consisted of three stages, which ran from the summer of 2006 to the spring of 2007. The first stage, Hera I, commenced at Tenerife, Gran Canaria, and Fuerteventura on July 17, 2006 (at which point over 5,000 illegal entries had been counted) and deployed experts from France, Portugal, Italy, Germany, the United Kingdom, the Netherlands, and Norway to identify migrants' countries of origin (Frontex 2006d). Representatives from Senegal, Gambia, Mauritania, and Frontex assisted the experts (Ministerio de Interior, Spain, cited in Carrera

2007, fn. 101). According to Frontex's curiously named Information and Transparency Unit (personal communication via e-mail on 29 January 2007), Hera I alone identified all of the 18,987 illegal migrants who arrived at the Canary Islands with about one-third being returned to their countries of origin (Morocco, Senegal, Mali, Gambia, Guinea, and others). Interviews conducted by the participating EU experts led to the arrests of human smugglers and the detention of an additional one thousand potential immigrants to the Canary Islands by the Senegalese authorities. Hera II and III provided operational support to prevent *cayucos* from leaving the coastal waters beyond Mauritania, Senegal, Gambia, and Cape Verde. These boats could be turned back to the transit country's shore, as they had not yet entered international waters. If apprehended in the open sea, the intercepting vessel would be required to bring the migrants on board and provide them with as much humanitarian assistance as they could. Participating member states supplied the operation with large-scale hardware including, for example, one vessel and one aircraft from Italy, one vessel from Portugal, and one aircraft from Finland (Frontex 2006d). Spain supplied two additional sea vessels to provide technical support to an Italian ship. It also supplied four additional patrol boats and two helicopters for air surveillance and support to maritime operations off the coasts of Mauritania, Senegal, and Cape Verde (Carrera 2007, 22).

What does a Frontex operation designed to stop "bad" circulation look like? Though many operational details remain classified, the EC released video footage of the patrol work on the Senegalese coast from Hera II. During the week of September 4, 2006, the Italian Guardia Costiera (coast guard) led surveillance runs off the coast of Senegal, which had already intercepted 586 people during the whole resource-intensive operation. This deployment included an ATR-42 twin-propeller surveillance aircraft with a crew of nine people (three pilots, three systems operators, and three technical staff). They fly for three to five hours a day covering about 1,200 sea miles. It also included a large Italian vessel weighing 500 tons, stretching 50 meters in length, and consuming 1,500 liters of fuel per hour. No fewer than thirty marines and commanders plus one Senegalese officer make up its crew. Only the Senegalese officer can order the interception and return of the *cayucos* within Senegalese territorial waters (European Commission 2006a). EU countries and the cooperating third countries have shared responsibilities to ensure that the human rights of any detained or deterred persons are safeguarded (Sirtori and Coelho 2007, 39–41). Otherwise, dangerous and humiliating situations for migrants emerge, as in early 2007 when Spain and Mauritania argued for thirteen days over who should take responsibility for 369 sea passengers held onboard in international waters during the dispute. The video footage shows the Hera II mission as follows (European Commission 2006):

> The crew of an Italian surveillance aircraft are preparing for takeoff from Dakar Airport in Senegal. Two Italian crewmen in the cockpit adjust dials and flip switches to the background hum of the engines. Four crew members dressed in army green are discussing plans in the galley. The ATR-42 begins its ascent with the camera showing the view of Dakar and the Atlantic coast. A radar screen shows the ATR's flight path, sets its current location in the center of the circular surveillance field, and reveals in a pinkish hue a longboat resembling a *cayuco*. The camera then shows external footage of the open sea with apparently nineteen *cayucos* moving through the water followed by interior shots of the crew tracking the boats with radar equipment and nautical charts. The map suggests that they are located in Senegalese territorial waters. A close-up shot shows a *cayuco*, carrying about ten people and mostly covered with a tarp, moving across a video screen in the surveillance plane. The Italian major Venditti calls out its location in the microphone on his headset while another crew member views the boat through high-power binoculars. A third crewman takes notes.

The video then cuts to the side of the Italian coast guard ship *Diciotti* on patrol near Dakar. It carries in descending order the Italian, EU, and Senegalese flags. Its crew also look for *cayucos* through binoculars and video surveillance and tracks them on maps. Commemorating this particular mission, they wear shirts with "Guardia Costiera Hera 2006" printed on the back. A crewman on *Diciotti* watches another *cayuco* on his video screen. A radio operator gives the *Diciotti*'s position and asks his colleague for the number of people on board. The *cayuco* appears again on the video screen as the operator writes down its speed and location.

The crew of the ATR-42 direct their attention to the *cayuco*. They track it with high-powered handheld cameras and on video surveillance, where it is microframed in white lines in the center of the screen. Close-up shots of the *cayucos* show over a dozen people on board. Back on the *Diciotti*, the ship's second in command, Pasquale Golizia, explains, "Our duty is to report any sight of the so-called *cayucos* to the Frontex coordination center in Canarias, Tenerife, in order they [sic] can arrange with Senegalese authorities to stop and repatriate them immediately before they leave the territorial waters." Then, the Senegalese officer discusses the *cayuco*'s location with an Italian officer.

The next scene shifts to the exterior of the coordination center in Tenerife. Inside the center the Spanish officers in charge view the *cayuco* on a large video screen. Elsewhere in the center Portuguese officers and staff discuss developments as they unfold in real time. In a meeting room, officers from Portugal, Italy, Poland, and Spain evaluate the current state of the Hera mission. Since the mission is based on Spain's sovereign territory, a Spanish officer leads the discussion in front of a large map that shows the position of aircraft and patrol boats along the West African coast.

The scene shifts to Los Cristianos Harbor in Tenerife, where tourists watch a Spanish coast guard ship pull a *cayuco* filled with about fifty suspected illegal migrants to the dock. Police secure the area into which the migrants will disembark, while coast guard sailors wearing facemasks to prevent the inhalation of viruses or bacteria help tie the boat to the dock. Spanish police and Red Cross workers wearing protective gloves escort weakened migrants onto the dock where they are given biscuits and beverages under a protective tent. The final scene shows them boarding a bus between parallel lines of polices officers that will take them to police headquarters.

Migrants, of course, have some agency in these encounters even if they maneuver from a desperately weaker power position. In an interview with me, one Frontex official explained some of their tactics:

> Some months ago, the *cayucos* going to the Canary Islands could make the crossing in four to seven days. We sent an airplane to check the position of the boats before they made the risk of crossing the sea. Then, they started going at night and we couldn't see them, so we sent planes with night capability. Then, they started something else. They moved migrants in small numbers and disguised them as fishermen as they shuttled them to a larger vessel waiting for them out in the sea. Mauritania gave Spain the right to sail their ships in its territorial waters [and to send them back to shore].

Another border patrol official explained that migrants in the eastern Mediterranean appropriate Frontex missions for their own ends. If picked up at sea, would-be illegal migrants must be rescued according to international law and taken into safety and custody. This obligation requires that they be brought into the EU if it is the closest point of disembarkation where they may claim asylum. The Greek border control authorities find this particularly problematic, as only 600 meters separate some of its islands from the Turkish mainland. One border control official explained that "[migrants] leave from Turkey in small vessels. When they see the Greek border ships, then they jump into the sea. Greece has to rescue [them]. Some know there is no cooperation agreement with Libya [so it is harder for Italy and Malta to return them]." (Libya and the EC signed a migration cooperation agenda in October 2010, over a year after this interview.) He added that if sophisticated smugglers and migrants "know that a Frontex mission is in operation, then they are attracted to it so they can jump in the water and get rescued." This knowledge generates precisely the opposite of the desired effect of the operation, namely to keep migrants out of the union.

RABITs

Not all Frontex operations benefit from as much lead time as Operation Hera. Some must respond to sudden "crises." What constitutes a sudden crisis? "Suppose that Jordan decides to release its two million Iraqi refugees, or there is a regime change in Algeria?" pondered one Frontex official. "We have Cyprus, which has had a real problem with Lebanese people coming during the war with Israel. Thousands of people coming to this small island," added his colleague. Southern EU member states first pointed to the need for rapid response capability as they complained that the EU-27 does not support them in preventing illegal border crossings (EurActiv 2007a). To manage these crises, they prompted the European Parliament to vote overwhelmingly for the creation of "rapid border intervention teams" (RABITs), with 526 in favor, 63 against, and 28 abstentions. Frontex is now empowered to mobilize these teams drawn from a reserve of over six hundred border guards and national experts to meet any sudden arrival of illegal immigrants at the EU's external border (EurActiv 2007b; Frontex 2009, 34). The teams complete training courses as well as "real-life" field exercises (Frontex 2009, 20). They are assembled according to competency in piloting ships and helicopters, controlling containers, detecting moving objects with radar technology, detecting forged identity papers, interpreting maritime laws, and understanding certain languages (20). Frontex establishes a five to ten day window to put them in place. "National resources could hold off [the 'problem'] until then, but it's difficult logistically to do," explained the Frontex official.

Scenarios

The first known Frontex mission began in October 2010 at the request of the Greek government. Approximately 350 migrants per day were attempting to enter Greece in the Orestiada area along the Turkish border (BBC 2010). Frontex deployed 175 RABIT officers from twenty-four EU countries along the border between Orestiada and Alexandroupolis. In addition to routine surveillance responsibilities, these officers interviewed migrants in order to determine their countries of origin and to collect intelligence on smuggling and trafficking networks (Frontex 2010, 2). Frontex announced that it has run at least three fictitious training exercises to prepare for such "crises" approaching the EU's external border. These provide a richer understanding of how RABIT missions are prompted, conceived, and deployed. The first training scenario took place in November 2007 in Porto, Portugal, at the Francisco Sá Carneiro Airport (Frontex 2007b). Agents from sixteen member states participated in a simulation involving the arrival of a plane from a fictitious Central American island republic. The plane is carrying a large number of passengers traveling on forged documents supplied by a criminal network operating in the country. The carrier, "Central American Wings," has announced the addition of more flights to Porto to accommodate growing passenger demand. The country's economic downturn has prompted many of its citizens to seek illegal entry into the Schengen Area to find work. The Portuguese border authorities are unable to handle the influx and will need assistance from other member states via Frontex. This exercise particularly tested capabilities in document security and second-line interviews for travelers whose answers to the first round of questions still suggest illegal intentions. In 2008, Frontex ran two exercises in southeast Europe. One exercise took place along the Romanian-Moldovan border. It involved forty-nine agents from twenty-three member states trying to prevent an exceptionally large influx of third-country nationals from illegally entering the EU (Frontex 2008). The other exercise tested border control capability on the Slovenian-Croatian border and included agents from twenty member states. It transpired as follows:

A crisis in the southeastern part of the Balkan Peninsula started to spread in the neighboring countries, which are not capable to handle [sic] incoming refugees any more. A sudden increase of illegal migrations through the "Balkans Route" has been recorded.

Most endangered is the Slovenian-Croatian border in the northeastern part, which is under the auspices of the police directorates of Maribor and Celje. Illegal migrants are crossing the border daily in large groups of 20 to 30 persons. Many cases of illegal migrants hidden in trucks and vans were detected at border crossing points Gruškovje and Zavrč. A huge increase of passengers using forged and counterfeit documents has also been noted at these two BCPs [border control points].

. According to intelligence information and risk analysis, the pressure of illegal migrations will even increase. Illegal migrants will try to enter the EU territory on the northeastern part of [the] Slovenian-Croatian border, and then travel further to Germany and Sweden, where a majority of illegal migrants have their relatives. The objective of the RABITs deployment is to reinforce the response capacity of the Slovenian authorities and to ensure that their security measures meet Schengen standards at the Croatian border.

The main operational aim is to avert threats to the external European Borders by: conducting border surveillance, conducting border checks (detecting forged and misused documents and thorough second-line interviews). In response to the specific situation and identified illegal immigration threat at part of [the] Slovenian external border, Executive Director of Frontex, Mr. Ilkka Laitinen decided to provide rapid operational assistance for Slovenia by deploying Rapid Border Intervention Teams to police directorates Maribor and Celje. (Parzyszek, e-mail to author, 25 April 2008)

This exercise involved thirty team members from twenty EU countries and took place specifically in the Maribor and Celje police directorates, which cover 160 kilometers of the Slovenian border with Croatia. Some of the skills used in the exercise were fraudulent document detection, observation with night vision equipment, and surveillance with thermovision cameras (Slovenian Presidency 2008b). The officers in the exercise carried firearms and pepper spray and possessed expertise in the surveillance of rural terrain (Lewis 2008).

Noteworthy in the description of this scenario is the flexible use of the term "refugee." The people with whom the hypothetical RABITs are concerned are called "refugees" when they remain in the politically and culturally indistinct Balkan Peninsula (Todorova 1997). We can evoke sympathy for the civilian victims fleeing what is commonly misunderstood as a land of eternal ethnic conflict. The label quickly changes to "illegal migrant" as these fictitious migrants wend their way to the EU border at Slovenia, the northernmost former Yugoslav republic and now EU member state. The individual's status fluidly shifts from a creature of sympathy to an object of threat as the migrant moves closer to EU territorial space. The migrants' helplessness derives not merely from the life-threatening circumstances of war, which will someday pass, but from their spatial relation to the EU itself. The degree of humanitarianism increases in inverse proportion to the migrant's impact on the EU polity, which is usually a function of geographic distance (see also Hyndman 2000).

This fictitious scenario has some basis in real illegal border crossings. The Slovenian-Croatian border stretches over two hundred miles through mountainous terrain and accounted for more than three-fourths of the illegal crossings into the EU through Slovenia in 2007. Nearly one thousand cases of counterfeit or altered documents were also detected during that year. The "Balkan Route" is a known pathway into the EU that runs from countries of origin such as Serbia, Macedonia, Albania, and Turkey across Kosovo to Montenegro, Bosnia-Herzegovina, and Croatia then into Slovenia in the EU. Slovenian authorities report that most migrants reach the Slovenian border far from official border crossing points in cars or minivans led by smugglers. They then cross individually or in groups of up to sixteen, sometimes with the smuggler and other times independently, in which case they meet a facilitator inside the country who takes them on to Austria or Italy. While the Slovenian government estimates that illegal entries decreased by 25 percent from 2006 to 2007, the "pressure on its border"—to use the official parlance—remains high compared to the size of the country (in terms of area and population). Between September 2007 and March 2008, Slovenian officials conducted 9.5 million checks on international travelers through the Schengen Information System (SIS), which produced 4,661 "hits" on wanted persons or missing persons or objects. Out of that number 3,187 persons were refused entry and 196 counterfeit travel documents were seized (Slovenian Presidency 2008a).

National border control agencies actively support the RABIT program even if they encounter difficulties responding to unforeseeable crises and managing complicated logistical coordination. Unlike operations planned in advance that emerge out of Frontex's Risk Analysis Unit (for example, Minerva, Poseidon, and Hera), member states request that the Frontex executive director initiate a RABIT operation as soon as possible. The executive director must decide within five days, and he usually honors the request. He asks participating EU states for a list of available RABIT members, from which he drafts a roster for the operation. He returns the list to the national border guard units, at which point the assembly of the team becomes qualitatively more challenging. The border official responsible for RABIT operations in one EU member state explained some of the hassles: "What if they are out of town, or on other assignments? What if I am out of town?" Tracking down RABIT members is only the first step. The team member must next reach the deployment location, which introduces additional obstacles:

> Then we have to get the RABIT to the destination. If they need to bring their service weapons, then this could take two days. We have to get airline approval per IATA [International Air Transport Association] regulations. Member states need to give their approval for us to bring our service weapons into their countries.

Language barriers are also problematic:

> [Frontex asks] for Farsi and Pashtun. . . . Frontex should contract its language interpreters. Belgian RABITs speak at least four languages. Sometimes RABITs from different EU countries need translators among themselves. This is a huge problem that can sometimes jeopardize the whole operation.

These problems do not deter member states from participating in any of the Frontex operations. This official explained that his country dedicated 4,000 hours to Frontex operations in 2008. He added, "That's 2.5 policemen you can't use. You have the operation, but you also have the things around it." Networking is most important. He continued, "If we need information from Spain, if you go through the official route for getting information, it takes too long. If you know someone personally, then it comes in minutes." Such networking expedites cooperation among national border control units. "We have specialized knowledge. We see things other countries don't know. [Our country] is especially good with fraudulent document detection. I've never seen a participant disappointed from his participation [in a Frontex operation]." This official is expressing an opinion evidently shared with his counterparts in other member states when he explains that

> For one thing, it is about solidarity. Even in meetings, you can feel the gratitude from other member states for your participation. It means your national training is working. We can say we intercepted the most people, that we are doing a good job. . . . The chain is only as strong as the weakest link. It's a hole in all of Europe. If we train them, then local border guards take pride in their work. Soon we will have the European Border Guards. You can feel it is going in that direction. Used to be short-term deployment for two to three months. If that works, then it will be six months. There will be a European Border Guard.

If this border official's prediction materializes, then two key features likely will have played foundational roles. First, such an integrated agency requires a large amount of standardization of policy outlook, compatibility of technical infrastructures, the linking of bureaucracies, and institutionalization of a common policy language. In addition to the examples already provided, Frontex recently produced the Common Core Curriculum, which it distributes to national border patrol agencies to establish common training standards. Second, the technological means for quick, spontaneous communication among relatively low-level officials dispersed through the EU is critical for bypassing the bureaucratic lethargy that such integration invites. Ironically, the informal networking serves the purpose of advancing the agenda that formal bureaucracy cannot advance on its own. The enthusiasm for work that such informality generates helps to move forward the broader project of convergence. These two features present in this border guard's professional experience are also key features in the work done in other migration policy domains such as that of the European Migration Network (Chapter 1) and of the biometric experts harmonizing national systems (Chapter 5).

The satisfaction that this border guard takes from the informal camaraderie with his counterparts in other EU member states is central to the production of a "nonce bureaucrat." This individual experiences a sense of self-fulfillment when collaborating with others who share unique skills that provide a crucial service to the larger mission they serve. This affective experience should not be described as self-satisfaction through a blind loyalty to the "system." Brenneis (1994, 33–34; see also Zabusky 1995) describes it subtly and accurately as "considerable social pleasure, pleasure of a type defined in terms of professional self-definition and satisfaction," along with "[the] enjoyment of technique, a sense not so much of responsibility as of successfully negotiating complex exchange relationships." Moreover, the nonce bureaucrat transforms into a nonce peer as the alienation of the former is replaced with the solidarity of the latter (Calhoun cited in ibid., 33) and injects the expert with a self-motivation at no cost to the apparatus.

THE VIOLENCE OF MARGINALIZATION

If banal technocratic practices advance the harmonization of EU border control policy, then how do they affect those whom the EU is trying to keep out? Many of these people, of course, embark on an illegal migration journey of unimaginable hardship. To be sure, respect for the migrants' agency should not allow us to forget the excruciating circumstances they face. The two most common clandestine routes to Europe from West Africa both end up in Spain, and both involve high risks and costs. Migrants from West Africa, who colloquially call themselves "adventurers," might take the overland route, which begins in Gao, Mali, and proceeds north through Algeria and into Morocco. From Morocco, either they try to enter Spain via boat across the western finger of the Mediterranean Sea to Costa del Sol, or they attempt to get through the land border to the Spanish enclaves of Ceuta or Melilla located on the shores of northeast Morocco. Other common overland routes begin at Agadez, Nigeria, and move either toward Sebha, Libya, then to Tripoli and on to Italian islands in the Mediterranean Sea, or toward Tamanrasset, Algeria, then Oujda, Morocco, before aiming for the Spanish coast across the sea (De Haas 2008, 17). Since 2001, increased sea patrols in the western Mediterranean and the now heavily fortified borders of the enclaves have forced more adventurers to attempt the sea voyage to the Canary Islands, the southernmost EU border (17).

But who are these adventurers whom policy officials see as statistics and as fluorescent objects on radar screens? How do they specifically reach the decision to take such a life-threatening journey? How is the journey organized? What is it like? And what effect does their decision to undertake it have on their families and home communities? While individual circumstances vary, three salient themes come through their testimonies: their obligation to support family and relatives and attendant sense of shame when failing to fulfill it; their vulnerable position with respect to their smugglers (though some studies show a more complex relationship; cf. van Liempt and Doomernik 2006); and the harsh natural environment through which they move. One individual who traveled covertly from Senegal to Italy told his tale to the BBC:

Mamadou Saliou Diallo, who goes by "Billy," is a forty-five-year-old from Guinea now working in Brescia, Italy. He undertook the overland route at the end of 1999. At age twenty-two he had moved with his family to the Senegalese capital, Dakar. He began working in a hospital, gained training as a nurse, and continued working there for seventeen years. Billy calculated that his monthly salary of $130 could not support his wife, Idiatou, and their children. Like anyone, all he wanted was to give his children a better start in life than he had. He concluded that immigrating to Europe was the best way to achieve that goal. Making the journey overland was both cheaper than flying and, according to rumor, required no visa. He thought that he would reach Spain in a week. When telling the story of his journey from Dakar to Brescia, Billy simply stated, "Little did I know how wrong that was" (BBC 2004a).

Billy left Dakar in November 1999, paying a man $1,300 to deliver him to Europe. With $90 in his pocket, he first traveled by train 650 miles east to Bamako, the capital of Mali. His contact there was never found. Billy met other migrants in Bamako who told stories of Algerian police shooting on sight for fear of Islamic radicals, and of armed robbers taking everything in a migrant's possession and leaving the migrant for dead in the desert. Terrified and a stranger in Mali, Billy phoned home for reassurance. His mother begged him to come back, but his father had a dream that all would end well. Billy then flew 500 miles northeast to Timbuktu with eight others, where they joined seven more migrants from West Africa. The fifteen of them traveled by night in a lorry 200 miles east to Gao, which was the last staging point before the journey northward across the Sahara. Thousands of migrants had congregated there waiting for transport in the same direction.

Billy and his fellow travelers bought bread and tinned sardines for the desert journey and carried water in the inner tubes of car tires. During the first afternoon, their driver showed them the graves of seven people who died of thirst after their lorry broke down. Billy himself developed diarrhea, probably from his own water supply, but he kept drinking it for fear of suffering the same fate. They traveled in the back of the lorry during the windy, cold nights and rested underneath it for shade during the hot days. They could hardly sleep, however, as sand blew everywhere around them and into their eyes, ears, and throats. Seven days after they left Gao, the group had moved 900 miles northwest to Tindouf, Algeria. Police beat them there and arrested their driver, who held their papers and money.

Luckily, a Nigerian man in their party had money hidden in his shoe and gave five dollars to each of his colleagues. They then bought trinkets to resell so that they could earn enough money to continue their journey, though four of them gave up in Tindouf. The remaining eleven traveled with a Senegalese guide over Morocco's Atlas Mountains, reaching a village two days later from where they took a bus to Casablanca some 500 miles north. Billy had not washed since he had left Bamako one month earlier. His body was covered in fleas. "It was terrible," Billy recalled, "we looked like mad men." In Casablanca, he and some of the others worked at building sites to earn money but could only afford one meal of rice and fish per day. He called home to have Idiatou sell the family television set and to borrow money from friends and relatives. She wired $700 to him from Dakar. For $600 a Moroccan guide agreed to take him to Europe, first traveling northeast along the Atlantic coast 200 miles to

Tangier where he first saw "the lights of the Spanish mainland twinkling on the other side" (BBC 2004a).

From Tangier, Billy and his fellow travelers made two attempts to smuggle themselves into Ceuta, the Spanish enclave in Morocco (BBC 2004b). They first dressed in black and entered the forest near the border. Rather than try to scale the barbed-wire wall, where many migrants get caught, they waited two weeks and tried to enter through a tunnel. However, the police spotted them before they reached the tunnel and beat them with their rifle butts. Billy lost a front tooth. A week later, they headed to the coast and boarded an inflatable raft. Everyone, except the guide rowing the boat, lay down on the floor to avoid the searchlights. Two hours and thirty miles later they made it to the Ceuta shore, successfully avoiding the police and arriving at the Calamocarro Red Cross camp. Billy argued that he was a refugee from Rwanda, knowing full well that if he admitted that he was from Guinea or Senegal he would have been returned home. That March 2000 night was the first night that he had slept on a clean and comfortable mattress for four months. Three weeks later he was given a residency permit and put on a boat for the Spanish mainland.

In Spain, Billy worked in the fields for a month to earn enough money to travel to Brescia, Italy. When he finally arrived in this northern Italian town, he could not locate the cousin he was supposed to meet there. He ended up living for a year with fifteen other migrants in the filthy crawl space of a single-room flat. He sold African trinkets and jewelry to make a living. Eventually a friend gave him his work permit as they looked similar, and Billy got a factory job making agricultural tools. In 2002, the Italian government legalized 700,000 illegal immigrants who had a job. In May 2003, Billy got his papers and could finally travel freely back home to see his wife and three children after four years of separation. The stress on his family had been tremendous. Of course he missed them very much. His daughter believed that her father was Billy's cousin who had been living nearby. Idiatou recalled having two breakdowns and worried "especially when people started saying that he must have a girl-friend in Italy" (BBC 2004c). Billy has been able to improve his family's living standards. His children now go to a good private school, and his family owns a plot of land. Were these gains worth the cost? Billy spoke with ambivalence on this point: "I went through hell to reach Italy and would never have left if I had known what the journey really entailed. But I don't regret it now because I can look after my family far better than when I was working as a nurse in Dakar" (BBC 2004b).

Billy's story, of course, echoes those of many others who managed an illegal entry. The risks are enormously high, as are the economic, social, and personal costs. This is the price that must be paid when trying to evade the migration management apparatus.

"Inside" the apparatus, many migration policy officials in the EU equivocate about its effects. Maria (Chapter 1) explains her internal conflict as someone who empathizes with the migrants whom she nevertheless manages. She laments that migrants "are just statistics. They are not real people, though some have psychological traumas. . . . I just get them on a piece of paper, just files and files and files. [But] I want to hear it from them. They can tell me if they have a mother and father or had to fight in a civil war." The contradiction between her professional obligations and her personal sympathies intensified when she started volunteering at a detention center: "My colleagues said don't do that. It is a conflict of interest." She nevertheless began offering English courses:

> The first course was offered for females but no one applied. So, we opened it for males. I was scared being a female. But the atmosphere was good. I became their friend. They gave me a birthday party, put candles in Coke bottles. They sang me songs. There aren't many people who do this for the simple reason—and I understand this—they don't want to catch diseases. I took the TB test. If these people arrive, you don't know who they are, what diseases they have. Outside the shelter, they have nothing and wander the country on their own. I don't see this as human. Yes, it is not human to keep them in tents but they need medical care, shelter, and counseling.

Unsure how to deal with migrants whose lives are held in limbo, Maria concluded that providing better detention facilities is the humane course of action:

> Build a structure—a closed detention center. They are overcrowded in [my country]. [The migrants] break the showers, the toilets. It is inhuman. In summer we have the tents, eighteen beds. The first time I see them I was shocked but they have shelter in the open center. They should have a proper shelter. . . . Put them through the process in a proper way. [Our] side is trying to do their best, but no one wants them back: Nigeria, China. . . . But what I don't like about the government is the mentality. The [professional colleagues] around me are scared to take steps. They wait ages just to get a paper signed. It's like this in everything.

Despite her higher hopes for migrants' well-being, this goal only increases the efficiency of the larger migration apparatus by treating the symptoms of illegal migration rather than its systemic causes. In any case, Maria's story makes clear that the EU's migration apparatus not only contains and regulates migrants; significantly, it regulates its own expert operators as well. Maria was simply unable to reconcile her personal disposition with the demands of her job. She resigned her post in 2008 to pursue postgraduate education. In similar frustration, an experienced project officer in an Austrian NGO concluded that "I'm not sure I want to take part in this. It's a cynical business. We completely rely on what the donors [EU member states] want." This individual also resigned to pursue postgraduate education.

THE MAINTENANCE OF DISPARITY

The harrowing situations in which illegal migrants find themselves cannot be separated from the enormous infrastructure that precludes their entry into the EU's territorial space. The "system of systems," which integrates national border control installations and facilitates informal communication among geographically disparate officials, decreases these migrants' chances of a successful entry and increases the risks incumbent in the journey. Frontex sea operations, RABIT land operations, EUROSUR, MEDSEA, and so on strive to render the EU external border nearly impermeable and the space beyond it almost entirely visible. The system of systems monitors potentially everything and everyone that moves within its scope. The sympathy that individual European officials qua individuals express toward migrants cannot override the apparatus's dehumanizing effects.

Part of the animus that invigorates the system of systems is located in risk analysis itself. For risk analysis, like insurance, is a political technology that generates a mediated form of social solidarity, at best, or at least precludes a social fragmentation that the state could not manage (Ewald 1991b, 207). That social solidarity appears in the form of national (and perhaps European) identity, which the system of systems juxtaposes against the threats it identifies in the illegal migrant. In so doing, risk analysis likewise elicits a national community, as it were, by creating "a close solidarity of interests" rather than a society of atomized individuals (207). The matter speaks to the consolidation of a national labor force as well if we apply Ewald's (204–5) argument that insurance covers not the loss of limb per se, but rather the indemnified's loss of profit-making capacity. Likewise, risk analysis in the form of border patrol protects the domestic labor market against the loss of (usually low-status) jobs thereby preserving the profit-making capacity of the domestic laboring class. The treatment of the alien as an external object of risk nevertheless generates an image of a world that is fortuitously connected rather than causally related (Brenneis 1994, 24), which thereby frees the risk assessor from responsibility toward that which is identified as a risk object. Similarly, officials routinely justify external border control measures as necessary practices to keep threatening objects out of sovereign space with no regard for how those objects are manifestations of issues relating that space to places beyond (Heyman 2008, 325).

While migrants are sometimes lucky enough to find ways to get in—as many academics and migration officials admiringly point out—appreciation of their ingenuity should not overshadow the gravity of their situation. Though particular legal channels are available to circulate through the EU, the apparatus functions to maintain a large-scale apartheid between the North and South precisely because the prosperity of the former cannot be universalized to include the latter, regardless of the hope invested in development projects (Chapter 6). Thus, while capitalist space is all but synonymous with global space in the post–Cold War era, human circulation is contained within subspaces that are actively forming along economic and geographic lines. In this regard, the official who reasoned that Frontex is not building Fortress Europe because of its partnerships with transit countries is partially correct. Those partnerships, however, are designed to restrict migrant circulation while the circulation of finance and commodities continues, most often in a North to South direction.

The problem of circulation posed by today's liberalized economy does not fundamentally differ from the opening of towns and hamlets in the eighteenth century as Foucault described. The lowering of barriers—either the town walls or the border check points—risks the entry of undesirable objects. Such entries cannot be completely stopped, but their probability can be significantly lowered through comprehensive surveillance, intensive mathematical analysis, and border control operations. These efforts grapple with questions of probabilities: What is the likelihood, for example, that more migrants will travel to the EU via the Libya–Italy route rather than the Senegal–Canary Islands route; or via the Turkish coast to the Greek islands versus overland through Serbia and Croatia up to Slovenia?

The many liberal-minded policy officials building the migration management apparatus do not justify their work in exclusionary terms—"they are different" or "they are inferior"—even though exclusion is the obvious effect of their labor. Rather, they largely justify their labor in terms of migrants' own good: "They have made the dangerous decision to risk their lives by trying to illegally cross the border. We must save their lives before it is too late. We are the innocent ones because of the position that this matter puts us in." The EU solves the humanitarian crisis at its doorstep with benevolent border control practices. Nevertheless, the efforts to develop such a thorough border control regime effectively reinforce Kennan's brutal point that "we"—the EU in this case—must maintain these current conditions of disparity. This situation likewise gives credence to Žižek's point that "unabashed economic egotism" prompted Frontex's creation and new border control practices more broadly (2002, 149).

However, the condemnation should be reserved for the practice not the practitioners, many of whom genuinely struggle with the moral contradictions involved in their work. Dispassionate rational calculations backed by implicit ideological assumptions ultimately sustain the apparatus: What is the likelihood that a mass of people on Libyan shores will embark for Italy? Do political developments in Morocco threaten the border at Ceuta? Do our multivariate analyses incorporate the proper data? Are our bureaucratic procedures sufficiently lean? Do we agree upon a template for sharing intelligence from maritime surveillance? Insisting on the humanitarianism of these policy rationales does not compensate for their dehumanizing effects, as Maria testifies. Allegiance to utilitarianism rather than irrepressible forms of nationalism might be the greater factor foreclosing discussions on more equitable approaches to migration management.

If these border control measures treat migrant populations as an anonymous mass of indistinguishable entities, then biometric technology individualizes the mass at official border crossing points. The next chapter shows how biometric control mechanisms both thwart illegal crossings and expedite desirable circulations. The organizational forms present in EU border control practices—the galvanizing power of "crises"; the dense networks of material infrastructure versus informal associations of nonce bureaucrats; the standardized policy outlook; and the objectified migrant for analytic purposes versus the humanitarian subject for rhetorical purposes—also play crucial roles in the integration of biometric systems. The chapter also shows how access to the EU is becoming even more explicitly a matter of income and education rather than nationality with the rise of the registered traveler program.

5 BIOMETRICS
Where Isn't the Security Threat?

Security is no longer a defensive measure. It's an enabling catalyst for achievement.

Unisys 2009

TO TRAVEL IN GOOD FAITH

Developments in border control described in the previous chapter and developments in biometric information systems operate in complementary policy spheres. While the former precludes the entry of proverbial masses of unwanted migrants, the latter scrutinizes the identity of every individual border crosser to ensure that only those with proper documentation can enter. When addressing industry leaders, the EC's top official for biometric IT systems, Dr. Frank Paul, alluded to the symbiosis: "Integrated border management is obviously very closely linked to identity management. You cannot think about proper border management if you do not at the same time think about proper ID management." This fusion of these policy spheres is inextricably linked to a larger moral narrative framing the relationship between the state, the citizen, and the third-country national. That narrative often downplays the importance of national identity and ethnic or cultural background, while celebrating the particular, individual cosmopolitan traveler in need of state protection from invisible transnational criminal networks. Government, the EC, and industry officials deploy this narrative to marshal citizens behind the biometrics cause. The narrative also justifies greater surveillance over the migrant, whose integrity also requires state protection from the threat of illicit trafficking and smuggling networks. That protection ostensibly secures the individual while his or her creativity and productivity benefits self and society.

Biometric information systems expedite the circulation of bodies through border control points first by recognizing the link between the traveler and the travel document and then by checking the traveler's identity against a central database to determine if entry is permitted. Biometrics facilitates state surveillance by isolating travelers and then dividing them into various categories of border crossers, for example, short-term labor migrant, tourist, or refugee. This power does not serve the state as an end in itself but rather the liberal economy, which the state's regulatory functions secure and sustain. Within the context of the territorialized social-democratic state, Poulantzas (1972, 131) argued that "this effect of isolation which is designated by the term 'competition' covers the whole spectrum of socio-economic relations." In today's global capitalism, biometrics helps to organize transnational labor circulation through such isolation and thus increases the availability of Southern labor at competitive, legal, and transparent prices. To ensure the integrity of labor circulation, however, these systems must check everyone (citizen and noncitizen) crossing an EU border control point in order to find the paucity of travelers who either deviate from or threaten the normative "virtuous traveler." The distinction between citizen and noncitizen blurs into the more inclusive category of mobile laborer, among whom security threats lurk. In fact, everyone is suspect until the database declares the person's innocence. The initial policy question then becomes, not where *is* but where *isn't* the security threat?

Jan de Ceuster, once head of the EC's borders and visas unit (now heading the Visa Policy unit since 2010), explained how biometrics allows border officials to sail between the rock of preventing undesirable entries and the hard place of admitting desirable ones:

> On the one hand, there are security considerations. It will be a means of permitting us to improve the fight against illegal immigration and threats to public order. But on the other—and this must not be forgotten—it will be a means of assisting the free movement of foreign nationals who need a visa, who travel in good faith. (Lobjakas 2005)

Biometric information systems should also stop the traffickers and smugglers who exploit virtuous individuals, and the tricksters who commit identity theft through the use of fraudulent documents. These miscreants jeopardize the circulation of bodies, cash, finance, and commodities upon which the global economy so fully depends. As a $31.6 billion global industry, human trafficking has become the third most profitable criminal activity in the world behind illegal drugs and the black market sale of weapons (Ramdas 2007). Fittingly, Franco Frattini, former European commissioner for justice, freedom and security, proclaimed in an EU ministerial-level conference on border management that "Europe needs a new approach to border management to better face the challenges posed by globalization, increased mobility and ever changing security threats. We need to be one step ahead to [sic] the increasingly better organised networks of terrorists and criminals who have discovered the lucrative trafficking in human beings, drugs and weapons." He is joined by Lin Homer, chief executive of the UK Border Agency, who made the point more robustly while illustrating the benefit of migration for the host country:

> The UK wants to realize successfully the many benefits of migration—economic, social, cultural—and to do that we think we need to protect the identity of individuals and to facilitate travelers we want such as business people, investors, students, and those who will benefit the UK economy. And whilst we do that we must protect public services against abuse and we must tackle the problems caused by people traffickers and illegal working . . . and we must also ensure that the public have confidence in our ability to protect them.

All in all, biometrics secures the mobility of the desired travelers and helps to sift out the illicit networks that steal their identities for illicit purposes, including the production of false travel documentation.

This chapter situates EU biometric systems in a historical context to examine how they function in migration management, how they encourage particular types of professional networks, how they objectify travelers and regulate them through different administrative techniques, and how they induce particular subject-positions that sustain the EU's current political economy. These investigations reveal rather bizarre situations in which loose, ephemeral professional networks create the conditions for the ever tighter integration of national biometric systems in which identities become alienated from individuals as they request permission to cross from one sovereign space to another. This chapter also describes the sheer volume of information capture at work, which involves literally scores of millions of personal files. Nevertheless, the champions of biometrics in EC, national, and industrial bureaucracies insist that biometrics secures travelers from the lurking threat of identity theft, thus allowing them to become creative globe-trotting individuals. The result is the strange marriage of liberal individualism and the advanced security state.

IMMUTABLE DATA

Broken down into its original Greek, "biometric" means simply "life measurement." Biometric systems are rapidly expanding in the fields of border control, business security (particularly banks and casinos), criminal investigation, and the administration of detainees of all types. Biometric data are information about an individual that does not change through time. It could include behavioral data, such as a person's gait and voice pattern; physiological data like hand vein patterns, iris patterns, retinal patterns, facial recognition, and fingerprints; and even genetic data in the form of DNA patterns. Motorola, a leading vendor of biometric information systems, explains that they are simply "pattern recognition" systems. These systems chart and institutionalize "normal" human circulation and thus allow "deviance" to be established, detected, and quarantined in relation to it. Biometrics emerged as an applied science at the end of the nineteenth century with the French anthropologist (and police clerk) Alphonse Bertillon developing a system to record anthropometric information for purposes of criminal identification. Anthropometry measured gross body parts, which rendered it relatively imprecise as advances in measurement capability took hold. The British anthropologist Sir Francis Galton determined that fingerprints were immutable and unique to an individual (up to 64 billion individuals). He identified patterns based on particular points of intersection among fingerprint ridges that he called minutiae, which remain the basis of fingerprint recognition, or dactylography, to this day. Through time, then, units of biometric data have become ever smaller, from gross anatomy to microanatomy to genetic structure. This shrinking of the size of the unit of biometric data captured corresponds to the exponential growth of the number of individual profiles that biometric information systems now process.

Electronic travel documents contain digitalized biometric information that corresponds to the traveler and any databases that may contain the traveler's biometric profile. The document mediates the relationship between the state and the traveler. The EU is now setting global standards through the International Civil Aviation Organization (ICAO). EU travel documents contain digitalized records of all ten fingerprints as well as facial images in a microchip, which is sealed in a travel document such as a visa sticker for third-country nationals or a passport (now called an "e-passport" for EU citizens). A border guard matches the information stored in the chip against the biometric data taken from a traveler at the border control point through fingerprint or facial scanners (see Thomas 2005 for a discussion on human rights, law, and biometrics). If a match between the two is not detected, then the border guard must proceed to a second level of inquiry to determine the traveler's identity. The traveler's biometric information is also matched against EU-wide databases to see if any entry restrictions are in place. The more technologically advanced fingerprint scanners monitor body heat and blood flow below the surface of the skin to detect any phenotypic discrepancies between the actual fingerprint and the digitalized record (Gleeson 2003). Though not infallible, biometric data offer a very high probability of determining the presence or absence of a one-to-one match between the traveler and the travel document. Exemplifying the use of mathematical rationales as much as any explicit ideology to organize society, algorithms are used to minimize the chances of a false positive or false negative reading. However, as one biometric consultant explains:

> The problem is that the better you get at rejecting [catching] criminals, the more likely you are to reject [catch] innocent people and the other way around. These rules and algorithms are influencing the lives of people. Imagine that you know you are innocent and you put your fingerprints on the detector and it says you are a criminal.

Indeed, while false positives are rare, border crossing is ultimately a game of probabilities.

One effect of biometric identification systems is the disembodiment of the individual traveler and the elimination of his or her qualitative personal history. Since the state recognizes the traveler through a digital representation, not only are bodies disappearing (Lyon 2001, 8), but border crossers become people without history, to reframe a Wolf (1982) title. For it is not the qualitative experience lived through a body that is the primary object of management but rather the status that the state attributes to the quantitative, digitalized representation of the body (for example, tourist, business traveler, citizen of a failed state). The individual's dynamic history is less important than the static category assigned to the individual's biometric representation. The consultant explained that biometrics has "shifted the emphasis from habeas corpus to 'habeas cognos.' Your existence was proved because you had a body. But today you only exist if you have information [about your body]." The European Biometrics Group, an industry booster, nevertheless celebrates this shift from the qualitative to the quantitative as a mechanism through which individuals assert themselves as unique actors:

> Biometrics is the most used way to identify persons: you recognize a face, a photograph, the sound of a voice, because it looks unique. Today, biometrics technology enables [sic] to capture this uniqueness and digitalize these various biometrics attributes: face, eyes, fingerprint etc. . . . With the venue of the information society, identifying yourself with biometrics seems the safest way [sic] safest means to protect your identity against theft. If a password is what you

know, if a smart card is what you have, biometrics is what you are! (European Biometrics Portal n.d.)

The fusion of one's identity to one's biometric data likewise fuses the state's objectification of the individual to that of the person's subjectivity.

Biometric information systems, moreover, effectively guarantee the eternal storage of biometric information, its instantaneous transmission across the EU's territorial space, and the near impossibility of sharing one's data with another person (unlike a passport photograph). Along with individualizing travelers, the system renders them legible across the state territory through dense computerized networks connecting border crossing points, police surveillance points, and any location where the traveler might come into contact with state-regulated institutions. How are biometric systems built in the first place?

SETTING STANDARDS AND LABORING ABSTRACTLY

Reminiscent of a Kafka novel, the permeation of biometric systems into the body politic sits bizarrely with the fact that the experts who make it happen rarely, if ever, meet each other in person. To be sure, the enormity of the social distance between the plethora of migration policy officials is only slightly greater than that between biometric IT workers themselves. Most of their expert labor occurs in cyberspace where they work to integrate, consolidate, and strengthen biometric information systems across the EU. Hardt and Negri (2000, 295–96) argue that this type of work exemplifies the "informational economy," where networks replace formal organizations and where proximity of workers to each other and to material infrastructure (railways, assembly lines, storage depots, and so on) is no longer necessary. Workers engage in "abstract cooperation" by communicating remotely, remaining unknown to each other, and interacting without a central agent. Hardt and Negri point out that in today's immaterial labor—labor that produces services, cultural products, knowledge, communication, and so on rather than durable goods— "cooperation is completely immanent to the laboring activity itself" and is not imposed from the outside (294–95). The European Biometrics Forum (EBF), an independent agency created by the EC's Directorate General Information Society, harmonizes biometric standards and applications. In the EBF's own terms, it works to develop "a secure, user friendly, socially acceptable and ethical use of biometrics in Europe" (European Biometrics Forum 2003). More specifically, the EBF is designing a road map for the industry to fill gaps in research, expand commercial applications, and develop new ways of integrating biometric information technology systems. Though headquartered in Dublin, the EBF is composed of a lean network of experts located across Europe and the world, acting as a forum for knowledge exchange, policy developments, and public awareness. Unisys manages their main communication venue called the European Biometrics Portal (EBP), which is a modest website providing information on news updates, events, links, resources, and contacts.

The EBF relies on no solid organizational structure but rather on a field of relevant actors that CEO Max Snijder can assemble according to particular needs similar to RABITs. Staff levels are determined according to each particular business plan, with extra help hired externally as necessary. With this approach, the "core of the EBF can stay small, cost efficient and flexible" (Snijder 2005). Snijder consults with many EU member-state governments and is a high-level member of many international biometric organizations, such as the Consortium on Security and Technology of the East/West Institute, the Porvoo Group, and the CEN Working Group on Integrated Border Management. He is also a founding member of the International Federation for Information Processing Working Group on Identity Management. He formed the Biometric Expertise Group (BEG) in 2004. The BEG consists of a small team of experts (about twelve to fifteen) that offers "knowledge and experience in building biometric business cases/models and implementation designs" (Biometric Expertise Group n.d.). According to its own self-description, it covers all aspects of the biometrics enterprise: "financials, business models, SLAs [service legal agreements], contract management, procurement, vendor selection, legal aspects, organizational processes, functional processes and designs, standardization, technology assessments, testing and evaluating, auditing etc." (ibid.).

Apropos of the industry's amorphous organization, the EBF itself does not offer the EC or EU member states a product as such. Rather, it *enables* the delivery of biometrics products. Speaking to the example of SC 37 standards (see below), which enable interoperability among separate national biometric systems, Snijder (2005) explains:

> We do not see ourselves actually doing the certification and testing, but helping to coordinate the process. This needs to be done very quickly. We have a lot of knowledge throughout our network and we can mobilize this in order to find organizations and help them create the appropriate test and certification centres.

He highlights the work of the Essen Group, composed of IT experts from the UK, the Netherlands, and Germany (discussed below). This group, he explains, "is working to create interoperability of ePassport solutions. They are very interested in sharing this information with other Member States. This is exactly the sort of role EBF can play."

While abstract cooperation enables the production of SC 37 standards, these standards are crucial for achieving "interoperability" between national databases, EU databases, and electronic travel documents. As Bowker and Star (1999, 13) put it, "A 'standard' is any set of agreed-upon rules for the production of (textual or material) objects." Standards allow things to work together across distance, through time, and through heterogeneous metrics (14). Their fusion effect across different communities of practice results from their being both ambiguous and constant as well as both abstract and concrete. Bowker and Star describe standards as "boundary objects," which can obtain common identities in different contexts because they are weakly defined in generic terms and strongly defined in particularized, tailored applications. They interlock systems that would otherwise fragment or never converge to begin with, and function as a countermeasure to the broader alienation of workers that occurs in abstract cooperation, and of mass society in general. As direct social relations become estranged, standards reconnect people through much more mediated and technologically driven forms of communication.

Standards also help the EC unify a hitherto fragmented biometrics industry. The four largest biometrics companies operating in Europe—SAGEM, Motorola, Cogent, and Gemalto—had been developing biometric systems for numerous clients in national and local governments. The EC now has integrated these various systems into such EU-wide entities as the Schengen Information System (SIS), the Visa Information System (VIS), or other registered traveler (RT) programs. More specifically, SC 37 standards will enable biometric IT systems produced by different vendors to exchange template fingerprint data rather than digitalized fingerprint images. The difference lies in the size of the latter at 15 kilobytes versus the former at 3 kilobytes; the smaller size allows the data to move more quickly through the network and take up less storage space on a travel document's radio frequency identification (RFID) chip. SC 37 standards facilitate the exchange of fingerprint minutiae points among the different national systems that store biometric information, allowing border guards to quickly match biometric information between the traveler, travel document, and the biometric database.

The name "SC 37" blandly refers to Subcommittee 37 of the Joint Technical Committee 1 (JTC 1) of the International Standards Organization (ISO), which is an international network of national standards institutes from 157 countries. The production process for SC 37 spreads far and wide, incorporating a diversity of disciplines and industries. JTC 1 consists of forty participating member states and forty-two observer states along with other partners such as international commissions and industry associations for banking, telecommunications, nuclear and geological sciences, and multimedia systems. It divides further into dozens of subcommittees, working groups, and specialty groups. JTC 1 holds an annual plenary meeting, but the bulk of its mutual cooperation takes place virtually on its website, where reports of all kinds are posted, some of which are publicly available. Other matters such as ballots, resolutions, and projects are discussed through "livelinks" on the website, which require passwords and login IDs. Ironically, the enduring aspect of its abstract cooperation exists virtually in cyberspace on its "Enterprise Workspace" for IT (Information Technology Standards 2003a). Since 1998, JTC 1 has published well over one hundred sets of international standards annually, mostly on information technology systems. JTC 1 draws on the talents of roughly 2,100 technical experts from around the world (Information Technology Standards 2003b). As of April 6, 2007, it had issued sixteen standards on biometric technical interfacing, biometric data interchange formats, and biometric performance testing and reporting. The names of these standards sound painfully tedious to the uninitiated, for example: "Informational technology—Common Biometric Exchange Formats Framework (CBEFF)—Part 1: Data Element Specification" (Information Technology Laboratory 2007).

The Essen Group further illustrates abstract cooperation, as it amounts to an informal network of IT specialists supported by governments and industry. The group exists in no core location, office building, or physical space. Instead, it created a website where it posts reports from tests and experiments on the interoperability of passports and e-documents. The name "Essen" simply refers to the German city in which the semiprivate secunet (Security Networks AG) is based. This IT security company provides the domain services and IT security for the Essen Group website on which the group's reports are posted (secunet 2008). One significant report sums up the results of a 2006 test workshop held in the Crown Plaza Hotel in Berlin (secunet 2006). The German Federal Ministry of the Interior hosted the event with further support and cooperation from the Brussels Interoperability Group, the EC, the ICAO's New Technology Group, and other public and private entities. In this event, titled the ePassport

Interoperability Test Event, IT experts spent four days testing the exchange capability of the ICAO's new digital information standards. The results of the test conference are available on the Essen Group website, along with other up-to-date results and notifications, for interested parties to study.

The test event illustrates the ad hoc and ephemeral connections that exist between actors in the biometrics field. Most of the communications, preparations, and preliminary work that formed the substance of the conference were conducted separately in dispersed labs and then communicated virtually. The actors know each other mainly through mediated forms of communication (e-mail, teleconferencing, website messaging, and so on). Their direct interpersonal contact composes nothing more than a hectic conference, the photographs from which show meeting rooms unceremoniously filled with computer equipment strewn across tabletops. Again, the enduring substance of their IT work—the very information about how to technically create interoperable systems to process the biometric data in e-passports—exists on a website. That substance is, ironically, virtual information rather than something material. It is thus similar to the bodies of border crossers themselves, which are represented through digitalized biometric information more than through their own corporeality (habeas cognos over habeas corpus).

Significantly, no formal organization was required to mobilize the vast array of expertise that contributed to SC 37's development. Specific location is a second-hand issue; it is decided on an ad hoc basis, and functional considerations are the main priority: where and how quickly can we assemble and disassemble our computer stations? Information laborers work in a plethora of private companies and public institutions and are drawn from these different locations to pool their knowledge around a collective "problem." It is the "problem" of irregular migration that animates the network and its "informational economy" more broadly even if information laborers have no vested interest in it. Nevertheless, like those working on the I-Map and the 3MP guidelines, the flexible and decentralized character of this abstract cooperation remains pivotal to the assembly of a very specific, centralized, and territorialized goal: the careful regulation of bodies across the EU's external border.

SC 37 signals both an assertion of the EU as a global leader in biometric technology and a major advance in the convergence of an EU-wide information exchange system. The EC's implicit reason for creating the EBF was to build a European industry standard that could improve upon and be independent of the more widely accepted US standards, according to one former EC official. The EU began pushing e-passport technology more quickly than any other country in the world. Another EC official responsible for integrating biometric information systems pointed out:

> We were the first in the world [on large-scale interoperability]. Now ICAO will take over our standards. The US [was] much later than us. They still have not decided if they will take fingerprints. NIST [US National Institute of Standards and Technology] standards weren't for passports. Some in Canada. EU has much influenced international standards. Balkan countries, Turkey, even US were looking at us.

"CLAIM AN IDENTITY"

In addition to those who produce the capacity for large-scale biometric information systems, others must justify those systems' social value. These justifications emerge out of discussions between small business leaders, big business leaders, industry boosters, and EC, national, and local officials. Though certain people among them possess the institutional capital and administrative talent to take the lead in moving this process along, they are not O'Brien-like Orwellian figures. Similarly, no éminence grise is pulling the strings from an undisclosed location. Instead, these individuals overall embody middle-class morality, liberal humanitarianism, and economic entrepreneurialism and see the role of the police, security, and defense establishments in migration management as a matter of common sense. The ethnographic question is how a rationale of governance functions in these officials' mundane practices to legitimize the isolation and securitization of the individual traveler, which in turn facilitates the management of millions of travelers. The rationale is not simply rhetoric that stands in contrast to material processes. Instead, the power of the rationale is that it fuses together "reasonable" opinion and material practices so tightly that mainstream debates cannot entertain their decoupling and the new ideas that might follow.

Like the different experts described throughout the book, these business and government professionals work in isolation of each other, so catching them in rare moments of dense interaction offers valuable ethnographic opportunities to learn how such a rationale appears in policy discussions. One occasion took place in a convention in London's charming Covent Garden organized by Science Media Partners, a consortium supporting the global biometrics industry. The event buzzed with five hundred participants, mostly government officials and industry leaders. They flocked around display booths to examine microcameras, facial scanners, dactyloscopic readers, and other Bond-like gadgets. These devices measure biometric data such as the diameter of one's iris, the distance between the tip of the nose to the corner of the jawbone, and the vein pattern in one's hand. Large companies like Raytheon provided pamphlets on information technology systems capable of handling millions of individual profiles at a time. These participants support national border control programs like the UK's newly created e-Borders Programme, or the EU's SIS, VIS, and European Dactyloscopy (EURODAC).

Two catch phrases emerged from the convention's plenary speeches, workshop discussions, and casual conversations: "claim an identity" and "identity management." Like the algorithms and technical language of IT experts, these phrases both organize work in the biometrics industry and contribute to the traveler's objectification as they separate an identity from a body and establish it as an object over which border crosser and border guard negotiate for control. The first phrase refers to what a traveler actually does when requesting passage into the EU at a border control point. A top industry official working on border control systems at Amsterdam's Schiphol Airport explained to the convention audience the bewildering challenge of verifying identities: "You will always have people from other countries wave a document at you and say 'Hey, I claim an identity.'" Flippant though his comment sounds, he actually synopsizes the experience perfectly. Travelers, and migrants in particular, stand immobilized at a controlled border crossing point and ask the state to recognize their identities. They cannot assert their identity but rather request that the state accepts the claim as if one were retrieving a lost possession. Our identities are effectively lost when we move from one sovereign space to another, and they must be reclaimed from the state at the journey's end. The phrase "claim an identity" betrays the alienation of the self from the state, as the state is empowered to decide if the biological traveler is entitled to own that political identity. Everyone is at least temporarily a stranger and a suspect for not being whoever he or she claims to be (Browne 2009, 145).

Nevertheless, many experts justify biometrics on the grounds that it protects, rather than alienates, the individual. I asked the marketing manager of a contractor for EURODAC why anyone should trust the state with biometric data. She replied:

> Many people say that "something is being taken from me" when they give biometric information, but I look at it the other way around. Biometrics protects

my anonymity. Has someone ever entered your home and taken something from you? This happened to me a week after my honeymoon. The police caught him six months later from fingerprints that they matched against his biometric information.

The irony of her argument that "biometrics protects [her] anonymity" is that each individual's personal security requires further isolation from others in the eyes of the security state. The more biometric information we bequeath to the state, the more individualized we become, and the better secured from other members of society. Biometrics thus generates a mere collective of individuals, simplifying the task of policing their social relations.

One expert who helped design the EURODAC system reached the same conclusion but through an inversion of the marketing manager's reasoning:

> If you have total privacy, then you have no identity, then [you] have no contact with any other organization. I can't have isolation. That's why I like biometrics: because it's a physical attribution. You can have only physical attribute[s]. No one can go against it. Given the complexities of modern life, I like biometrics. You can't get money, you can't transfer money, you can't pay for things, you can't cross a border, you can't have a life event without documentation: birth, marriage, divorce.

For this individual, biometrics activates social life rather than segregates social actors, even if the social is mediated through state surveillance to prevent identity theft and other forms of deviance. These two advocates of biometrics can reconcile their opposing starting points quite easily through Arendt's observation on the "public," which requires socially constructed things to mediate human interaction: "as a table is located between those who sit around it; the world, like every in-between, relates and separates men at the same time. . . . The public realm, as the common world, gathers us together and yet prevents our falling over each other, so to speak" (1958, 52). For the marketing manager, biometrics guarantees the sanctity of her separation and privacy so the public cannot violate that privacy and inhibit her from participating in the social world on solid footing. For the EURODAC expert, biometrics provides her the means to establish her connection to the public. The two views fit together because the social integration described by the latter presupposes the separation, isolation, and individualism described by the former. However, these complementary processes objectify the individual to preclude the threat of qualitative difference between individuals in mass society. Biometrics celebrates plural-ism as a unique but quantitative matter of biological difference—fingerprints, faces, and irises. As such, it suppresses the uniqueness of the individual's quali-tative personal history, which is a pluralism that can very much change the social world (Arendt 1958; see also Žižek 2002, 11).

Another business representative, who used to work in biometrics and now runs a document security company, quite readily recognized the objectifying effects of biometrics. "I used to use the term 'material biometrics' . . . but it wasn't politically correct [in the industry]," he remarked. I asked him why, and he responded:

> Purists get upset because "bio" is Greek for "life," and therefore biometrics means the measurement of life . . . they said that biometrics is about life and people. . . . Since material is not live it's deemed to be an incorrect use of the word. My view [however] is that the expression "material biometrics" sums up in only two words exactly what's going on.

If his point holds that biometrics simply measures inert material rather than something alive in a socially meaningful way, then the gentleman evokes the ancient Greek distinction between mere biological life (*zoē*) and qualified po-litical life (*bios*) (Agamben 1998). He effectively argues that biometric informa-tion systems reduce human life rather than enhance it, thus undermining the entire moral narrative of biometrics. Following this businessman's logic to the end, one can conclude that the social is made possible through the reduction of the individual's life from a set of qualitative experiences to an immutable quan-titative representation. As discussed below, however, the discourse normalizing the expansion of biometric technology frames the issue in precisely the op-posite way: biometrics allows the state to liberate (not reduce) the individual's qualitative capacities.

"IDENTITY MANAGEMENT": POSTMODERNISM MEETS THE SURVEILLANCE STATE

The phrase "identity management," which also circulated through this conven-tion, describes IT systems that process biographical information on very large numbers of people. In the case of migration management, the EU renders mil-lions of travelers comprehensible as temporary laborers, asylum-seekers, stu-dents, and others through the processing of their "identity claims" at border crossing points. An estimated 140 million third-country nationals legally enter the EU every year while 160 million EU citizens do the same (Europa 2008b). Corporations from the US military-industrial complex, such as Lockheed Martin, Motorola, and Northrop Grumman, along with major European companies such as SAGEM, Cogent, and Gemalto possess the technological capability and the experience to cope with the sheer volume of information involved in identity management systems. In the wake of declining orders for military hardware in the post–Cold War era, these companies found an expanding market in the fields of criminology and migration management. One "solution architect" for a major defense contractor explained that "the steps from defense contracting to migration go through criminal justice with advanced intelligence work, facial and other forms of identification, and systems integration." The transition proved relatively smooth as these companies already possessed the relevant experience in systems engineering, data storage, personnel training, budget management, and so on. One industry consultant hired from a national defense background explained:

> How do you bring all the stuff together, biometrics at 250 locations, communications networks so information comes in three seconds on request? How to schedule control of your program? The hardware for that could fill up a whole building. [Border control] is a natural extension of the intelligence business. If you look at it from the system perspective it is the same thing. The tracking doesn't matter if it is a migrant, a MiG [Soviet fighter jet], or a terrorist.

Identity management for border crossing purposes involves a huge amount of biological information stored in EU databases that is instantly transferable across EU space. The labor power of postmodern, deterritorialized IT networks is now fused to the modern state project of protecting territorial integrity. While the work of Frontex and its affiliated institutions monitors space at the EU's external border and beyond, in complementary fashion biometric information systems begin at the border to monitor incoming human flows through controlled crossing points.

One example is Raytheon, a multibillion-dollar company with offices in nineteen countries that is best known for designing weapons systems. It leads Trusted Borders, a group of seven companies, in the £650 million e-Borders project for the UK's Home Office. (Lockheed Martin and Northrop Grumman led unsuccessful consortia in the competition.) Perhaps the most comprehensive border control program in existence, e-Borders operates at all points of entry into the UK—rail, sea, and air—to gather information on domestic and international passengers. It checks both arriving and departing passengers on domestic and international flights. Through enhanced communications and information management technologies it can combine the service of several law enforcement agencies including police, customs and excise, and security services. Trusted Borders aims to identify those who "have no right to be in the UK and [to] assist in the fight against terrorists and criminals" (United Kingdom Home Office Press Office n.d.). Lin Homer, chief executive of the newly formed UK Border Agency, proudly announced in April 2008 that since the start of e-Borders earlier that year 23,000 alerts appeared in the system; 1,700 arrests took place; and many football hooligans were prevented from leaving the UK for other countries. She also announced that the Biometric Visa Program has been catching 150 cases of identity swap per month.

The EU's major IT systems such as SIS, VIS, and EURODAC grew out of earlier multinational efforts in Europe to share information on deviant individuals such as criminals, terrorists, spies, and refugees. In the 1970s, west European police agencies relied on early versions of fax machines to transfer information about socially marginal travelers. As technologies increased the scale of information capture, so European governments widened the net to enclose the entire population of travelers. Interior and justice ministers from the then European Community held regular meetings beginning in 1975 to discuss international cooperation between their respective national police forces. They found motivation in acute security crises such as left-wing Europe-based terrorism and the Palestinian attacks on Jewish athletes at the 1972 Munich Olympics. The first intergovernmental group of ministers to formally organize around such information-sharing was called TREVI. "TREVI" stood for the French acronym Terrorisme, Radicalisme, Extremisme et Violence Internationale, though it might also signify the famous fountain in Rome. This allusion also coincidentally referred to the surname of the then director-general of police in the Netherlands, which was "Fonteijn" (Benyon et al. 1993, 152). Though TREVI originally focused on terrorism, prompted by talks of a common European market it expanded into other areas of law enforcement. Four working groups soon composed TREVI: (I) antiterrorism; (II) public order, equipment, and training; (III) drugs and organized crime; and (IV) the abolition of borders. The EU's current definition of terrorism ranks as one of Working Group I's enduring contributions to transnational surveillance: "the use or attempt to use violence by an organized group to achieve political goals" (154). Working Group II focused on the technical challenges of information exchange among hitherto incompatible national databases. Its first major opportunity to harmonize communication arose in the aftermath of the 1985 Heysel football stadium tragedy in Brussels. The rowdy behavior of Liverpool supporters resulted in the collapse of a stadium retaining wall that crushed thirty-nine fans to death. The working group organized a network of permanent correspondents in each country to share information on hooligans suspected of committing violence and vandalism as they followed their favorite clubs around Europe. This surveillance and monitoring of such class-based violence led to agreements on common reporting formats that facilitate information exchange (155). Working Group III also led to the standardization and harmonization of information exchange as well as investigative techniques and criminal analysis. It also absorbed the responsibilities of Working Group IV.

These efforts to combat terrorism, criminality, and political violence set the precedent for the foundation of the Schengen Information System (SIS), which records information about goods and people as they cross the Schengen border (Joubert and Bevers 1996, 38–39). The Schengen Area (Chapters 1 and 3) functions as a homogenous block of space collectively monitored at external border control points, thus forming an internal complement to Frontex's surveillance of the EU's external space. The group's 1985 founding members—Belgium, France, Germany, Luxembourg, and the Netherlands—abolished their common borders to permit the free movement of goods and persons, a move that spawned efforts to create common visa regimes and a common asylum policy. Italy joined in 1990, followed by Spain and Portugal in 1991 and Greece in 1992. Now all EU countries are members of the Schengen Group, though the UK, Ireland, and Denmark participate only on matters of police cooperation rather than the free movement of persons. The Schengen Agreement was transposed into EU law in 1999. The Schengen Group similarly established four working groups: (I) policy and security; (II) movement of persons; (III) transport; and (IV) customs and movement of goods. Whereas TREVI focused on the criminal and terrorist dimension of cross-border flows, the Schengen Group started the comprehensive process of monitoring flows of all kinds. Schengen's remit, therefore, includes everything from harmonizing police communication procedures to reducing the risks of global flows including agricultural products, ship cargo, illegal drugs, and the various categories of international travelers. To meet the needs of intensified communication, the Schengen Group was among the first organizations to develop and systematically use an electronic mail infrastructure (141).

Following close in the footsteps of that revolutionary form of communication, the Schengen Group first developed SIS to process and share travelers' personal data, though it has yet to make the planned switch from alphanumeric to biometric data. Updated every five minutes and with seventeen million entries, SIS keeps data on people's name, nationality, place of birth, and known aliases and on lost, stolen, or missing firearms, documents, motor vehicles, and money. The Schengen Agreement ensures intra-EU cooperation on investigations of illegal migrants, on tracking and extraditing criminals, on filling European arrest warrants, and on monitoring "asylum shoppers." By the end of 2011, SIS II will include biometric facial images and fingerprints, with some states considering iris or retinal scans. As of 2005, it utilized six different "alerts," including people wanted for arrest and extradition, people refused entry into the Schengen Area, missing or dangerous persons, people wanted in court, people placed under surveillance, and lost and stolen objects. The charter for SIS II allows for the creation of new categories of alert including "football hooligans" and "protestors" set to be included under the category of "violent troublemakers." SIS II had obtained one million records of persons under this category as of 2005 (Hayes 2005). Seven member states have finalized SIS III, also known as the Prüm Treaty. Nine more states have declared their intention to sign. With sixteen member states on board, they can have SIS III transposed into EU law, which would permit the sharing of DNA, fingerprint, and license plate information among participating states. Authorities in one signatory state will have access to the relevant databases in others so that information can be matched for identification purposes (Council of the European Union 2007). In effect, the Prüm Treaty further collapses the distinction between citizen and noncitizen as it monitors EU and third country nationals alike.

The EU's first large-scale biometric information system grew out of the Dublin Convention (signed in 1990 and coming into force in 1997), which created common procedures aimed at stopping asylum shopping. This convention addressed public allegations that refugees were in fact economic migrants who abused national asylum systems by placing claims in multiple countries or applying in subsequent countries after a denial. Out of the convention emerged EURODAC, which went live in January 2003. The EURODAC biometric information database stores generic personal data like name, date of birth, sex, and home country as well as biometric data in the form of ten rolled fingerprints and three slap prints. The applicant submits this information when claiming asylum, and it is then matched against a central database to determine if the applicant has made a prior claim in a different EU country. In 2008, EURO-DAC processed 219,557 sets of fingerprints, of which 75,919 belonged to people illegally present on the member state's territory and 61,945 to people trying to cross borders irregularly (Europa 2009a). It is the first large-scale biometric information database that overcame the problem of interoperability described earlier. While lower-caliber systems existed in the US between the FBI and local police forces, "EURODAC was really pushing the boundaries," as its chief architect concluded in an interview. The technical requirements for EURODAC are now being used in SIS II, VIS, and the Biometric Matching System.

The "problem of visa shoppers" prompted work on the Visa Information System, scheduled to go live by 2012 at the earliest. The EC described VIS as necessary "to prevent threats to internal security of any of the Member States" (Commission of the European Communities 2004, 12). Since admission to one Schengen Area country provides easier access to others, visa applicants might apply in multiple countries to increase the likelihood of acceptance. Currently, citizens from 134 countries require visas to enter the Schengen Area, and about five million of the approximately twenty million annual visa requests are rejected (Lobjakas 2005). New applicants for a Schengen visa must travel to an EU consulate in a third country and supply a digitalized facial scan and ten digitalized fingerprints taken flat. Exceptions are made for children under six years of age and individuals who cannot physically present the biometric information to a scanner (European Commission 2006b). The European Commission maintains the Central Information System, the National Interface in each member state, and the communication infrastructure between them (Commission of the European Communities 2004). VIS will process five types of visas including short-stay visas, transit visas, airport transit visas, visas with limited territorial validity, and national long-stay visas. Visa applicants will submit the information according to the regulations of the state to which they are applying. The national authorities will create a file and link it to any other files on that individual that might exist in the VIS. The file is to consist of the application number, information on the visa status, and the authority to which the application has been submitted. Also included are personal data such as surname (and surname at birth); additional names; sex; date and country of birth, current nationality, and nationality at birth; type, number, date of issue, and date of expiry of the travel document; place and date of application; and type of visa request. The system also records the details of the applicant's sponsor who will bear financial responsibility during the stay. Data are also gathered on reasons for a visa rejection, annulment, revocation, or extension. Finally, a photograph and fingerprints are also entered in digitalized, biometric form. The data, stored for five years, distill a three-dimensional life into a two-dimensional digital representation.

The potential numbers of non-EU citizens absorbed and abstracted into biometric information systems are legion. VIS will likely become the world's largest biometric database as it stores data on people from over one hundred countries across the globe. A high estimate for the number of profiles to be stored in VIS reaches seventy million people. As of 2003, police officers, border guards, immigration officials, intelligence officials, security officials, vehicle registration authorities, judicial authorities, and customs officials had an astonishing 125,000 access points to SIS, a figure that includes only the fifteen pre-2004 EU member states (Council of the European Union 2003, 11). New member states implemented the system in 2007, increased the tally to over 500,000 (Council of the European Union 2009, 3). The decision to provide security agencies with access did not occur through the requisite legislative procedures outlined in the Schengen Convention. Rather, according to Statewatch (n.d.), SIS working groups composed of officials from member states agreed informally to reinterpret Article 93 of the convention, which says that SIS is "to maintain public order and security, including State security." The change exemplifies the ease with which key security decisions are rendered as technical rather than political matters.

REGISTERED TRAVELER PROGRAMS:
FROM NATIONAL TO CLASS DIFFERENCES VIA INDIVIDUALIZATION

EC officials also design biometric information systems to expedite the circulation of "wanted" travelers. These registered traveler (RT) programs facilitate border crossing for individuals who have relatively high economic capital, a move that emphasizes the individual over the collective, and class over nation. EC and industry officials justify these programs as the next reasonable step forward. Dr. Frank Paul, the EC's unit head for Large-Scale Information Technology Systems, oversees the administration of SIS, VIS, and EURODAC. He projects a commanding but not egocentric presence, which suggests a dispassionate but not callous competence. His demeanor conveys to an audience of industry leaders and government officials that he is a man "we can do business with." Much of his work focuses on the EC's developing relations with the biometrics industry. His dry wit and down-to-earth style help when he tells a group of industry leaders that the EU's plans for an RT program will take time: "Folks, we're talking about government activity here. OK? So, this is not gonna happen tomorrow." He added with a laugh, "That's very difficult to explain to people. I sometimes get calls from industry and people say 'So, Mr. Paul, are you rolling this out globally by the end of the year?' No we are not, no we are not. We definitely are not."

However, the low expectation that Paul sets for a delivery date belies the unit's ambitious plan for supporting RT programs. EC officials and industry leaders in biometric and information technology envision these programs as eventual replacements for what they see as an outdated visa system. They argue that today's visa programs place all travelers requiring visas into the same category with the same prerequisite security clearances, which presents an unfair hassle to the virtuous traveler. RT programs can rectify the obstacles that this individual faces. Traditional visa policy in this view is too unsophisticated to expedite border passages and identify "high risk" travelers. The solution lies in shifting the emphasis in border regulation from nation to class by applauding the virtuous traveler and by acting on simple common sense. As Paul explained:

> Basically what you want to do is to allow those people who are low risk . . . you want to allow them a speedy passage through the border. Now, "low risk," what does that mean? If you take a look at visa policy as such, and this is part of a broader debate, we are basically looking at an outdated concept. Visa policy today is country-based. And why do you ask for a certain nationality to have a visa? Because you have found out that for a variety of reasons . . . there is a risk of terrorism, economic migration, whatever . . . for a variety of reasons a certain nationality needs a visa. That doesn't make sense. That doesn't make sense.
>
> So you say, for example, all Lebanese for whatever reason need a visa. That doesn't make sense. That doesn't make sense. Because a visa is an additional security layer, you do a more thorough check than you normally do . . . when someone pops up at the border [by] checking him beforehand. But it doesn't make sense to ask a visa from every Lebanese citizen because it means that everyone is put into one pot and you apply the same rule to everyone in that pot. And that means that the person who might indeed be a security risk has to apply for a visa. That's fine. That's fair enough. You might also catch the one person who is a terrorist—that's fine—but it also means the same rule applies to the rich businessman who just wants to take his wife to Paris six times a year to go on a super-shopping spree. That means that the most welcome to come to

the European Union also need to apply for a visa and they'll just say "what the heck, I'll go somewhere else where I don't need a visa." And thirdly, it means that people who just want to visit their children who are studying in the European Union all need to go through the same procedure and that doesn't make sense. So long term, and I think everyone agrees at least at the European political level, we need to move away from the country-centric approach and to the person-centric approach. It's not the country, the nationality as such, that causes a risk, it's indeed the person, your behavior, what you're doing in your life. This is what causes a risk or not. Registered traveler programs are the first move away from the country-centric approach to the person-centric approach where you look away from the country and you look at the person and that person's history.

The goal of expediting the travel of high-end consumers (the "most welcome" in Paul's parlance) and international students' parents utilizes a neoliberal discourse that further individualizes mass society. Yet it also goes one step further by pushing a transnational class agenda that admits travelers on a basis of spending capacity rather than nationality. Lin Homer, chief executive of the UK Border Agency, similarly remarked, "We want to make it easy for legitimate travelers to the UK: businesspeople, students, investors." Paul explained to a different industry audience how RT programs are an integral part of the EC's Integrated Border Management Strategy. As they were originally known as "trusted traveler programs," he struggled to dispel the notion that the EC maintains a distinction between desirable and undesirable travelers. "In our perception, the trusted traveler doesn't exist. It doesn't exist because it is politically incorrect. It implies that there are trusted travelers and nontrusted travelers, which is not quite the way we see it. The way we see it is that there are trusted travelers and travelers we trust even more." Through ironic laughter he admitted that it is difficult to put into a term, "so this is why we moved to 'registered traveler.'"

As Paul indicated, this increased individualization deployed to separate and mobilize "wanted," "trusted," "business," and "educated" travelers requires further streamlining of the visa application process. Elaine Dezenski, a senior vice president for Crossmatch Technologies, argued in April 2008 that even though current enrollment in RT programs has reached only 700,000 out of a billion travelers a year, "we can still make the argument that RT is entering the mainstream." This mathematically questionable statement nevertheless signals the modes in which certain factual observations are normalized—that is, through sheer repetition by actors endowed with the requisite technical knowledge and administrative capital. The wealthy traveler appears as the norm, and is thus mainstream, while the low- or middle-income traveler or illegal migrant is removed from sight as a deviant or at least as abnormal. The economics support her argument better than the mathematics. According to one biometrics consultant, "RT travelers are only 16 percent of travelers to Europe [and] 80 percent of the business of travel is supported by that 16 percent . . . so RT makes it easier for those people. It's [about profit] with the excuse of terrorism."

Dezenski also deploys the argument of convenience that highlights how apparatuses designed for different purposes in one historical moment can transform to take on a broader suite of regulatory functions. Speaking at the same event in a talk called "Registered Traveler: A Path to Technology and Policy Convergence?" she casually said, "Let's have a think," to show the simplicity of the reasoning that had hitherto evaded the policy conversation:

> What normally happens when you apply for a visa? You provide ten fingerprints, at least when you come to the US. You go through an interview with a consular officer. You provide a significant amount of biographic data. Your fingerprints are checked against a relevant database or two or three. And a decision is made. What happens when you typically apply to a registered traveler program? You provide ten fingerprints. You go in for an interview. You provide documentation . . . lots of biographic data. Those biometrics are run against a relevant database. So, you are seeing the point here. I think that there is a convergence of processes. And one question that perhaps, again, we can think about for our panel discussion is "at what point does an RT process look like a visa process, and at what point do we see a convergence of these processing activities that are taking place in advance of the actual travel?" If the goal is to make the passenger processing run as smoothly as possible to get the most out of our infrastructure . . . to use the available technology for multipurposes, we need to be thinking even beyond where we are now as to how we get to that convergent point, if that is what we want.

Registered traveler programs in Europe are currently designed to expedite border crossing for travelers who do not need a visa to enter the Schengen Area. (The EC aims to extend these programs for qualified travelers who do need them.) Travelers who qualify for these programs can pass through automated border crossings at an average speed of eight seconds since the process requires no interaction with a passport control officer. "If you are a businessman, then you know it very well . . . every minute counts. Whether you have to queue two hours or ten minutes makes a huge, huge difference in your schedule," Paul explained. RT programs provide members with cards containing the required biometric information. Schengen passport holders would submit the biometric indicator chosen by their particular program. In the case of third-country nationals this would include digitalized recordings of the traveler's facial scan, fingerprints, and flat prints (recordings of the four fingers on each hand and each thumb lined up next to each other).

The Automated Border Passage Project at Amsterdam's Schiphol Airport, also known as the Privium Program, is a leading example of an RT program available to travelers not requiring a Schengen visa. It serves "trusted travelers" across the internal borders of the European Economic Area (Airport Technology 2008) and exemplifies the hyperrefined strategies at work in expediting their circulation. Privium offers three categories of membership: Basic (€99), Plus (€119), and Partner (€55), the latter being an extra membership attached to either Basic or Plus. Basic membership entitles the traveler to pass through border control with an iris scan while Plus membership includes several extra features: parking in Schiphol's P2 car park adjacent to the arrival and departure halls; business class check (even with an economy class ticket) with eighteen participating airlines; discounted valet parking at Schiphol Airport; discounted rates on mobile phone calls; discounted rates on luggage sealing; automatic check-in and seat selection; and discounted wireless Internet rates at 32,000 hotspots with a single password and user name. Special offers are also available to Privium members, such as discount rates at airport spas and on Italian jewelry (Schiphol Airport n.d. a). "Airports are turning into shopping malls; by every thousand people we get through quicker, we make that much more money," remarked another EC official working on biometric information systems. The Privium Program not only creates frictionless travel for passengers with economic capital, but it also pads that experience with extra comfort. Indeed, as global capitalism continues to eradicate barriers to the movement of commodities and financial capital, the travel experience of capitalism's technocratic elite must create a sense of privilege and entitlement lest travel begin to feel burdensome and mundane. Gold-level travelers receive personal greetings from flight attendants (even when seated in economy class), and red carpets often resembling worn doormats are provided when they step through the boarding gate to the jetway.

Applicants accepted to the Privium Program make a fifteen-minute appointment at the Privium Service Point at Schiphol Airport. (Acceptance requires only a payment of the membership fee, a valid passport, and a height of a meter and a half.) A representative then scans the passenger's iris to digitally record the spatial geometry of 256 measuring points. These are used to reproduce the lightness-darkness patterns unique to each individual. The scan is preserved in a biometric chip sewn into the Privium card. The one-and-a-half-meter height requirement ensures that the iris scanner, fixed at 130 centimeters, can read the traveler's eye. The border passage reader scans the iris and photographs the eye four times in a second. These images are compared against the digital image stored in the card to verify identity. Border crossing through the Privium Program takes an estimated ten to fifteen seconds. The surveillance of the individual traveler, moreover, occurs with as little intrusion as possible. No blinding flash is used to photograph the eye, only three "weak" red lights positioned at different angles. Neither eyeglasses nor colored contact lenses need to be removed when facing the automatic border passage reader. Iris scans require no physical contact with the scanning equipment, unlike fingerprinting, which risks transmitting bacteria or viruses left on the finger scanner. The only possible inconvenience is bending over to position one's eye within ten to fifteen centimeters of the scanner. If the scan fails to work, then an agent will escort the traveler to the front of the line for a border crossing using a regular document check (Schiphol Airport n.d. b). In effect, the Privium Program exemplifies the marriage of liberalism and advanced state security; the traveler's border crossing experience is free from the state's physical intrusion while still meeting its security conditions.

The EC envisions a sea change in overall border management practices along these lines that would allow for massive financial savings. Paul announced boldly, though in a subdued tone:

> In a way we are introducing a revolution, we are introducing a revolution at the border. Border checks [have remained] relatively unchanged . . . we are introducing a revolution where most of the checks will be done automatically. . . . We have shown in our studies that huge investments in a fully automated system would pay itself off in less than two years, because the savings would be so huge because you need much less people at the border. At the time being, we believe that one border guard will be sufficient to supervise up to eighteen e-gates.

He drew on the example of the administrative border between Hong Kong and mainland China where a million travelers arrive each morning and are processed through approximately eighty fingerprint-based e-gates requiring only five or six border guards. "It's absolutely amazing. So border guards can be freed up to really focus on the risk cases so that at the end of the day we will enhance security while making it easier for bona fide passengers to cross borders," Paul explained. He concluded the point by stressing, "If we don't do anything, we will have chaos in our airports in five to ten years." The fact that he highlights China—as did the official in Chapter 3—as a model for successful border management suggests eerie similarities in regulating mass society between two politically opposite polities. Both polities appeal to the same normative border crosser in the form of the frequent business traveler, from such places as Hong Kong or Lebanon, who bring in large amounts of cash but stay for short periods of time. This new subjectivity, of course, contrasts quite sharply with the border crosser of lesser social status or economic means. While some travelers may experience a sense of liberation, others confront serious restrictions.

"A CHAIN OF TRUST":
THE NORMATIVE BIOMETRIC SUBJECT AND OTHERS

Biometric IT systems do not just encourage particular social categories and hierarchies. They project a new normative subjectivity backed by the power of the state, inclusive of its formal governing institutions, business lobbyists, technical experts, marketing specialists, and so on. Of course, the extent to which people actually internalize this subjectivity remains an empirical question, but they must contend with it in one way or another. While understanding the policymaker as a subject is crucial in comprehending the emergence of the EU's migration management apparatus, no less important is drawing out the archetypical migrant that this system demands.

A video presentation of the Portuguese Electronic Passport (PEP) best illustrates this normative subject (Portuguese Consulate in Sydney 2007). Since April 2005, the Portuguese government has been issuing state-of-the-art electronic passports that fully comply with EU and international standards and have become a model for other national governments. Currently, EU passports must contain a digitally scanned facial image and two digitalized fingerprints, usually from the right and left index fingers (Europa 2009b). The video shows a merger of the biotechnical and the qualitatively unique individual in which the former is necessary to liberate the latter from criminals and terrorists lurking in a sea of anonymous travelers. The effect is to meld the self-actualized individual with the high-tech security state. Against a soundtrack mixing the noises of jungle animals with mysterious melodies, the video begins with blurry footage of travelers moving through airport corridors. The narrators, who alternate between a male and female voice, explain that "in order to answer the citizens' needs as well as issues of free circulation and collective security, the European Union and other international organizations have defined a new security policy for travel and identification documents." The video then shows the EU flag (a circle of thirteen gold stars against a solid royal blue field) from which a new PEP emerges. The passport draws closer to the viewer, and its personal identification page opens. The viewer then sees a close-up shot of the bearer's photo before the video segues to a collage of heterogeneous people moving through their daily lives, most of them with smiles or looks of compassionate concern. The narrator says, "A passport that serves the citizens! A safe document!" The video then shows a digital representation of a human body, a photograph of an actual human face, and the contents of the carrier's personal information, all inside the circuitry of the PEP's microchip. The narrator explains its ability to withstand forgery and counterfeiting by detailing its graphic paper, polycarbonate coating, digitalized photographs, security threads, geometric lathe patterns, and other security features. He punctuates the list by asserting that "Personal elements are visible, yet secure! In a nutshell, a process that ensures a valid document, in the hands of the right person!" This point is made against a soundtrack of dramatic and uplifting techno-rhythms.

To retain national identity in a world of globalization and hybridity, the passport remains faithful to Portuguese culture by incorporating sketches of the great poets Luis de Camões and Fernando Pessoa. The video shifts back to technical matters by introducing a data-gathering system that is "fast and clear," demonstrated by a passport control officer easily processing information stored in a PEP. It explains how the traveler's digital facial image can be matched against an image of the bearer taken at a border crossing point. The narrator assures the viewer of the PEP's reliable data protection systems, which allow the passport to "defeat identity usurpation, data theft, and illicit practice." The narrator then explains that the PEP "articulates" with other e-government programs in Portugal and meets the standards for the US Visa Waiver program. Returning to a full shot of the passport, the narrator says the "PEP helps create a chain of trust between public administration and citizens, as well as stronger bonds with other countries and international organizations." Reinforcing the Portuguese-ness of the document, however, the video simultaneously shows a handsome, rugged, and individualistic image of artist Júlio Pomar. It also presents the PEP pages that feature maps of Portugal's historic voyages around Africa's Cape of Good Hope, of the emigration routes of its diaspora, and of Internet communication routes. The video concludes with "The New Image of Portugal in the World."

The PEP video showcases a subject whose life chances, creativity, and self-actualization are enhanced precisely through the state's use of advanced technology. Neoliberalism is fused to the police state and integrated into an international surveillance system. Biometrics ensures the individual's safety from the external threats of identity theft, fraud, terrorism, and human trafficking. Protection against a loss of the self requires a union between the state's (or the EU's) public administration and the citizen, which allows the latter unique creative expression, as exemplified in the artist Pomar. Furthermore, the liberated self is set free to travel and to circulate. Concealed in the apotheosis of the normative subject are the travel restrictions placed on people from poorer countries and countries suspected of harboring terrorists or international criminals. The racialization built into this norm will in theory be eradicated as RT programs become institutionalized as the EC hopes. At that point, discrimination will be class-based, with easy border passage made available to anyone with economic means or educational level regardless of cultural-cum-racial background.

However, the link between class and racial background is evident in the difficulties faced by skilled workers immigrating to Europe. While the rhetoric surrounding biometric data and e-passports celebrates the expedited flows of creative individuals, the experience of submitting one's personal information to the authorities feels like the same identity theft that the state is trying to prevent. Dr. Melek Doğru, the Turkish scientist working in the Netherlands mentioned in Chapter 1, explained:

My parents visited me for the Xmas holidays. If you could see the information that they had to hand over to a private company that the Embassy hired in Ankara to manage the visa applications you would not believe in your eyes! Copies of credit cards, bank accounts, papers to prove ownership of housing, their jobs, income, insurance papers, health papers, papers from the employers to say that they are aware of this trip, etc. etc. . . . Plus the papers that we had to sign over here . . . no privacy at all! I called the Embassy and protested. I mean, you hand over information to the Embassy, I understand, but who can guarantee the security of this information in a private company? The answer I got was expected and simple: if you want your parents to visit you, you have to go through this.

Doğru sees this as a global problem reflecting growing disparities between the North and South. She continued, "I guess it is not very much known how little privacy we 'non-Europeans' have and how much we go through to get visas and how much we are humiliated in border checks even far before 9/11 and yet today all around Europe."

More drastic are the stories of those lacking a promising future outside the EU who succumb to human traffickers to bring them inside the union. Prostitution is a depressing example. While extended participant-observation with migrant street prostitutes is a difficult proposition (though see Lindquist 2009 for an illuminating ethnography), undercover police officers investigating illegal migration and transnational crime exposed me to the decrepit material circumstances in which these prostitutes live and the horrific impact that prostitution has on their lives. "It was there," officer Ricardo said while pointing to an old town outdoor café, "where the boss told her that she will have to prostitute herself." "She" is a teenager from Romania now working in a southern EU member state for a transnational crime ring. "Romanian bosses threaten to harm the girls' family back home if they do not comply," explained Ricardo, who has been working undercover for five years. "She broke down in tears after he told her that. We had it on video and audio. She might get 30 percent of her pay and will give over 70 percent to the pimp."

Street prostitutes in this national capital work from about 11:00 P.M. to 4:00 A.M. and may see as many as ten clients a night. Cars drive slowly through the seediest parts of town, surveying the selection quite literally on the basis of national background. "Nigerians run the area near the technical university," Ricardo explained as we watched a male figure approach a woman standing just far enough from a bus stop to suggest that she was not actually waiting for public transportation. Making our way out of that district, we moved through a narrow street strewn with trash but home to a number of night clubs out of which Ukrainian bosses run prostitution rings. Not much further away was an intersection populated by Brazilian prostitutes. "Since the US started tightening its border, we've seen an increase of illegal Brazilian immigration in southern Europe. Much of it starts in Portugal." Waiting in pairs in doorways and alleys, these women glance discreetly at the potential clients driving by:

> If they accept a client, then they go to a nearby pension run by the ring. There, the pimp can protect them from violent clients and make sure that they do not run away. Most don't, though, because they have nowhere to go and they fear for the families back home. If he is a regular client, then the pimp might let her go somewhere else with the client but he'll have to pay more.

The usual pensions where prostitutes take their clients are dilapidated buildings that one would expect an EU municipality to condemn as unfit for habitation. Moreover, these are often the same types of buildings in which the prostitutes live. "Pull over there," Ricardo asked his partner driving the car. He then got out of the car and hung his police officer's badge around his neck. Crossing the street, Ricardo looked into the front door of a seven-story building, one of many in a row. His partner then got out and encouraged me to come along. The foyer stank of mildew, and trash and debris were piled in the corner. A bank of mailboxes dangled from a few odd nails in the wall. As we ascended a narrow and dirty staircase, Ricardo's handgun was visibly tucked into his belt. The floorboards at the base of each flight of steps had broken through, and flimsy sheets of plywood were placed on top of the holes. Plaster had fallen from the walls. Some doors to the flats were smashed, but as we climbed each flight it was clear that no one lived, or could live, in this building. One could see through the cracked doors that most of the rooms were filled with debris. However, at the seventh floor, we stopped in front of one door, beneath which light was shining out. "Four or five prostitutes live there," Ricardo explained. "If you go in there, it will stink from the dirty dishes and rotten food in the kitchen. You wouldn't want to live there."

The contrasts are clear between the virtuous PEP-carrying traveler, the Turkish scientist working in the Netherlands, and the street prostitutes trafficked in from abroad. The desired migrant is a person of honest individualism, deserving of efficient service and in need of protection from lurking identity thieves. This person is also implicitly an individual of economic means who lubricates the flow of cash and capital. RT programs assume the normality of that individual even though registered travelers constitute a small percentage of total travelers. Some travelers are subject to a higher level of scrutiny when entering the EU; others are forced into a dangerous and unsavory life in the EU underworld.

THE ALTRUISTIC STATE AND THE HELPLESS INDIVIDUAL

European Commission officials well know the hardships that so many migrants face. They nevertheless rely on key rhetorical devices to argue that the benefits of properly managed migration outweigh the costs in human suffering. This justification involves a deft weaving of many disparate aspects of migration management that show how the individual is to be protected from all possible crises, how this goal requires ever more surveillance, how the sanctity of the law is maintained, and how the state remains innocent through the entire process. Frank Paul shows empathy in the face of a human crisis, an empathy that quickly transforms into suspicion:

> You have all seen those terrible pictures of people drowning in the Mediterranean trying to reach . . . Lampedusa and then in the Atlantic as well to the Canary Islands, etc. These are absolute tragedies. We have to do everything to stop it. And one of the ideas is the need to develop a very sophisticated maritime surveillance system that will allow us not only to detect those movements as early as possible but also before actually people really . . . get to the Mediterranean, have more intelligence on their whereabouts. Today as we speak there are an estimated 250,000 people—250,000—who are hanging out in Libya basically just waiting for passage to Europe. And we know more or less about their whereabouts but we would like to have more information, more intelligence about what exactly they're planning, when they're planning to go to Europe, how do they do this, when do they embark . . . and by doing that and having that information we would be able to intervene much earlier and then not only with idea of building . . . an absolute fortress around Europe because this is not our intention, but it is simply to save lives and make sure that these people don't drown and direct them to legal ways of emigrating. Because today the biggest problem is that it is very difficult to legally emigrate to Europe and therefore organized crime today has a higher revenue . . . a higher revenue . . . very few people know this . . . from smuggling people, from trafficking people than actually they have from drugs. Today smuggling people is a much more profitable business.

Paul's narrative morally justifies the displacing effect of narrowly defined legal migration channels; that is, the production of ambiguous geographic spaces like deserts, seas, and decrepit urban areas and of a dispensable labor force willing to traverse those spaces at all costs. The state—in the form of cooperation among EU member states—innocently strives to save the lives of people who have made "bad choices," in a neoliberal register, or who are passive victims of invisible evildoers such as smugglers traveling incognito. As such, the invocation of the maritime surveillance system and biometric identification systems is justified as a humanitarian measure to protect, rather patronizingly, individuals from themselves, invoking a neocolonial register. This is the only conclusion Paul qua EC official can reach, because he must avoid two things: one, portraying the migrant as an evildoer, which is not politically correct; and two, acknowledging the structural inequalities at work, because this could lead to a moral justification for illegal migration.

Skepticism of these large-scale population management systems can be found at high levels. Baroness Sarah Ludford MEP argued that "the VIS is a border management system, and its principle is not to combat terrorism and crime. Let us remember that 99.9 percent of visitors to the EU are legitimate travelers who do not have any connection with criminality whatsoever, nor indeed do illegal immigrants or unauthorized entrants." An EC official who drafted legislation for biometric standards on EU passports similarly confessed that "all of this is done for .001 percent of travelers. For me, it's something like [firing] a cannon to a fly. It's not my decision." The former EC official who spearheaded the creation of EURODAC explained her motivation in terms of protecting the reputation of asylum applicants from neo-nationalist defamation:

> When I started I was naïve because I thought EURODAC would validate the true asylum-seeker and challenge the bad reputation they were getting in the press ... I think EURODAC did prove that there is an underclass of people who move around, but it is much smaller than imagined. This helps manage migration because we need migrants to produce wealth because we are not producing babies. EURODAC actually changed the discussion this way and rather quickly. Only 230,000 a year in the thirty countries. Are you really being swamped? The neo-Nazis [now use] the expansion eastward—Poles, Estonians, etc.—in their diatribes, not so much Chinese and Indians.

Despite their intents, none of these high-status individuals can impede or refine the proliferation of biometric information systems. This process happens in a political context that allows border management to be treated as a technical problem. The ultimate concern at stake shifts ethics (the terms in which people should relate to each other) to administration (the most efficient procedures for managing a mass of undifferentiated people).

. . .

The EU's large-scale biometric information systems complement the Frontex mission described in Chapter 4. While the latter monitors all incoming travelers located in the space beyond the external border, biometric systems regulate all travelers crossing controlled checkpoints to circulate within the space of that border. As a technical endeavor these systems result from the labor of loosely affiliated workers in the informational economy, all of whom engage in abstract cooperation. Standards, functioning as boundary objects, enable these systems to fuse together across vast geographic settings and disparate policy arenas (Bowker and Star 1999, 15–16). The ephemeral character of networks of IT experts belies the synthetic strength of the surveillance systems that they build. Advocates in the European, national, and industrial bureaucracies insist that biometrics guarantees individual security, enables individuals to participate in social life, and allows them to activate their creative potential. In effect, however, the pluralism of peoples' biology is substituted for the pluralism of their personal histories, thus neutralizing any given individual's potential for social transformation for the sake of public administration.

Biometric systems objectify travelers by reducing their identities to digitalized information, by separating identities from bodies and storing them in electronic travel documents as biometric data. Those data then mediate relations between the individual travelers and the state; the former must regain their identities at border crossing points in order to move from one sovereign space to another. Border crossing proceeds not only along national lines but also along class lines; wealthy travelers are encouraged to submit biometric data to RT programs as part of a sustained effort to increase the speed with which they consume goods and stimulate the EU economy. Biometrics thus helps divide global space into vertical layers in which the wealthiest can move relatively easily throughout the top strata. Those in the lower strata must either travel under tight restrictions or clandestinely cross the external border only to live a life in the underworld. The next chapter demonstrates how those restrictive conditions fit into the EU's circular migration agenda through which migrant labor power is extracted at minimum cost and with minimal presence on EU territory.

6 THE RIGHT SOLUTION, OR, THE FANTASY OF CIRCULAR MIGRATION

We have a responsibility. The key continent we need to work on is Africa.
We contributed to the problems it is facing. Africa has always been
Europe's problem.

former European Commission migration official

THE IDEA OF CIRCULAR MIGRATION AND THE ENTERPRISE-UNIT

"Migration to another country is not a decision for life," announced a jovial
state-level minister in Germany to a Metropolis delegation (Chapter 2). "We
need to improve the conditions for mobility . . . and prevent brain drain. . . .
Let the Malian doctor work in Manchester and at home." Along with "circular
migration" and "temporary migration," "mobility" has become a choice buzz-
word in migration policy discussions, not least because it implies permanent
circulation rather than permanent settlement. The idea of circular migration
holds that migrants do not wish to settle in their destination countries. Rather,
they wish to travel to wealthier countries to remit higher wages and to gain
skills that will help them return home better equipped to develop their communities and countries. The increase in these migrant-entrepreneurs' human
and financial capital also better supports development in the global South than
centrally planned programs conjured up in distant European capitals. Furthermore, this idea of circular migration allows migration policy officials to
speak for the good of the South's poor migrant masses, to be cognizant of their
dignity, to work to provide them opportunity, and to appear to transcend the
parochial nation-state. Posing as a great equalizer of economic inequalities, it
is not simply an idea but rather a fantasy that EU policymakers must appear to
believe. Yet more pragmatically, circular migration functions as a tacit compromise between nationalist conservatives (neo-nationalists) concerned that migrants will become permanent fixtures of society and economic conservatives
(neoliberals) concerned that cheap labor will not be available for economic
growth. It resolves their most significant disagreement, specifically the length
of time a migrant should be permitted to stay on national soil. It serves as
the "right solution" (pun intended) to their basic disagreement, allowing the

broader architecture of migration management to remain intact. Given how it ties together the loose ends of so many policy problems, circular migration functions as the conceptual lynchpin of the EU's efforts to harmonize migration management.

This chapter examines the institutionalization of neoliberal economic rationales in EU circular migration policies that result from negotiations between EU member states and migration-sending and transit countries. Officials from countries located along all points on the transnational migration chain cooperate to build a regime of manageable, transparent, and efficient circulation of labor often with the support of NGOs and IGOs in the process. Their efforts aim to empower migrant laborers with increased human capital so that they can both contribute to the receiving national economy and return home to develop their home countries. The supporting infrastructure lubricates not only migrant circulation but also the attendant flows of cash, finance, and technical knowledge. The chapter then investigates how efforts to build a circulation regime shape different institutions and programs that encourage temporary labor migration and discourage attempts at illegal border crossing. These range from the creation of migration information centers in Saharan Africa, to the signing of "mobility partnerships" with third countries, to the uploading of web-based job portals that match non-EU temporary laborers with EU employers. Drawing on the Blue Card debate in the European Parliament, the chapter also demonstrates how a conservative political discourse contains the range of opinions impacting EU migration policy.

Unlike in years past, today's circular migration programs cast individual migrants as potential entrepreneurs. Officials shift the object of policy analysis from the laborer as a resource between capital and production—or a passive object of planning—to the laborer as one who uses the means available to him to achieve policy goals—or as an active subject in planning (Foucault 2008, 223). The laborer is now recognized as a bearer of capital to be encouraged and rewarded with more knowledge, skills, and income. Moreover, the laborer is, conceptually speaking, an "entrepreneur" in a (global) society made up of "enterprise-units" (225). Far from symbolizing *Homo economicus* of classical theory, who is an actor embedded in relationships of exchange, the entrepreneur-unit exists for himself: for his own capital, his own earning, and his own production, especially the production of his own satisfaction (225–26). This shift also reinforces the commodification of not merely the worker but rather the worker's various skills and thus reduces this individual to a skill set to be sold on the labor market (Urciuoli 2008, 212). It also functions as the dominant policy paradigm between EU policy officials and their counterparts in third countries with whom circular migration programs are developed.

CELEBRATING THE CIRCULAR MIGRANT
IN INTERNATIONAL POLICY DISCUSSIONS

Circular migration programs draw on new strategies in organizing labor forces through the individualization of the migrant workforce. Like so many policy initiatives in adjacent domains, circular migration programs work by creating the conditions for the delivery of the product rather than the product itself. Recall that the EBF did not aim to produce biometric devices for the EU or its member states. Rather, it organized the experts in the field to do so on an ad hoc basis. The EMN strives only to create a common vocabulary with its Asylum and Migration Glossary so that member states can coordinate their particular policy-making endeavors. It does not aim to deliver policy solutions from the center to the member states. Rather than asserting what constitutes better border control practices, 3MP's I-Map is only a clearinghouse to be used on an "as needed" basis for border control. In the case of circular migration, the EU creates the conditions to generate a locally defined labor migration objective rather than dictating the specific need and delivering the solution. This move transpires through a widespread adherence to a liberal rationale about economy, subjectivity, and mobility that can be incorporated into disparate migration projects pertaining to remittances, development, knowledge enhancement, and so on. Its plasticity accounts for its polymorphic appearances. This rationale furthermore assumes a migrant-subject who is an active, self-starting entrepreneur rather than a mere worker selling his labor to the highest bidder. Foucault describes the situation as follows:

> The mobility of a population and its ability to make choices of mobility as investment choices for improving income enable the phenomena of migration to be brought back into economic analysis, not as pure and simple effects of economic mechanisms which extend beyond individuals and which, as it were, bind them to an immense machine which they do not control, but as behaviour in terms of individual enterprise, of enterprise of oneself with investments and income. (2008, 230)

The whole strategy of organizing circular migration in such a way as to minimize the length of a migrant's stay needs justification to the European public, third-country governments, and the labor migrants themselves. Like the German official's call to "Let the Malian doctor work," liberal migration officials adopt a populist stance in their implicit battles with neo-nationalists. Franco Frattini (2007), former European commissioner for justice, freedom and security, invoked "mobility" to announce that a wholesale new paradigm of migration thinking was necessary:

> We have to shift—even if not completely—our traditional way of thinking of migration as a world of loss and sorrow. Let us be realistic in a visionary way. Let us try to use, a new expression: EU mobility. We have to look at immigration as an enrichment and as a [sic] inescapable phenomenon of today's world not as a threat.

Frattini was quick to link this new vision to the global North's internal competition for labor from the global South:

> We should take more account of what statistics tell us: 85 percent of unskilled labour goes to the EU and only 5 percent to the USA, whereas 55 percent of SKILLED labour goes to the USA and only 5 percent to the EU. . . . Europe has to compete against Australia, Canada, the USA and the rising powers in Asia.

The increased market value of migrants qua laborers mixes with a broader narrative of valuing migrants qua vital human beings. However, statements about the value of the migrant's life carry ambiguously coded messages. Officials, on the one hand, can speak of migrants in positive terms as "contributors" and "resources" and, on the other, support policies that recruit migrants for particular short-term labor needs. A blurry line separates the claim of cherishing individual migrants as global entrepreneurs from a policy effect of extracting maximum labor gain at the lowest possible cost. The average of these two positions might be an agreement among liberal officials to discard the condescending term "illegal" in favor of the more neutral term "irregular." Migrants are thus not "bad" in a legal or moralistic sense, but they are not "normal" in an administrative sense. One OSCE official explained in an interview with me:

> "Irregular" is a broader term. Some states like to use the term. This is of concern to many of our participating states. The political environment may not be conducive to migration. But, it might be of interest to the business community. Sometimes a more liberal approach is better.

By illuminating the individual migrant as a positive economic force, liberal officials can avoid referring to the negative structural factors that systematically degrade poor migrants' material well-being. The framing of the migrant as global traveler also provides crucial support to EU efforts to globalize migration policy or, in practice, to integrate the policies of transit and sending countries into its own. Reasoning through a similar neoliberal perspective, the Global Commission on International Migration (GCIM), established by Kofi Annan at the very end of his second term as UN secretary-general, reported that "the international community [should] capitalise on the resourcefulness of people who seek to improve their lives by moving from one country to another" (Global Commission on International Migration 2005, 5). It is the "people" in the form of a mythical group of migrants who would otherwise uplift themselves if nation-states only overcame their parochialism. The passage calls only for the opportunity to circulate—not to resettle—and plays right along with circular migration's compromise between neoliberals and neo-nationalists.

Lant Pritchett of the Center for Global Development offers the most liberal argument for circular migration to have entered the policy debate. In a book with the Moses-inspired title *Let Their People Come*, he argues that if the world's rich countries would allow just a 3 percent rise in temporary labor migration, then the world's poor countries would receive $300 billion in return (2006, 3–5). This yield would far exceed the annual $70 billion in aid and development funds. Moreover, this small increase in labor migration would yield $50 billion to the rich countries that admitted the additional migrants. According to Pritchett, public officials should tackle political reluctance by arguing that freer labor mobility is no more dangerous than the rich world's current free trade regime. Morally framed in terms of the well-being of everyone living below the poverty line of rich countries, "which is the large bulk of the world's population" (2), this book has excited officials working in international organizations who feel much less pressure from neo-nationalists than their counterparts working in national government ministries. "We think it is a great idea but try getting states to go along with it," explained one such official based in Vienna.

This idea of circular migration shapes formal cooperative agreements between top-level EU and African migration officials. In lofty preambles to international agreements, acknowledgment of structural inequalities often precedes more detailed references to neoliberal solutions. For example, the Joint Africa-EU Declaration on Migration and Development (2006), announced from Tripoli on 22 and 23 November 2006, affirmed the new priority of linking these two "problems" in a trans-Mediterranean relationship. The declaration opens: "RECOGNISING that the fundamental causes of migration within and from Africa are poverty and underdevelopment, aggravated by demographic and economic imbalances, unequal terms of global trade, conflicts, environmental factors, poor governance, uneven impact of globalization and humanitarian disasters . . ." The declaration of the 2006 Euro-Africa Ministerial Conference on Migration and Development held in Rabat, Morocco, further codified the union of these two policy priorities. At the meeting, more than fifty foreign ministers and other high-level officials from Europe and North, West, and Central Africa stressed the necessity of making "better use of the potential of migration as a factor for the development, modernization, and innovation of the societies of origin, transit and the host societies." They also affirmed their concern with "the phenomenon of brain-drain which holds back the development of countries of origin by depriving them of quality skills, leadership and experienced workers" (Euro-African Partnership on Migration and Development 2006). The IOM puts the tenets into practice through its *Handbook on Establishing Effective Labour Migration Policies in Countries of Origin and Destination*, which was written in cooperation with OSCE and the ILO. The handbook elaborates three reasons commonly heard in migration policy discussions why circular migration presents a win-win situation for the three involved parties (OSCE/IOM/ILO 2006, 113). First, receiving countries meet their labor needs and avoid the problem of long-term migrant integration (a tip to the neo-right). Second, countries of origin do not suffer from brain drain and benefit from the transfer of knowledge and remittances. Third, migrant workers and their families benefit from the increased wages and increased human capital.

This idea of circular migration was further ensconced in Article 13 of the Cotonou Agreement, which helped to finalize a Joint Declaration on "Migration and Development" signed by France, Spain, the Economic Community of West African States (ECOWAS), the European Commission (EC), and Mali on 8 February 2007. Article 13 captured a familiar gamut of policy arenas. It called for the signatory parties to protect human rights and eliminate racism; to treat third-country nationals fairly and integrate them on terms comparable to citizens; and to consider strategies for reducing poverty, improving living and working conditions, and developing training opportunities—all of which should contribute to "normalizing" migratory flows. These stipulations match the circular migration narrative as they uphold the right of any individual to flourish, even if these are intended to keep people within their national borders, as stated in the fourth point: "the Parties shall ensure that such action is geared towards the vocational integration of ACP [signatory African, Caribbean, and Pacific states] nationals in their countries of origin" (Cotonou Agreement 2000, 22). The policing of illegal migrants, however, is also written into Article 13. It asks for a committee to develop policies to prevent illegal flows, without specifying what these policies might entail, and for a humane return policy that respects human rights. It asks that African countries readmit their nationals without further formalities. The commitments outlined in these international agreements set the direction of circular migration programs, as shown below. As a result, liberal economic policy emerges as an essential part of migration management, even as the individual migrant upon whom the economic growth rests is encased and monitored through such police procedures as humane return for illegals and enhancement of the border police.

Security has not been removed from the agenda, but it is moved to the background and interwoven into a comprehensive approach to migration management. A quote from the director-general of the International Centre for Migration Policy Development (2008, 2) illustrates the discretion with which security backstops the migration and development paradigm:

> Considering the nexus between migration and development, we are also exploring how to make development work for better managed migration. The question obviously has, and still does, alert the attention of policy makers and administrations dealing with asylum and migration policies in countries of destination. Some answers do suggest that in many cases economic development increases the propensity for migration for a sustained period. Experience also shows that dialogues and capacity building efforts supporting good governance in areas such as migration and security are indeed quite often preconditions for enhanced inter-governmental co-operation. This will lead to genuine migration partnerships for the benefit of the countries concerned and, last but not least, for the migrants themselves. ICMPD draws this conclusion out of its numerous activities to back up structural reforms.

The passive voice reporting that "migration and security are indeed quite often preconditions for enhanced inter-governmental co-operation" is the voice of Europe, which makes its cooperation on migration-cum-development conditional on African cooperation on migration-cum-security. The hidden security premise conditions the migrant's own beneficial experience similar to the policy justifications found in the domains of border security and biometrics.

Industry leaders augment the narratives of creating opportunities for individual migrants and building a global infrastructure to regulate their circulation. Unisys Belgium, a high-tech business services corporation, and the Migration Policy Group (MPG), a prestigious migration policy think tank, are jointly developing a web portal to inform potential migrants about EU and national migration policies, legal migration opportunities, and the risks of illegal migration. According to Ann Mennens, project manager of the Immigration Portal, "People who are thinking about moving to EU member states deserve the most up-to-date information on opportunities, requirements and processes. This portal will provide potential immigrants with a comprehensive tool that will support them when making the decision to move abroad" (Unisys 2008). Much like the Portuguese electronic passport, industry leaders conceive of the Immigration Portal as an enterprise uniting all stakeholders—industry, government, and migrants. Patrice-Emmanuel Schmitz, Unisys director of EU management consulting, made the point:

> Immigration management is one of the EU's major challenges in the years to come. Europe will need to invest significantly in order to manage existing migration flows and deal with new waves of migration. Together with our partner MPG, Unisys intends to create a portal that gives all stakeholders a clear, cross-community understanding of the benefits and implications of immigration in the EU, without forgetting the risks and consequences of illegal immigration. (ibid.)

The above quotes, spoken and written by disparate policy officials at disparate times and places, are not random and disconnected. They must be read synergistically in all their appearances in policy documents, in newspaper articles, at migration conferences, and in public statements from officials at all levels. When they are stitched together, a picture emerges of who the ideal migrant actually is and what kind of political economy sustains that idealization. Again, the point of this exercise is not to determine empirically if this ideal migrant corresponds to the modal migrant that might emerge out of the millions traveling annually through the EU. In other words, the point is not to ask, "Do the policymakers understand the proverbial 'on the ground' reality?" Similarly, the question here is not, "Will circular migration programs work per se?" Rather, the task is to tease out what officials assume about these migrants when producing circular migration policies and, in turn, what type of subjectivity migrants actually confront when engaging with these policies. It is furthermore to ask, "How does the concept of circular migration hold together the broader migration management apparatus and the EU's contemporary political economy?" It counts as a victory for neoliberalism that the ideal circular migrant and the ideal citizen-traveler carrying an e-passport are almost entirely identical subjects. Both are cast as creative individuals trying to maximize their capacities through global travel; both are endangered by nefarious transnational networks; and both find security and protection from the surveillance state and well-managed borders. While only one benefits from citizenship in a wealthy country, both are reduced to circulating objects whose value is determined by their productivity and entrepreneurialism.

CIRCULAR MIGRATION IN PRACTICE

Circular migration is not new. As the French sociologist Philippe Fargues explained to an audience of policymakers, NGO leaders, and academics at a 2008 Metropolis International conference, circular migration was invented by migrants themselves. Chinese migrants between 1860 and 1920 evaded the US Exclusion Act by smuggling themselves into the US and then back to China only to be replaced by younger migrant workers. This steady supply of replacement labor kept cash flowing back home indefinitely as it maintained a stable age pyramid in the US. Moch (1992, 76–88) documents a host of temporary and seasonal migration patterns throughout the regions of western Europe during the second half of the eighteenth century. These systems took hold as land enclosures forced the conversion of peasants into proletarians, as population increased in industrial areas, and as rural manufacturing expanded as a result of new production processes. Middle East and North African countries have a long history of circular migration throughout these regions well predating colonization. However, the arrival of Europeans drastically altered these patterns. For example, French *colons* (settlers) in Algeria, including Algerian coastal cities, drew seasonal and circular migrants from Morocco throughout the second half of the nineteenth century and into the twentieth (de Haas 2005). During and after the French colonial period, Malians migrated throughout French colonies and France itself. One particular form of circular migration involved Malians working seasonally on the peanut plantations of the Senegambia and the cotton and cocoa plantations of the Ivory Coast (Findley 2004). In short, migration has played a central role in the making of Europe for centuries despite nationalist myths to the contrary (Sassen 1999; Zolberg 1983). The policy challenge for European officials has been directing migratory flows to serve the purposes of nation-states.

Today the EU is moving vigorously to regularize, encourage, and direct circular migration in order to meet its own economic needs. Advances in travel and communication technologies allow many migrants to maintain contact with their countries of origin, a fact which the EU and some sending-country governments hope to use in support of development and foreign policy agendas. The EU meets this goal in three steps: first, it defines the term "circular migration," then normalizes it through institutional practices, and finally exports the new norm to third countries through mobility partnerships and other initiatives described below. The evidence that circular migration programs will narrow structural economic inequality is lacking. For example, Saskia Sassen (2008) points out that the low-end jobs available to migrants in the North are concomitant with a relative loss of household income for the families receiving remittances back home. This vulnerable position is hardly an endemic condition of a poor country; rather, it is a consequence of economic restructuring programs imposed on Southern countries by Northern-dominated institutions such as the WTO and IMF. The reliance on remittances is doubly problematic. Families in sending countries are dependent on impermanent, low-end jobs, which add up to major portions of poor countries' gross domestic products; for example, Tonga (31.1%), Moldova (27.1%), Lesotho (25.8%), Haiti (24.8%), and Bosnia-Herzegovina (22.5%) (ibid.). The narrative that circular migration solves an economic problem external to the EU by empowering the migrant, however, glosses over these economic relations between the EU and its migrant-sending countries. Sassen calls the bluff in no uncertain terms:

> Stances that regard immigrants as exogenous to our own global practices are not going to help us develop a better immigration policy. Our starting point should actually be: how do we address the massive economic losses we have imposed on global south countries through our unremitting pursuit of IMF and World Bank restructuring programmes. (2008)

Nevertheless, the EU buries these structural problems in a series of programs designed to address their effects rather than their causes.

The EC modestly defines circular migration "as a form of migration that is managed in a way allowing some degree of legal mobility back and forth between two countries" (European Commission 2007, 4). It divides circular migration into two types that are "most relevant in the EU context": circular migration involves either third-country nationals settled in the EU who can temporarily return to the home country to transfer their professional skills as a step toward development, or people living in third countries who temporarily work, study, or train in the EU. The EC funds numerous projects for both types of circular migration that are usually carried out through an implementing partner—an NGO, IGO, or an agency of the third country's government—in cooperation with migration-sending countries. Most of the circular migration projects ongoing through 2007 supported efforts to institutionalize the movement between the EU and countries in its "neighborhood"—that is, adjacent to its external border—such as the western Balkan countries, Morocco, Tunisia, Egypt, and Ukraine, and also countries such as Colombia and those in the Caucasus. The IOM served as the implementing partner for four of the nine projects (European Commission 2007).

The EC invested €10 million from the European Development Fund and opened CIGEM—Migration Information and Management Centre—in Mali's capital city, Bamako, as a pilot project, which could lead to similar centers in countries geographically close to the EU, or in the "European neighborhood" as the EC now calls it. The first center of its kind, CIGEM provides information for Malians and other West Africans about the EU labor market and the risks associated with illegal migration to the EU. The EC strategically chose to locate it in the Malian capital because it is one of three nodal cities on West African illegal migration routes. (The other two cities are Gao and Tessalit, both in Mali.) CIGEM establishes a model for partnership between the EU and a country that itself is the home of a large number of illegal migrants in the EU. More than 1,500 Malians were returned in 2007 alone. The EC would prefer the less expensive proposition of better regulating immigration from Mali, on the assumption that readily available information would discourage potential illegal migrants, rather than the costlier option of apprehending, detaining, and returning illegal migrants. Through information centers like CIGEM, the EC will try to export managed migration to third countries by appealing to European neoliberal norms. Arguing that managed migration has been crafted to improve the situation for Malian migrants, Giacomo Durazzo, head of the EU delegation in Mali (European Commission 2008), explained that

> The situation became dramatic because no one wanted to manage the phenomenon. And now we find ourselves in situations where people are forced to leave [the European Union]. Actually if we developed and structured immigration properly ten or fifteen years ago we wouldn't be in this situation today.

Diplomats and high-level migration officials typically use the passive and collective voice when championing managed migration. This grammar allows them to objectify the problem, separate the EU from any responsibility for it, and claim common cause with migrants.

In keeping with humanitarian rationales of managed migration, CIGEM's (2008, 13) own promotional materials explain that its primary aim is "to define a Malian migration policy addressing the concerns of potential migrants, returning migrants, and migrants residing outside Mali. It will serve as a one-stop shop for information and guidance for migrants." Its mission reflects the EU's comprehensive approach to legal, managed migration as explicated by EC official Ilse Cougé (Europafrica 2008):

> The CIGEM is a pilot project. For the first time the EU will help a sub-Saharan African country to solve its problems of both legal and illegal migration, by approaching the phenomenon in all its aspects. The centre aims to promote the mutual gains of legal migration, to discourage illegal migration, to profit from the transmission of diasporas' funds and knowledge and to strive for a better understanding of the migration processes to develop an adequate policy.

If successful, the EC will have created a Malian counterpart that has empowered itself to run its own operations—but on the EU's terms, thus exporting a liberal rationale of economic and population regulation. No less significant, CIGEM will help Mali "to define and implement [its] migration policy and 'adapt' it to international, regional, and national dynamics" through the exportation of European norms on managed migration (European Commission 2008). Equally concerned with the recirculation of people and finance back to Mali, CIGEM also informs would-be migrants about the potential role of the diaspora in local development and provides advice about one's return migration to Mali. CIGEM's proindividual rationale grew out of a concerted effort among European and Malian policymakers to refrain from "demonizing" migration and to shift the discussion to the question of how to make migration "work" for everyone involved. Indeed, Malian officials reinforce the same neoliberal discourse used by their European counterparts. Badra Alou Macalou, minister for expatriate Malians and African integration, argues, "This illegal migration is currently prospering because legal migration is not sufficiently available to users. By that, I mean potential candidates" (European Commission 2008). Abdoulaye Konaté, director of CIGEM, similarly explains, "Today we would not be able to deal with migration questions in a sustainable way without taking into account people's desire to develop themselves and find employment and training, which largely explains the reasons they want to leave" (ibid.). Thus, the migrant-entrepreneur is celebrated across an international field of strategically located policy players. That individual's success assumes well-lubricated systems to circulate migrant labor across the Mediterranean and to transfer remittances from the EU back to the sending country.

CIGEM's inaugural press release mentions that "partnerships on mobility are also envisaged—agreements would include commitments in terms of re-admission as well as opportunities created by legal migration" (CIGEM 2008, 15). CIGEM symbolizes global cooperation on migration management in the form of cooperative agreements between nation-states. However, as noted, European officials and African officials diverge sharply on the issue of development. The former make any financial support for economic development contingent on the latter's improved performance in accepting return migrants and tightening border control. (EU member states have become particularly averse to paying for migrant detention and return.) The EU, through Frontex, is exporting policing methods to North African countries, particularly Morocco, Libya, and Algeria.

As a technology of public administration, CIGEM resembles Portugal's Centro Nacional de Apoio ao Imigrante (CNAI) known colloquially in EU policy circles as a "one-stop shop" for migration. Free from the legislative and policy decisions structuring the country's intake, CNAI's function is to manage migrants as efficiently and humanely as possible. It is housed in a single building in downtown Lisbon. Upon arriving at the center, immigrants are directed to a room by the front door called the "sorting office" where they talk to a "sociocultural" mediator. Almost always an immigrant and usually a woman, the sociocultural mediator explains which office will serve the visitor's needs and what documents he or she will need to present. All the offices are located in the three-story center. These include education offices for issues about children's schooling; health care offices for direction on obtaining medical attention; an office for legal advice on such matters as employment, housing, and discrimination; an intercultural office that puts migrants in contact with immigrant integration programs; and the Serviço de Estrangeiros e Fronteiras (Immigration and Border Control Service) office that processes the paperwork pertaining to their status in Portugal. CNAI also hosts a bank branch designed especially to help migrants open an account.

On most days a mass of immigrants fills the center. The waiting room sits in the building's atrium on the ground floor, open to the third-floor ceiling above. It is equipped with a large play area for children, lest they get bored while their parents are occupied. Immigrants also wait in the open corridors of the upper floors, peering down over the railing as they wait for their number to be called. Though crowded, CNAI is efficiently run and is perhaps the most sophisticated center of its kind in the EU. However, while employees treat migrants with individual respect, the migrants themselves feel the degradation of being processed as case numbers and living outside the pale of law. "Useless. That is how it feels to be illegal. You can be fired from your job. You cannot complain. You cannot take care of your family," explained one sociocultural mediator, a former illegal immigrant herself. She expressed the frustration illegal immigrants feel when they stop her on the street where she lives to ask questions. "They think I can do more, but I can't." To demonstrate her point she thrust her arms forward and crossed them at the wrists as if to say that her hands were tied. Of course, CNAI's sociocultural mediators cannot change a migrant's legal status in Portugal. At best, they can provide help in adapting to those conditions.

As a regulator of labor circulation, CIGEM traces its roots to Morocco's ANAPEC (Agence Nationale de Promotion de l'Emploi et des Compétences), which established an agreement with the Spanish government to run bilateral circular migration programs. By the end of 2006, approximately 31,000 people had received jobs in ten thousand businesses with the assistance of four hundred advisers. Seasonal work in agriculture, restaurants, and food markets comprised the majority of job offerings (González Enríquez and Ramón 2010). One circular migration program illustrates an increased gendering of the international migration-development nexus (Bailey 2010). From 2001 to 2007 it recruited about one thousand Moroccan workers to Spain for six-month seasonal employment planting and harvesting fruit and berries (Touahri 2007). Only women from the countryside with families are eligible to participate. The choice of laborer, of course, is intended to maximize the chance that the fruit gatherer returns home so that the benefit of the individual's labor is not offset by the cost of policing visa-overstayers. No explicit mention is made of the social and even economic costs of removing a mother from her family or the possibly discriminatory labor practice of hiring workers on the basis of their family status rather than their own qualifications. Proponents point out that Moroccan workers received training, health care, administrative support for paperwork, and Internet facilities to communicate with families back home (González Enríquez and Ramón 2010). Moreover, proponents can celebrate the woman's "choice" to improve her family's material condition through participation in the program.

Despite institutional efforts to increase workers' human capital, criticism of circular migration programs is readily available. The Malian Association of Emigrants, which by some estimates could claim to represent one-quarter of Mali's twelve million people, has opposed CIGEM and warned about the rise of disposable "Kleenex workers" who are tossed aside after one use (Anrys 2008). Other refugee organizations refer to CIGEM as an "outpost watchtower of Fortress Europe" (Europafrica 2008). Still others argue that the point of CIGEM—and circular migration in general—is to provide the EU with "migration à la carte" paid for out of its development fund (No-Racism 2008). Individual Malians who have unsuccessfully attempted to enter the EU also voice doubts about CIGEM's efficacy. Nouhoum Diaby, a recently repatriated Malian migrant, told the IRIN news agency that he tried to enter Libya three times without a visa, and that CIGEM cannot influence people intent on migrating: "I have not heard about the centre. But that will not change anything. If I could get the money tomorrow, I would leave immediately. . . . Europe can post a security guard at each metre of its borders and we will gladly pay each of them a visit" (IRIN 2008). Offhand remarks from European officials suggest skepticism on their part as well. A UNODC delegate indicated that CIGEM would also function (intentionally or not) as a data-collection center that would support mapping exercises such as those described in Chapter 3 (Hess 2008). Another IGO project leader sighed with futility: "To be honest . . . there are a couple of terms in the migration world that I don't understand: circular migration; migration and development; global approach to migration."

Nevertheless, a significant part of the infrastructure of a trans-Mediterranean economy is advanced through information centers like CIGEM. Proponents of circular migration programs argue that secured borders throughout North Africa would help to regularize flows within that continent as well as curtail illegal flows across the sea to the EU. The human and financial capital accumulated by circular migrants would augment, and increasingly replace, development aid that would increase as the borders are "normalized." While this policy wish might not materialize as neatly as planned, it nevertheless directs the fusion of a migration management apparatus toward the EU's interests while claiming to serve the needs of Malian migrants.

MOBILITY PARTNERSHIPS

Policy initiatives called "mobility partnerships" help to put the apparatus infrastructure into place. On behalf of particular EU member states, the EC negotiates agreements with third countries in order to gain their cooperation in controlling illegal migratory flows in exchange for more favorable conditions for legal migration. This broad scope grows out of earlier policy statements such as the "Global Approach to Migration," which calls for international cooperation to manage migration in all its facets. The partnerships are also designed to serve the EU's development policy agenda as well as its "external dimension" of immigration and asylum policy (see Boswell 2003). One veteran EC official involved in the early stages of harmonization conveys the daunting challenge:

> We need to look at incentives to make it worthwhile to legalize illegals, and to make it attractive to business to not exploit cheap labor. In the long term, we may be desperate to get the people we need [even though] the public doesn't want Africans looking after their mothers. People want Christians, Filipinos, Brazilians, etc. There will be global competition for these people. On the other hand, we don't want to be seen as exploiting the sending countries so we [need to] get our development agenda working properly. We have to go back to a partnership without it being a colonial practice. At the moment, Europe is the only immigration "country" linking immigration and development, not the US, Canada, Australia, and certainly not the Asian countries. China and India are not going to be worrying about this.

While partnerships would vary, the list of potential commitments from any third country is long. The EU is likely to ask for cooperation in identifying and readmitting their own nationals, and for assistance in determining the nationalities for unidentified migrants. Many third countries have shown little interest on this score, thus complicating matters for member states intent on carrying out the returns. Third countries could be asked to participate in information campaigns to discourage illegal migration and to cooperate with Frontex to improve border control. Also, they may be required to improve the security of the travel documents they issue to protect them against fraud and forgery or make them biometrically compatible with EU databases. The EU or a member state may require that the third country cooperate in information exchange for security purposes or take increased measures to fight human trafficking and smuggling. The third country may also be required to make economic adjustments that might help reduce the incentive to migrate to the EU. Mobility partnerships thus play a central role not only in creating the conditions for a neoliberal mobile workforce but also in a bourgeoning EU foreign policy (Hess 2008).

EU member states and the EC also have commitments in mobility partnerships. First, EU member states might offer better opportunities for third-
country nationals by giving them favorable treatment in certain visa categories.
Second, a member state could assist legal migrants coming from the third
country. This could include providing information about a member state's
labor market, job-matching services, or technical or linguistic training. Third,
the EU can support measures to reduce brain drain from sending countries,
which usually entails a commitment to support circular migration. Fourth,
visa-processing procedures for short stays can be eased or improved, and similarly, consular services in the third country can be better organized. The terms
and conditions of any given mobility partnership can draw from a range of options according to particular needs, thereby allowing EU officials to argue that
these agreements are tailored to the third country and not constrained by a
one-size-fits-all model.

The EC is running mobility partnerships as pilot projects with Moldova
and Cape Verde. Other specific projects will likely be incorporated to create
full mobility partnerships. The EU-Moldovan mobility partnership illustrates
the comprehensive and decentralized character of these agreements. Much of
its content draws upon existing projects with EU member states. For example, the Swedish Employment Agency works with its Moldovan counterparts
to strengthen the latter's ability to accept returned migrants and reintegrate
short-term labor migrants back into the Moldovan economy. The Polish Ministry of Internal Affairs and Administration supports Moldovan measures to
detain illegal migrants and to cooperate in the fight against human trafficking.
The Portuguese Serviço de Estrangeiros e Fronteiras (Immigration and Border
Control Service) cooperates with the Moldovan Ministry of Internal Affairs
to incorporate EU standards on unspecified migration issues. The Moldovan
Border Guard Service signed an agreement with Frontex to implement procedures for risk analysis, planning and participation in joint operations, training
of personnel, and research and development. Portugal and Moldova signed an
agreement on social security as part of the broader package (Republica Moldova 2009). Moldova's biggest incentive is to increase its own capacity to secure
its borders, to manage flows through its territory, and to create more efficient
mechanisms for remittance transfers. It can also realize one of its fundamental
foreign policy goals as it moves away from the Russian and into the EU sphere
of influence. EU integration allows, again, for the exportation of EU standards
on global matters ranging from trade practices, to border security, to absorbing

foreign investment, to government downsizing and support for nongovern-mental organizations. In short, it liberalizes Moldovan society on terms favor-able to the EU.

Cape Verde's mobility partnership features a similar framework, with the goals of facilitating legal migration flows, linking migration and development, and countering illegal immigration. The EU will pay €51 million out of the Eu-ropean Development Fund from 2008 to 2013 for this partnership, which is co-ordinated from Lisbon by the Portuguese Institute for Development Support (IPAD). A major aspect of facilitating legal migration is the creation of centers similar to CIGEM. Located in Praia, these centers accept applications for short-term stays in the EU and function as clearinghouses of information to provide order and clarity to potential migration. This information might include mate-rials on job opportunities, on migrant workers' rights, and on the rights of re-turned migrants. The centers also support migration and development, which would heavily involve the Cape Verdean diaspora. Both EU and Cape Verdean officials see the diaspora as a resource, especially as its numbers equal those of citizens living at home (De Queiroz 2008). After the signing of the partnership, IPAD director Manuel Correia was quick to point out that it aims to "stream-line the migration process, but not to eliminate the need for EU visas for mi-grants from Cape Verde, nor to establish an extraordinary legalization process for undocumented migrants" (ibid.). He also added this refrain commonly heard in high-level policy circles:

> The idea is also to provide Cape Verde with well-qualified workers from among its own nationals living in other countries. A Cape Verdean medical specialist working in Europe would be able to go home for a while without having to worry about getting back into the EU. [Circular migration would enable] better control of the flow of migration, which, as is well known, includes illegal traf-ficking and subsequent exploitation of human beings. (ibid.)

The Cape Verdean president, Pedro Pires, echoed the positive feelings, announc-ing in June 2008 that he hopes French president Sarkozy will offer solid support for his country's work in "creating the conditions for legal Cape Verdean mi-gration" (ibid.). Pires also reiterated that Cape Verde will cooperate in prevent-ing the island country from being used as a "trampoline" for illegal migrants to jump to Europe and will provide Europe with another ally in the global fight against illegal migration (ibid.). Cape Verde Properties Direct saw the mobility partnership as a marketing asset in attracting tourists and investors to its beachfront locales. Its website announced the partnership as a sign of further assurance to potential clients that the country is "economically and politically stable, the country is rapidly gaining increasing interest from investors searching for high potential capital gains along with a growing tourism market" (Cape Verde Property 2009a,b). In its "Country Brief" the World Bank also mentions the Cape Verde mobility partnership with the EU as one sign of prosperity, others including having pegged its escudo to the euro, having an 80/70 percent export/import relationship with the EU, having joined the WTO in 2007, and having 80 percent of its economy in the service sector, around which most circular migration programs are designed (World Bank 2009).

DEVELOPMENT AND DIASPORAS

The IOM also places great faith in circular migration and "co-development" with respect to seasonal agricultural labor (OSCE/IOM/ILO 2006, 124). In 1999, the Uni de Pagesos (Farmers' Union) of Catalonia, Spain, in cooperation with farmers' unions of Valencia and Mallorca, began managing the recruitment of labor from Colombia, Morocco, and Romania for work in the fruit-growing sector. By 2008, the program provided 5,250 housing units for the more than eleven thousand migrants. The program evaluates labor needs in the sector and, along with the Catalonian Ministry of Labor, determines quotas and deals with the logistics of issuing visas, arranging transportation and housing, and monitoring work conditions. The union's philanthropic arm, Fundació Agricultors Solidaris, provides migrants with an orientation on services such as health care and language training, on remittance transfers, and on labor laws, and it organizes social and cultural activities. It also supports codevelopment opportunities in the migrants' home countries with cofinancing and technical assistance for the creation of small businesses, agricultural enterprises, and civil society organizations. For example, it provided additional support to build a women's information center, an association of small milk producers, and a cooperative on the marketing and selling of fruits (ILO 2009). The IOM draws on these examples of development to justify circular migration to policy officials. It explains that

> Co-development begins with the movement of seasonal workers between origin and host communities. They remain, on average, six months in the host society and six months at home. As a result, two parallel flows are created: [first] An economic flow: seasonal workers contribute with their work to the sustain-

ability of the fruit sector in the host country. In return, they receive wages, which, to a large extent, become remittances for their families [; second] A more intangible flow, namely the interchange of knowledge and experiences. In host countries, the presence of seasonal workers approximates citizenship with the realities of less favoured and vulnerable communities. It promotes the development of these communities with collective projects co-financed by the host communities. (ibid.)

Another example of institutionalizing informal circular migration routes is found in the Integrated Management Information System (IMIS) cofunded by the IOM, the Egyptian government, and the Italian government. IMIS functions to circulate specifically targeted Egyptian labor to fill particular labor niches in the Italian economy. The program serves the aim of "regularizing" illegal Egyptian migrants in Italy but also of facilitating the return of detained illegal migrants, as the two countries signed a readmission agreement in 2007. Over the following year 2,400 Egyptians were returned (ILO 2009, 7 fn. 30). According to data from the Egyptian government, in the year 2000 around 90,000 Egyptian migrants were living in Italy, while the OECD reported that only 32,800 Egyptians held residence permits in the same year. This left some 60,000 Egyptians living in Italy without documentation (Roman 2009, 91). Italy has attracted both high- and low-skilled Egyptian labor because of high unemployment rates in Egypt since 2000, the loss of jobs in the Gulf oil economies due to the arrival of cheaper labor from Southeast Asia, and the relative ease of traveling to Italy from Libya via boat (90). Rafaat Radwan, chairman of the Information and Decision Support Centre, a government agency supporting economic and social development in Egypt, praised IMIS as a chance to "bridge the gap between North and South" and play a role in the "dialogue of civilisations" (Abdou 2003). The IMIS project moved in two phases (Roman 2008, 3). The first, which ran from 2001 until 2005, established the program's infrastructure. Egypt's aptly named Ministry of Manpower and Emigration built the employer-employee information exchange website and supporting systems, and the IOM informed Italian entrepreneurs of the IMIS system.

In this international job seeker's website Egyptian workers upload a user profile including a current résumé. They then select two job titles from a menu of fifty and have the option of choosing up to ten job specializations (Egyptian Ministry of Manpower and Emigration 2009a). To complete the online application, the job seeker should read and write in both Arabic and English. The ministry examines each profile and provides the Italian employer with those that match the job description. Employers must also create accounts to post job openings and learn the characteristics of the available Egyptian labor pool. The employer then short-lists the top candidates and can interview them directly or indirectly through an Egyptian recruitment firm. The ministry ensures the validity of the job seeker's profile. The final match is made with almost no contact between the laborer and the employer.

IMIS is mainly designed to promote seasonal migration (such as agriculture, tourism, hotels), about which the Italian government has strict policies. The temporary permit is valid for twenty days to nine months, after which employees must return to their home country. They will be given priority to return next year if the terms of the permit have been met, which includes having promptly left Italy by the visa's expiry date. The permit allows work only in the specific job for which it is granted, though a worker can change employers with their consent. Employers seeking temporary foreign labor must be registered with the Italian Ministry of the Interior. The IOM stresses in its description of the IMIS project that it "does not create a binding relationship between the employer and the potential candidate. Foreign employers reserve the right to choose the employers [sic] according to their recruitment needs" (IOM 2008, 1). The online system functions to erase nearly all contact between the employer, the employee, and the managing agency. The indirect angle from which it works increases its efficiency by removing the unpredictable element of human interaction.

IMIS's second phase, which ran from 2008 to 2010, created mechanisms to facilitate remittances from Italy to Egypt and to strengthen links between the Egyptian diaspora in Italy and Egypt itself. This phase was carefully calibrated in light of global economic trends. While global remittances have increased tremendously over the last several decades—from $2 billion in 1970 (Zohry 2003, 48) to $280 billion in 2006 (Migration Policy Institute 2010)—Egypt has experienced a slight downturn in its own intake since 1992. In that year it received its peak amount of $6.1 billion, though it would suffer a greater than 50 percent reduction of $2.8 billion in 2001 (Zohry 2003, 50). This decline is no small matter when considering that along with receipts from the Suez Canal and tourism revenues, remittances are one of Egypt's largest sources of foreign currency. The 2001 remittance figure equaled $42 per capita in Egypt and 4 percent of its GDP (50). Remittances support families back home at a subsistence level, that is, with food, medical expenses, clothes, and home improvement rather than with investment income. While the figure in the overall GDP is rather low, the funds received by families are vitally important. Zohry (2003) reports that the fall in oil prices early in the new millennium caused the decline, as did the aftermath of the 1991 Persian Gulf War. Both episodes correlate to a reduction of both emigration to and remittances from Saudi Arabia and the Gulf region in general.

Through its Prevention of Irregular Migration Project (IDOM), the Egyptian government is attempting to compensate for the loss in remittances by transforming transnational migrant networks into a formal labor circulation program run by the governments of Egypt and Italy. The IOM, the Italian government, and the Emigration Sector of the Ministry of Manpower and Emigration of Egypt cooperate on the Information Dissemination component of IDOM, which broadly aims to coordinate legal labor emigration from Egypt to Italy. Like CIGEM and the Praia information centers, Information Dissemination aims to "positively" influence Egyptian migration choices by notifying people of the opportunities and procedures for legal migration and alerting them to the threats of human trafficking and smuggling as well as the consequences of illegal migration (Zohry 2007, 40). Egypt and Italy have complementary interests in the project: Italy lacks labor in many economic sectors, largely because of an aging population, while Egypt has a large unemployment rate and a younger, poorer, and underemployed population. IMIS and IDOM, with the IOM's help, effectively arrange for an orderly transfer of labor and remittances across the Mediterranean Sea by appropriating organically formed transnational networks into their own programs.

Working in concert with the IDOM project, the Emigration Sector of the Egyptian government has been authorized to develop a comprehensive emigration strategy, which suggests the desire among officials from all sides to establish a steady migratory stream of labor from South to North. The stated aim on the Egyptian side is not only to "encourage Egyptian migration . . . on the assumption that emigration is a natural and stable phenomenon" but also "to achieve the maximum capitalization on Egyptian potential abroad, where in relation to scientific and research knowledge transfer or to the contribution in savings to Egyptian development strategies; to support capacities inside and outside Egypt" (Egyptian Ministry of Manpower and Emigration 2009b). Elsewhere the Emigration Sector states that it is "encouraging the Egyptian labour migration, especially among youth, as a security valve for the economic and social conditions in Egypt" (2009c). A further planned usage of the

IDOM is to examine labor markets abroad for emigrating Egyptians and to influence migration legislation in destination countries (2009b). The overall Egyptian emigration plan aims to stabilize the conduits for young Egyptians to move abroad and still retain their Egyptian identity by supporting émigré-related NGOs and facilitating their continued contact with the homeland. In one manifestation of what Glick Schiller and Fouron (2001) have called "long-distance nationalism," the Egyptian government is actively fostering Egyptian nationhood abroad to augment the state's own development strategy, appropriating an organic economic process. Much of migration management thus involves governments actively building what Coutin (2007, 4) terms "nations of emigrants" to resolve demographic and economic challenges.

In addition to supporting the circular migration of migrants to Europe, the EC supports the circulation of diasporas on its soil back to their sending countries. The Migration for Development in Africa (MIDA) Great Lakes project illustrates the strongly neoliberal character of such managed migration in what is known in migration policy circles as "knowledge creation and transfer" (Williams 2006). The Belgian government funds the project while the IOM manages it on behalf of Belgium (as the host country) and Burundi, Rwanda, and the Democratic Republic of the Congo (as the targeted sending countries). MIDA handles the applications from migrants residing legally in Belgium and willing to temporarily return to their homeland to train people in their area of technical expertise. These professionals include biostatisticians; lecturers in law, economics, and agricultural sciences; and specialists in public health, hydrogeology, chemistry, and international relations. The project experienced difficulty finding suitable candidates from Rwanda, as the IOM could not find enough professionals among the diaspora in Belgium and concluded that Rwandans do not want to return despite government encouragement. Only one candidate was selected out of thirty-nine.

The skilled migrants' home countries determine the kinds of professionals admitted to the program. In Rwanda these include engineers and technicians; in Burundi and Rwanda, professionals in justice, education, and health are in short supply; while the government of the Democratic Republic of the Congo (DRC) requested expertise in health and education. IOM Brussels seeks women candidates in particular to equalize the gender imbalance among highly educated professionals in the sending countries. The host institution in the sending country writes the terms of reference for returning migrant workers while IOM Brussels assembles their selection committee. The committee consists of one representative from the Belgian Ministry of Foreign Affairs, two representatives of the Belgian interuniversity council, one Great Lakes specialist, three nationals of the three Great Lakes countries, two representatives of umbrella organizations, and one IOM representative. The selection committee chooses candidates and oversees the implementation of the program. Chosen participants are given an average of €5,000 to cover the cost of transportation, meals, accommodation, and other incidental expenses.

All participants agree that the MIDA Great Lakes project has a positive impact, though the extent of its significance is difficult to gauge. Given participants' high levels of education (60% held either master's or doctoral degrees) and understanding of the local situation compared to European professionals, they believe they have improved the targeted institutions' performance. Furthermore, the project frees the employer's resources for investment in other areas, since the Belgian government covers the participant's cost (including the salary). For example, at Burundi's Ngozi University eight lecturers taught 525 students, saving the university €4,200; at the Studio Ujambo, also in Burundi, one journalist benefited eight local journalists and saved €1,340; at the DRC's University of Lumbumbashi eight lecturers benefited 337 students and 12 engineers, saving €2,400; and at its Ministry of Labour and Social Security one specialist benefited four local specialists, saving the ministry €320 (MIDA 2002). The project disseminates these figures to show "concrete" results of a development program operated by indigenous experts with Western education and "local" knowledge. The MIDA project also manages a "Diaspora Database" helping governments, private sector employers, and NGOs find diaspora members with the requisite skills, education, and experience to support particular projects aimed at developing sending countries.

In the last ten years, Northern states have been keen to draw the diasporic populations living on their territories into their development policies aimed at the diasporic homelands. The diaspora serves as a vehicle to transfer funds, skills, and knowledge gained in the host society to the sending country. From a neoliberal perspective, this move frees up the creativity of the ambitious individual for the benefit of everyone: the individual develops his or her full ability and enjoys the chance to "self-actualize"; the host country receives a temporary solution to its labor needs; while the sending country benefits from the inputs delivered by the diaspora. Moreover, politicians and senior officials can explain to voters how their efforts decrease immigration as they cut off migration's root cause through development.

BLUE CARD

Functioning in tandem with circular migration is the EC's Blue Card initiative, which aims to standardize, simplify, and expedite procedures to bring in highly skilled labor from abroad. Like registered traveler programs (Chapter 5), it would circulate travelers and migrants of high economic or educational capital throughout the union. Frattini's worry, mentioned above, is that 85 percent of unskilled labor goes to the EU versus 5 percent to the US, whereas the US absorbs 55 percent of skilled labor including engineers, technicians, and information and communications technologies specialists. As Euractiv, the EU's news organization, puts it, "The Blue Card is the EU's main policy initiative in the global competition for the best, highly mobile brains" (2008a). The EC hopes to attract twenty million highly skilled workers from outside the EU with an offer that is more open-ended than formal circular migration programs (ibid.). However, its more restrictive conditions might hamper it in competition with the US's Green Card. While the Blue Card is valid for two years and does not give automatic permanent residency, the Green Card is valid for ten years and includes permanent residency. While the Blue Card provides the opportunity for permanent residency after five years, the Green Card offers citizenship after the same amount of time. A Blue Card applicant must possess a recognized diploma, proof of three years' professional experience, and a one-year EU-based job contract with a salary three times greater than the minimum wage. The Blue Card is attached to the individual rather than the job thus allowing some labor mobility. An applicant for a Green Card has five routes to obtain the card: employment, family links, a lottery, investment, or residence since before 1972. One advantage of the Blue Card over the Green Card is that the former also allows the holder's family to live, work, and travel in the EU. The Blue Card at least offers a path to permanent residency in an EU member state, unlike the circular migration programs, which are designed to preclude permanence altogether. Like all efforts to institutionalize certain forms of migration to the EU, individual rights are sacrosanct. The Blue Card Directive guarantees: (1) working conditions, including pay and dismissal; (2) freedom of association; (3) education, training, and recognition of qualifications; (4) a number of provisions in national law regarding social security and pensions; (5) access to goods and services, including procedures for obtaining housing, information, and counseling services; and (6) free access to the entire territory of the member state concerned, within the limits provided for by national law (Delegation of the European Union 2009).

The European Council issued the directive for the Blue Card on 25 May

2009, and it obligates member states to transpose its conditions into national law within two years. (The EU's job portal for online registrations opened in January 2010 at www.apply.eu.) In fact, the Blue Card does little to reduce a member state's control over its labor admissions. It harmonizes admission criteria rather than admission rates or recruited job categories. The criteria are rather minimal, consisting of the need for a work contract, relevant professional qualifications, and a minimum salary level (Delegation of the European Union 2009). The member states decide for themselves how to recognize skills and educational credentials, and they decide what their own labor needs are. The Blue Card holder may work in a single member state only and must apply separately (though through an expedited process) if he or she wishes to work in a second member state. Therefore, the flow of even highly skilled labor is contained within national borders, or at the least the holder is permitted to cross those borders only after a careful vetting process. Given the wide range of average gross salaries among EU members states—Luxembourg and Bulgaria were €43,000 and €2,000, respectively, in 2006—EC officials do not want the Blue Card to permit intra-EU labor mobility for third-country nationals (Collett 2009). The European Parliament voted to support the Blue Card initiative, though with reservations and recommendations beyond the EC's own proposal. The initiative passed with a majority of 388 to 56 (largely due to a pact between the Party of European Socialists and the center-right European People's Party). The Liberals and the Greens led an abstention of 124 votes. While the European Parliament's vote is only consultative and not binding, it still succeeded in persuading the EC to increase the requisite number of years of an applicant's prior professional experience from three to five and to increase the salary threshold from 1.5 to 1.7 times the average national wage (EurActiv 2008b).

The contours of the debate in the European Parliament reflect the discursive field within which political alliances are formed and counterarguments made. Conservative members of European Parliament (MEPs), through their spokesman Phillip Bradbourn, argued that the Blue Card initiative is entirely secondary to the need for tighter border controls, which must stop "the wave of illegal migration into the EU before we tackle skills shortages" (EurActiv 2008a). He then mustered an argument that combines neo-nationalist fears with liberal humanitarian sentiments:

> The proposal as it stands will open a Pandora's box to those who seek to migrate to the EU without any of the controls necessary to ensure that those who em-

ploy illegal migrants are tackled and those illegal migrants who are caught are sent back to their country of origin. The proposal will encourage more people to undertake hazardous journeys from all corners of the world in the hope that they will get a work permit which once issued will give them free range to move across the whole of Europe. (ibid.)

Manfred Weber, German MEP from the center-right European People's Party (European Democrats Group), insisted that "the new rules must not put additional pressure on the millions of unemployed in the EU member states. In addition, only member states must have the competence to decide on the size of immigration flows" (EurActiv 2008a). Sverker Rudeberg of Business Europe argued that the Blue Card should contain provisions for swift family reunification and avoid setting a minimum wage level "that was far too high and exclude some people from jobs without any reason" (ibid.). The fact that the Liberal faction abstained does not suggest a retreat from this position but rather a stated concern that the initiative does not sufficiently protect migrants' rights. Their spokesman, Dutch MEP Jeanine Hennis Plasschaert, argued that the Blue Card would lead to "all kinds of restrictions and bureaucracy, rather than opening the doors to highly skilled workers" (EurActiv 2008b). Another significant criticism came from the European Trade Union Confederation, which argued that it is difficult to justify such a plan for immigrant labor while many member states face high unemployment rates. Catelene Passchier, the spokeswoman for the confederation, also noted that "people are concerned that high-level positions will be occupied by migrant workers who are paid less than Community citizens. Equal treatment is very important, to prevent unfair competition." She "would have preferred a horizontal directive" rather than a sectoral approach, as the former would have prevented employers from favoring cheaper immigrant labor in particular niches while overlooking the needs of domestic labor in others (EurActiv 2008a).

Perhaps most significant were the positions of the European Commission president José Manuel Barroso and Socialist MEP Claudio Fava. Barroso, understandably, sought to appease as many factions as possible, arguing that the Blue Card will boost economic competitiveness by encouraging labor migration while also solving the EU's demographic problem with its aging workforce. To satisfy the pull of the neo-right in national labor policy debates, he added, "Let me be clear: I am not announcing today that we are opening the doors to 20 million high-skilled workers. The Blue Card is not a 'blank cheque.' It is not a right to admission, but a demand-driven approach and a common European procedure." Barroso continued that "member states will have broad flexibility to determine their labor market needs and decide on the number of high-skilled workers they would like to welcome" (EurActiv 2008a). Fava argued against myopic national barriers that preclude both easy mobility throughout EU territory and "an economically and competitively advanced Europe" (ibid.). He pushed even further to open the Blue Card for low-skilled workers to avoid the exploitation of immigrant labor on the black market, a cause which liberals also champion. One key issue left ambiguous is the threat that the Blue Card program will encourage brain drain by offering a chance at permanent residency and family reunification. Barroso was cryptic on this score:

> With regard to developing countries we are very much aware of the need to avoid negative "brain drain" effects. Therefore, the proposal promotes ethical recruitment standards to limit—if not ban—active recruitment by member states in developing countries in some sensitive sectors. It also contains measures to facilitate so-called "circular migration." Europe stands ready to cooperate with developing countries in this area. (EurActiv 2008a)

The contours of the Blue Card debate reveal the salient role of liberal rationales with some strategic nods to neo-nationalist interests in managed labor migration. First, those contours push out neo-right arguments by allowing even highly skilled labor to compete against domestic labor. Again, the Blue Card holder's minimum salary is calculated on the basis of the average salary of the national workforce, so that the holder can easily work for less than the average highly skilled (and relatively highly paid) domestic worker. Recalling from Chapter 2, the ranks of Europe's neo-right are filled with the highly educated and highly skilled younger workers now disaffected by liberal economics, as much as they are filled with blue-collar workers abandoned by fractious and indecisive social democrats. Second, socialists and liberals share a common cause in encouraging free movement of highly skilled third-country nationals within the EU. The former see it as a worker's right to as wide a labor market as possible, while the latter believe that increased labor mobility stimulates growth. Third, while the conservative MEP decried the Blue Card's lack of attention to stopping illegal flows, he failed to recognize that member states in fact cooperate easily on that matter, as shown by EU-wide developments on border and passport control policy. He also introduced a curious blend of xenophobic paranoia and sentimental liberalism to argue for border restrictions for the sake of nationalism and the safety of the migrant. This position signifies again the marriage of neoliberals and neo-nationalists. In sum, the Blue Card debate illuminates the parameters through which disagreements on such matters are contained.

A REDEMPTIVE IDEA

The fantasy of circular migration presupposes the self-starting, industrious migrant animated through neoliberal economic opportunities and enlightened state policies. This individual will have done the necessary research either online or at EU information centers abroad to discover the legal channels leading to work in the EU. He or she is an enterprising soul who scans the horizon for opportunities rather than waiting for the state (sending or receiving) to provide assistance (Rose 1992). Like the global traveler protected and enabled by the e-passport, the migrant can ostensibly improve his or her own situation, as well as society more broadly, if only granted the opportunity to freely circulate across borders to exploit opportunities. Policymakers now frame migrants not simply as laboring resources between capital and investment but rather as entrepreneurs increasing and diversifying their own capital through higher wages, knowledge gains, and skills development. Migration officials located in countries along the transnational migratory chain jointly institutionalize conditions of labor circulation that render this narrative an obvious interpretation of an objective economic situation. As a result, a transnational regime of labor mobility is emerging that is backstopped by EU border control practices and exported to sending and transit countries. The EU achieves greater control over these flows through the global adoption of its norms and regulatory procedures.

Circular migration also functions as the conceptual lynchpin of the EU's efforts to create a harmonized, comprehensive migration policy: it solves the problem of the EU's aging workforce because it recruits labor; it solves the problem of brain drain out of developing countries because migrant labor returns home; it solves the root economic push factor of South–North migration because low- and high-skilled laborers bring their European experiences back to their home countries; and, thus, it reduces the EU's need to police illegal migration and to directly fund development projects because migrants contribute to economic growth at home in their own countries. Most crucially, circular migration policy resolves the conflict between neoliberals, who wish to circulate labor migrants into the EU, and neo-nationalists, who wish to keep them out—thereby functioning as the "right" solution to the migration "problem." All mainstream policy perspectives in migration discussions are accommodated, clearing the path to develop a harmonized migration management system. Given the vital importance of the Global Commission on International Migration in this entire discursive edifice, it is little wonder that it celebrates mobility, but not settlement, as a fundamental attribute of human nature. Its report asserts that "The human race has always been curious, and eager to visit different places, gain new experiences and encounter unfamiliar cultures. As a result of the globalisation process, much larger numbers of people can realise those ambitions" (Global Commission on International Migration 2005, 6–7).

According to this historically Western perspective, circular migration allows people the world over to liberate their exploratory soul in the openness of globalization. However, the very fragility of the circular migration concept perhaps demanded this naturalized conceptual anchor, just as any ethical system must ultimately appeal to a god, a moral imperative, or a prime mover lest the whole enterprise become a castle made of sand.

Outside their conferences, meetings, and offices, few mid-level policymakers see circular migration as the silver-bullet solution to Europe's "migration problem" and Southern poverty. Nevertheless, the fantasy of circular migration still commands the policy process with its promise of a new world order. The costs of migration are steep but remain outside the purview of the neoliberal lens, which sees individual achievement and occludes social obligation. For example, the loss of daily wages that the would-be migrant would incur to travel to the embassy or to an Internet station would appear inconsequential; the migrant's family would not appear to suffer economically from his or her absence because the remittances would far exceed the migrant's local wage; the social cost of separating people from their families, kinsfolk, and other social networks would appear to be of secondary importance. When in the host European country, migrants would work dutifully and never stray in thought or deed from the terms of the contract. If problems were to arise, the policy response would be simple: "the sooner we get these systems working properly, the better off migrants will be." The fantasy itself is not the problem but rather the obstacles to its materialization.

7 WHEN THERE IS NO THERE THERE

Nonlocal Ethnography in a World of Apparatuses

It is in the nature of the human surveying capacity that it can function only if man disentangles himself from all involvement in and concern with the close at hand and withdraws himself to a distance from everything near him.

Hannah Arendt 1958, 251

THE CRYSTALLIZATION OF A RESEARCH OBJECT

This nonlocal ethnography of the EU's migration management apparatus has not primarily traced connections between actors, places, and events. An apparatus cannot be adequately explained as a series of effects triggered in sequential order or as the product of tightly woven social networks. The primary ethnographic challenge was not to connect the dots of an unknown picture but rather to determine how an apparatus crystallizes out of ubiquitous rationales, discourses, and narratives as well as dynamic forms of technical and bureaucratic organization. These intangible phenomena inform work in disparate policy settings so as to generate family resemblances in multifarious policy outcomes. The resulting variation testifies to human creativity while the familiarity facilitates these outcomes' articulation into a larger apparatus. At once ephemeral and convergent, the apparatus requires a nonlocal ethnography to illuminate its organizing logics and heterogeneous practices even if these do not lend themselves easily to thick description. Where depth is lacking—and policymaking is a superficial practice by design—nonlocal ethnography allows us to move across domains to examine an apparatus's emergence in, and fusion of, disparate spheres and domains.

This book showcases the converging EU migration management apparatus, composed of a bewildering array of actors, knowledge practices, technical requirements, labor regulations, security discourses, normative subjectivities, and repurposed institutions that create the conditions for the orderly movement of bodies by the millions. Though the vast majority of its officials, technocrats, and other specialists do not work together in face-to-face settings, one still observes among them a great policy conversation taking place indirectly, in dispersed sites, across many policy domains, and in many venues (policy statements, public statements, press releases, government brochures, national legislations, international conferences, and so on). The apparatus serves a drastically imbalanced global economy, the displacing effects of which are treated through negative border control measures, narrowly defined visa requirements, and pervasive biometric surveillance. However, its legitimation is framed in such positive terms as safeguarding the creative entrepreneur, preventing brain drain, enhancing migrants' skills, and saving people from smugglers, traffickers, identity theft, and risky clandestine border crossings.

The negative and positive measures complement each other in the EU's effort to plug the holes in its aging workforce through temporary work visas. Backstopping circular migration programs are enhanced border protection measures like RABITs, integrated radar systems, satellite surveillance of offshore embarkation points, and patrol missions on the edges of international waters. Biometric information systems make illegal transgressions at controlled border points virtually impossible. Unique and immutable physical attributes are recorded, transmitted, and shared instantaneously among police authorities across EU territory, thus matching a traveler to a document that itself was issued under tight conditions. To help guarantee that only potential immigrants with the desired skills apply, the EU establishes job mobility portals in immigrant-sending countries. The apparatus does not of course materialize in such a complete, enclosed, and totalized form, but the full weight of mainstream discourses of public order, vast arrays of institutional resources, and established political and economic practices strongly push it in that direction. All travelers must deal with it even if some successfully evade it.

A speech by Graham Watson, MEP and group leader for the Alliance of Liberals and Democrats for Europe (ALDE), shows how the diverse parts of such a monstrous social construction work together as an integrated moral whole. He weaves in key themes such as security, humanitarianism, and economy that compose the broader migration debate while wrapping them around a specific crisis. The fusion does not indicate that a unified bureaucracy or singular policy exists (or will exist) but rather that similar rationales of governance can be applied to different migration policy domains. From the floor of the European Parliament in Strasbourg he gravely recalled the 2007 case of Tunisian fishermen arrested for human smuggling, when in fact they had rescued migrants, as required by international maritime law, from drowning in the Mediterranean Sea. Watson (2007) began the speech by asking, "Mr President, what could better illustrate the need for a common European immigration policy than the case of the Tunisian fishermen?" He then explained, "Everything about that tragic event—from the migrants on a rubber boat on the high seas, to the people smugglers who put them there and the authorities who jailed their rescuers—is testament to the failure of Europe's approach to migration." Pumping a clenched fist in the air, Watson continued:

> With every human tragedy, during a desperate do-nothing decade, Liberals and Democrats have asked one simple question: how many people must perish before governments see that lifting the drawbridge of Fortress Europe serves nobody's interests? Managing migration is as much in our interests as in the interests of those seeking our shores or prepared to die trying. While populism has propelled a policy forged in the furnace of fear, let us face the facts. Let us make no mistake: the Commission's cozy calculation that we can take the best and leave the rest will not work. Pushed by poverty, hunger, squalor and war, people will keep crossing the Mediterranean whether they fit our criteria or not. Why? Because our agricultural and fisheries policies are out-pricing their products and raiding their natural resources. Of course we must patrol Europe's borders. The Moreno Sánchez report is right to demand that Frontex be given the budget, the staff and the equipment needed to do its job. . . . Longer term, however, only a comprehensive EU policy that punishes the people smugglers, provides legal routes in and creates hope where there is despair can counter prevailing trends.

Pushing for the easy circulation of goods and people, Watson also condenses key themes into a single speech and wraps them in a blanket of outraged humanitarian concern: protecting people who risk their lives trying to enter Europe (humanitarianism); economic opportunities for European and migrant prosperity (liberalism); tighter border control to prevent illegal entries (security); fighting human smuggling networks (legality); and Europe's responsibilities to the South (development). He globalizes the migration problem by upholding its humanitarian and economic dimensions, distances himself from neo-nationalism by subtly condemning the impact of "populism" (the liberal code word for neo-nationalism) on EU migration policy, and announces his continuing support of Frontex to ensure an orderly framework for the circulation of individuals. The crisis of the Tunisian fishermen serves as a centripetal force that fuses these themes together. Politicians, policymakers, business leaders, and various sectors of the general public might disagree as to how much weight any given theme should carry. Nevertheless, the fact that they fit snugly into a single speech at the European Parliament suggests their compatibility in a harmonized EU migration policy. Uplifting and enabling Watson's high-scale morality, which conceptually integrates such a wide variety of global problems, is a social construct that is available to empirical study. The remainder of this chapter reviews recent ethnographic trends to set up an argument for nonlocal ethnography as a methodology for studying global regimes of governance, or apparatuses.

FROM METHODS TO METHODOLOGY
IN AN ETHNOGRAPHY OF MASS SOCIETY

By the late 1980s and 1990s, anthropology fully recognized globalization as much more than a force that acts upon the local. It blasted away the concept of the local as a bounded, self-contained, ahistorical unit (Appadurai 1996; Hannerz 1996). This created space for significant reflection on the role of ethnography in a world where social connections stretch around the globe rather than re-main presumably trapped inside territorial containers. Two subsequent develop-ments have been particularly influential in realigning ethnography for the global arena while retaining its key traditional elements. First, in American cultural anthropology George Marcus's (1995) multisited ethnography remains the sa-lient methodological response to globalization. This approach firstly focuses on connections between people geographically separated and highlights circulation over singular location: follow the people, the commodity, the story, the meta-phor. Secondly, it regards the system (or context) in which these actors operate not as a reified container but rather as a construction of those actors' own mak-ing. Multisited ethnography self-consciously collapses the distinction between lifeworld and system in order to retain the actor's agency (98). Like traditional participant-observation, it "is designed around the chains, paths, threads, con-junctions, or juxtaposition of locations in which the ethnographer establishes some form of *literal* presence" (105, emphasis added). Invaluable in illuminat-ing social connections not confined to singular places, multisited ethnography remains committed to the empiricist conviction that knowledge obtained from direct sensory experience leads to the most insightful conclusions. Crucial in contrasting actual human practice against theoretical imposition, it nevertheless risks inverting the problem it aims to solve: instead of positing a system that con-tains the individual, it posits a system that emits directly from the actor's agency.

Second, for sociology and social anthropology Michael Burawoy (2000) suggests the return and revision of the extended case method originally dem-onstrated in Max Gluckman's 1940 seminal piece *Analysis of a Social Situation in Zululand.* Among other virtues, this method accounted for an indigenous group's integration into wider colonial capitalism and can explain how micro forces are structured in relation to macro forces (Burawoy 2000, 16). Indeed, "the discovery of extralocal determination is an essential moment of the extended case method" because it recognizes the inseparability of the local and the global and hence the invalidity of the distinction itself (27). To update the extended case method, Burawoy offers three modes of problematizing global forces. The first follows an ethnographic chain from a high-level public or corporate official to a local resister. The second tracks how global forces are constituted through specific connections. The third examines how images of globalization are produced and distributed, and how their effects are instantiated (29–32). These modes directly address the local, lived experience, as Burawoy urges the traveling ethnographer to focus on how "global domination is resisted, avoided, and negotiated" (29). Where firsthand observation is obscured, measured theoretical insights are invoked to fill in the blanks, nodding to Abrams's (1988, 62) point that "when the gaff is blown" state secrets turn out to be trivial or theoretically predictable anyway. Evens and Handelman (2006) further advance the call for a revitalized extended case method. They note that American anthropology has somehow forgotten the Manchester School's foundational work in ethnographic praxis theory, which has much to offer the task of unpacking the interplay between individual agency and structural forces.

Multisited ethnography and the extended case method have emerged as datum points in the discussions on adapting ethnography to the global arena (Amit 1999; Faubion and Marcus 2009; Gupta and Ferguson 1997; Tsing 2005). As such, attention continues to focus on the problem of tracing tangible connections between actors, as in classic ethnography, and so most efforts continue to privilege evidence obtained through direct sensory contact and try to link actors through discrete, cause-and-effect connections. These new approaches revise earlier ethnographies that depicted communities as bounded, timeless, and unaffected by colonial and capitalist systems, though we should recall that the earlier ethnographies did so to counteract the determinism of nineteenth-century evolutionism. These updates in method reflect updates in moral commitment. If cultural relativism had been deployed to illuminate the blind spots of European and North American ethnocentrism, then today's ethnographies expose its global consequences.

However, the crucial change in the new world order to which ethnographers must adapt is not necessarily the globalization of social connections that directly link people through bartering practices, rituals, rites of passage, and so on. Rather, the disorienting change has been the institutionalization of social relations mediated by abstract third agents such as statistics, policy representations, exchange value, high-scale morality, and so on. This fact raises the question of whether our commitment to highlighting direct connections is a sufficient strategy in a world operating through mediated communications, alienated relations, estrangement of individuals, and ever-shifting social organization.

By the late 1990s and the early 2000s some anthropologists began to argue that equally significant efforts at state, international, and corporate regulation were rivaling the color and chaos of globalization (Comaroff and Comaroff 2009; Friedman 2003; Perry and Mauer 2003). What Zygmunt Bauman (1991, 7; see also Douglas 1966) had earlier described in philosophical terms—that the negativity of chaos is unintelligible without the positivity of order—many anthropologists began to take more seriously through studies of how the state orders global flows and thus defines disorder and chaos in the very act. The ethnographic work of Brenda Chalfin (2006; 2010) in Ghana and Yael Navaro-Yashin (2003) in Cyprus are cases in point. Yet, an explicit methodology is still needed to help identify what are casually called large-scale "regimes" or "systems" that regulate global flows; and to help us select the right methods to get a handle on them. *Where*, for example, do we study the problem of how a "migrant" gets framed as a particular policy problem requiring a particular policy solution? *What* is the object of study to answer such a question? Most of the thousands of high-level bureaucrats, Members of European Parliament, experts and officers on border controls, labor officials, academics, IT experts, health officials, and countless others involved do not know each other, do not work in the same policy domain, do not possess any significant influence as individuals, and do not even occupy the same moral universe as private individuals (Shore and Wright 1997, 14). Furthermore, policymaking often involves a strange process of coauthorship whereby multiple and disparately located authors contribute to a document—for example, administrators, oversight committees, academics, and consultants—yet their varying viewpoints are limited by the document's a priori framing (Brenneis 2006, 42–43). This situation highlights a strongly ungrounded dimension of policy processes.

Xiang Biao acknowledges this problem of ungroundedness in his study of a multinational IT labor system. He confesses that his ethnography of a system "does not contain much material to bring to the reader a flavor of the research sites and a sense of 'being there' as most ethnographies do. For the same reason,

[his] informants' experiences are fragmented in different chapters to serve [his] thematically organized argument" (2007, 117). As in the present ethnography of a migration management apparatus, we find that grounded, individual experiences quite often contribute to the fusion of larger systems of population regulation that a person effectively upholds. In this vein, Biao correctly notes the limits of anthropology's stress on local "embeddedness" and its insistence that concrete human connections still shape economic processes no matter how global, virtual, or abstract (3). He writes that "people may need to be told that ethnic networks still matter in migration, but they are keener to know why, say, IT professionals were constantly on the move and why they made a fortune by creating nothing but Web sites" (3). Riles (2000, 21) also argues that transnational legal networks simply defy "context" as the term is understood in traditional ethnographic parlance. From the ethnographer's standpoint, the intangibility of these kinds of social processes means—either worryingly or opportunistically—that there are no core locations, or even particularly good locations per se, in which to do participant-observation. "Being there," as Clifford Geertz once said of ethnographic fieldwork, is rather difficult because, as Gertrude Stein famously said about Oakland, California, "there is no there there."

Nevertheless, the ethnographic response to globalization and to the formation of decentralized regimes of power still assumes, if only implicitly, a directly connected set of practices appearing in discrete moments of space-time in which the ethnographer can be immersed. We still retain—or at least have not fully situated—the ethnographic premise that extended immersion in particular places is possible, that social connections are ultimately mappable, and that this approach can adequately illuminate contemporary power structures. This leaves ethnographers in a double bind: we must track ethnographic chains that wrap around the globe while simultaneously insisting that we immerse ourselves in every link along the way. The observations of Gupta and Ferguson (1997, 4; see also Amit 1999) speak to the issue:

> On the one hand, anthropology appears determined to give up its old ideas of territorially fixed communities and stable, localized cultures. . . . At the same time, though, in a defensive response to challenges to its "turf" from other disciplines, anthropology has come to lean more heavily than ever on a methodological commitment to spend long periods in one localized setting.

The point here is not that it is wrong to follow the object of study, that directly linked chains are not at work, or that one should not immerse oneself in a particular place. Rather, the point is that this strategy alone does not fully appreci-ate how globalization has generated qualitatively new forms of social regula-tion, economic transaction, governance, and identity production, all of which evade "location" as conventionally perceived and, by extension, participant-observation, even if the ethnographer has a limitless supply of time, tenacity, and travel funds. The global is more than local writ large. Contemporary eth-nography must grapple with how amorphous regimes of global governance ab-sorb millions of people within their purview—that is, indirectly, with extreme decentralization, and through powerful rationales that integrate what were once described as autonomous ethnographic circuits. Therefore, the problem before us is more than (and not even fundamentally) the logistical problem of chasing our object of study around the globe. Rather, the problem is how to create an ethnographic account of *empirical* processes that cannot be fully ap-prehended through *empiricist* methods, or through direct sensory contact with the processes in question (Feldman 2008, 315–18; 2011).

Challenges to contemporary ethnography are readily understood when placed alongside the changes in sovereign power outlined by the likes of Fou-cault and others interested in the power/knowledge nexus. As has been well ar-gued, sovereign power no longer resides in the body of the king, the prince, or the emperor who rules the polis from an external position of authority through traceable Machiavellian relations of co-optation, coercion, and reward. Like-wise, power cannot be reduced to the interplay between the headman and the villagers or between the corporate CEO and the workers and consumers. Nevertheless, as Jean and John Comaroff remind us (2003, 153), ethnography was born from the idea that a full picture of power relations can be mapped if one stays long enough with the proverbial tribe, or any other social network or system. In contrast, modern sovereignty draws on technical expertise to regu-late the population by isolating and collectivizing it, a process which transpires through countless policy domains often sharing neoliberal rationales of gover-nance (Ferguson 1994; Li 2007; Mitchell 2002; Trouillot 2001). These practices occur over wide geographic spaces and with the input of dispersed and nomi-nally connected actors, thus raising the question of where to do ethnography.

Indeed, these difficult empirical situations have prompted some anthropol-ogists to directly question the limits of empiricism in global ethnographies. Gavin Smith (2006, 621) points out that anthropologists must develop meth-ods that will expose the material conditions of capitalist reproduction, which are not immediately available to experience. Greenhalgh (2003, 210) argues that anthropologists have overwhelmingly focused on the micropractices that discipline individuals, as these are amenable to participant-observation, while the more elusive processes of population regulation have "languished in disciplinary obscurity." In positing an ethnography of the state in the global era, Trouillot (2001, 135) cautions that reducing "the object of study to the object of observation . . . reduces matters of methodology to matters of research techniques and mistakenly assumes all empirical studies to be necessarily empiricist in one form or another." Most assertively, Jean and John Comaroff argue that anthropology's response to globalization and the power regimes it engenders "has been conservative" and dogged by a "hidebound empiricism" (2003, 154, 155). They explicitly add that "anthropology has, for the most part, remained unrelentingly positivist in spirit" (153). Answering these critiques requires a clear epistemological basis for an ethnographic methodology that guides the selection of particular research methods, participant-observation among others, for any particular research agenda. This methodology should account more for enduring (but less tangible) rationales and processes generative of an apparatus than for tangible (but less enduring) objects and locations symptomatic of an apparatus.

NONLOCAL ETHNOGRAPHY AND ITS OBJECT OF OBSERVATION

Foucault's notion of the apparatus (*dispositif*) is directly apposite to the challenge of identifying an object of observation that is not easily captured in a singular place or series of places. Rabinow (2003, 50–51) describes it as a patchwork contrivance that produces docile bodies, orderly populations, and economic productivity. Its disparate elements fuse together in moments of "crisis." Indeed, today's regular identification of crisis—financial crisis, health care crisis, crisis in the Middle East, and so on—justifies and sustains the integration of national systems as a positively humanitarian, or at least humane, effort rather than a negative police effort. Furthermore, these acts of identification are necessary to legitimize state apparatuses, which effectively renders *security* rather than *insecurity* the state's greatest source of worry (Campbell 1998; Grinker 1998; Weber 1995). If security is achieved, then there is no need for the apparatus. Those pushing for a common EU migration policy identified crises in the illegal migrations to the Canary Islands, the case of the Tunisian fishermen, the aging of the EU's own workforce, and the preying of human traffickers upon innocent victims. The apparatus's technologies work by "first specifying (and to that extent creating) those targets and then controlling (distributing and regulating) them" (Rabinow 2003, 50–51). Crucially, its elements are "resolutely heterogeneous," incorporating "discourses, institutions, architectural arrangements, policy decisions, laws, administrative measures, scientific statements, moral and philosophic propositions" (Foucault cited in Rabinow 2003, 51; see also Collier, Lakoff, and Rabinow 2004). More than a collection of political technologies, however, the apparatus is "the network that can be established between these elements" (Rabinow 2003, 51; see also Agamben 2009).

That said, how does this "network" manage to connect these different elements to give an apparatus such powers of integration and convergence? How, for example, is the EC's "system of systems" welded together? How are global relations held together? There are several mechanisms that generate the network effect for an apparatus. First, certain technical devices function either as "boundary objects," that is, devices that travel across social worlds (for example, policy domains) and retain a constant identity while satisfying particular policy needs (Bowker and Star 1999, 15–16), or as "immutable mobiles," which create links between different places in time and space and transmit data and images for a synoptic presentation with "fantastic acceleration" (Latour 1990, 32). These devices share a certain plasticity that allows them to be applied to diverse policy contexts and a certain generality that allows them to integrate these contexts into a larger apparatus, often by default. For example, rationales of governance are ubiquitous because they are simple, convenient, and sufficiently vague to allow officials to work them into countless different migration policy situations. These require no abstract thinking, second thoughts, or central enforcer, so local actors can become active agents in their operationalization. These devices also include IT technical standards that disparate officials can adapt to their national databases but can still function to integrate those contexts into a larger system of population management. Similarly, IT systems virtually organize the information flows of massive numbers of unconnected officials without the friction built into social connections. Linguistic devices like "shifters" function similarly: these phrases—"migration that works for everyone"; "humanitarian approaches to border control"; "enabling migrants to help themselves"—are conspicuously vacuous yet possess an ability to integrate disparate discursive fields (see Brenneis 2006, 45; Urciuoli 2008, 214; M. Silverstein 1976).

Second, people themselves can be circulated rapidly and organized as needed, whether they are technicians or targets of circulation migration programs. "Nonce experts" work according to immediate need in ad hoc networks (for example, RABITs and EMN members) that offer greater labor flexibility than white-collar workers in top-down bureaucracies. Such experts find the work to be a fulfilling and organic experience, which simplifies the extraction of their labor and facilitates the proliferation of the apparatus into new domains. This spontaneity, as it were, creates a pleasurable community of experts of like talents (Brenneis 1994, 33–34). The possibility for an enriching experience facilitates their call to action, reduces labor costs and worker disgruntlement, and merges the laborer's moral universe with that attributed to the apparatus. Furthermore, as workers are increasingly identified as (and reduced to) carriers of a skill set, they must make themselves available for new tasks with increasing frequency. For high-skilled workers in particular, their "skill referents" are ways of speaking about an inchoate set of skills that they must sell in the diverse labor markets as they constantly readapt to shifting modes of production. Therefore, "the noun *skill* once denoted a specific manual or machine operation and now denotes any practice, form of knowledge, or way of being constituting productive labor" (Urciuoli 2008, 212). Skill referents are organized more by loose associational chains, in which the elements can be rearranged according to immediate need, rather than by a coherent, more determinative semantic field (LaDousa cited in ibid.). As a result of these forms of labor organization, the apparatus's material infrastructure is more tightly connected than the social relations among the individuals it employs (either as laborers or as objects of regulation, or both).

Third, apparatuses also constantly realign people in relation to ever-changing norms for the sake of expediting public administration. Whereas the norm once referred to a standard from which conformity and nonconformity could be distinguished, the reference point is now simply the "average" or the "play of oppositions between the normal and the abnormal or pathological" (Ewald 1991a, 140). No longer seeking the "good" but merely the functional or the utilitarian, the apparatus never risks obsolescence. Defense corporations can shift the object of surveillance from MiGs to migrants, and the TREVI group can expand into SIS as needs change and proliferate. The apparatus needs only to transmute to encourage behavior that contributes to the goals of social tranquility and economic productivity. In the process, it identifies and objectifies risk as the opposite of those two goals: unidentified people are thus potential security threats in the form of criminals, terrorists, or illegal laborers. The first group threatens property; the second, life and limb; and the third, equal opportunities for sustenance (in the cultural space that the apparatus serves anyway). All individuals within its purview are analyzed through quantitative means to determine the extent to which they threaten these objectives.

Fourth, and related to the third mechanism, documents ensconce the guidelines for producing such norms in the policy lexicon, giving those guidelines (or discourses more fundamentally) a sense of factuality and consistency in an otherwise vast field of writing (Dreyfus and Rabinow 1983, 159). For this reason documents are quintessentially "paradigmatic artifacts of modern knowledge practices" (Riles 2006a, 2). When we compare such artifacts to the function of documents in Fijian gift-giving ceremonies (Miyazaki 2006), we better see their role in mass society. Gift exchange among Fijians entails a period of uncertainty while the giver hopes that the receiver will find the gift worthy of the social connection that it is supposed to cement. The process works similarly in reverse: the gift-receiver must send a thank you letter to the gift-giver to express due appreciation and to honor the significance of the giver's clan. Until the moment that full acceptance occurs, social continuity remains in doubt. Miyazaki demonstrates that documents serve the purpose not only of recording the exchange but also of replicating the forms of rituals, which hold the social field together during the hiatus. In other words, documents do not simply record gifts but also are the aesthetic forms through which gift-giving transpires. Documents therefore function as a "meta-level objectification" of processes of social replication processes (222–23). Following Miyazaki's suggestion that we consider how documents serve this purpose across different forms of knowledge (223), we see that in highly technocratic settings the document still functions as an objectifier of replication, but it does so as a second-order, rather than first-order, agent in social mediation (Der Derian 1987, 7). In other words, in the Fijian example, the documentary record helps people arbitrate their relations directly, as parties can determine the relative value of the recorded gift and the character of the exchange ritual. However, in a mass technocratic setting, individuals are not positioned to use documents as part of direct interpersonal negotiations. Instead, each person must always situate him- or herself in relation to abstract social norms or commodity values expressed in law, policy, or the market, which in turn mediate relations between isolated individuals (for example, a judge arbitrates on the basis of a legal code, which the disputants themselves cannot manipulate, revise, or edit). Individuals appeal to an external abstraction to mediate the given issue rather than resolve it directly between themselves. Therefore, while in both cases documents are central agents in social replication, in the Fijian case their role is combined with the direct social engagement between the actors themselves, while in mass technocratic society their role is to mediate socially estranged actors who cannot mutually dictate the terms of their engagement. Documents therefore codify the technical and moral means through which an apparatus indirectly relates estranged individuals to each other.

Getting a handle on the "network"—or the network effect—that pulls an apparatus together makes for an unusual ethnographic challenge. However, given the organizational power of apparatuses and their ability to absorb countless people and resources, we would be wise to take them seriously and approach them confidently. Recent developments in global ethnography provide key tools to take up this task even if it requires applying them in fairly novel ways. Nonlocal ethnography shifts the accent of analysis from location-specific practices to rationales that enable, organize, and effectively integrate many disparate practices, in order to identify *unmappable* ethnographic terrain, as it were. "Nonlocal" describes rationales and practices that are present *in* multiple locations but are not *of* any particular location. In other words, it does not call for the ethnographer's immersion in "place" per se but rather in rationales that enable the apparatus—a situation leading to both real places (meetings, offices, events, conferences, and so on) and virtual places (websites, circulating documents, video representations, media outlets). Studying the formation of an apparatus requires that we shift the ethnographic focus from objects and structures to processes that create the conditions for certain kinds of objectifications and institutional and network configurations.

The example of commodity production in a neoliberal economy illustrates the point. As production is coordinated remotely among multiple locations, communication follows a generic template so that dispersed and unconnected workers can organize themselves ad hoc, remotely, and virtually through IT systems (Hardt and Negri 2000, 295–96). EMN's migration glossary, 3MP's I-Map, the Italian-Egyptian job portal, and Frontex's risk analyses exemplify the point with respect to migration management. Generic templates compensate for the policy group's inability to develop its own idiosyncratic traditions and communicative practices for lack of personal connection, shared history, and close physical proximity. A generic template also ensures that the group will not stray from the apparatus's demands. With the decline of pyramid bureaucracy and the stand-alone factory, flexible labor practices are decidedly vague in appearance and evade efforts to map their direct connections. Yet far from creating a disorderly economy free from regulatory intrusions, this kind of neoliberalism requires that the state—in whatever form it operates—provide optimal conditions for the productive behavior of the entrepreneur-unit rather than specific instructions for the subject to follow. This situation requires a constant adaptation, for example, "of the legal order to scientific discoveries, to the progress of economic organization and technique, to changes in the structure of society, and to the requirements of contemporary consciousness" (Foucault 2008, 161–62). (Neo)liberalism has hardly resulted in unrestrained circulation; rather, it involves "imposing a *Highway Code* while accepting that at a time of faster means of transport this code will not necessarily be the same as in the time of stagecoaches" (162, emphasis original).

Ananya Roy (2010, 34) finds an apt metaphor for this bizarre ethnographic terrain in Kandinsky's compositions, particularly *Small Worlds IV*. These works capture the "ensembles of centralities and multiplicities" of monopolistic forms of power/knowledge that are reproduced though mutated in varied locations. Riles (2000, 20), likewise utilizing the metaphor of modern art, describes the ethnographic endeavor of explaining familiar, modern, transnational relations not as a matter of detailed, thick descriptions of foreign lifeways but rather of selectively erasing detail so as to expose the contours of modern social constructs, which consume the ethnographer and the ethnographic subject alike. The resulting terrain includes an ever-shifting collage of institutions, offices, and organizations, of omnipresent prescriptions for a normative life, of appropriations of local practices, of imitations and reinterpretations of high-level policy prescriptions, and of the subversions of laws and norms that usually confine transgressors to lives in the margins. This terrain may seem superficial and insubstantial, but again, that appearance is the ultimate embodiment of the very superficiality that policymaking actively generates. It reduces the complexities of social life to thin representations of people as policy targets, statistics, and stereotypes, and it demands little substantial connection among its coordinating policymakers, officials, and technocrats. How such superficiality manifests an enormous hold over millions of people is the frightening ethnographic question to be asked.

NONLOCAL ETHNOGRAPHY AND THE VIRTUES OF DISPLACEMENT AND CONTINGENCY

When anthropologists have pursued the study of institutions or of hard-to-access elites, they have often developed a pragmatic ethnographic approach: choose any method that suits the research question and do not anguish over participant-observation. Indeed, forty years ago Nader (1972, 306–7) compellingly argued that if we are to address the most important contemporary problems, then we might have to "study up" and "shuffle around the value placed on participant-observation that leads us to forget that there are other methods more useful" for the problems we need to investigate. To deal with the problem of access, Gusterson (1997, 116) suggests "polymorphous engagement," which involves meeting ethnographic informants "across a number of dispersed sites, not just in local communities, and sometimes in virtual form; and it means collecting data eclectically from a disparate array of sources in many different ways." Shore (2006; see also Amit 1999, 15) argues that social anthropology should not be equated with ethnography, so that it may bypass the constraints of empiricism and better capture wider social processes. Gupta and Ferguson (1997, 37) suggest demoting "the field" (that is, the commitment to particular places) to just "one element in a multistranded methodology for the construction of what Donna Haraway [1988] has called 'situated knowledges.'" This move would create space for additional methods such as archival work, statistical analysis, media analysis, and interviews (38; Shore 2000, 7). This pragmatic and welcome use of varied methods still needs a clear epistemological basis lest we ignore the troubling question of what *isn't* ethnography. The pivotal question here is not how to compensate for participant-observation when access is impeded. That is a technical question of *method*. Rather, the key question is what kind of knowledge we seek through ethnography. That is a logically prior question of *methodology*, the answer to which suggests the most suitable *methods* for any particular research program.

To cope with this challenging and surreal terrain, nonlocal ethnography must avoid two pitfalls: on the one hand, it must not equate itself with participant-observation and thus start from an empiricist premise; while on the other, it must not fetishize documents, knowledge practices, and virtual forms of data and thus fail to see how these actually mediate social relations in the empirical world. To be clear, nonlocal ethnography does not involve the abandonment of participant-observation. Rather, it calls for a review of the *kind* of knowledge that participant-observation traditionally delivered in order to create a flexible methodology that can still retrieve it, even if place is far less stable than it appeared in anthropology's classic field sites. Traditionally, participant-observation has served the dual purposes of (1) *displacing* the ethnographer in order to break down preexisting biases for better reception of alternative ideas, values, practices, and so on; and of (2) showing the importance of *historical contingency* in either reproducing or altering the status quo. A review of these key assets of participant-observation suggests how we can equally incorporate additional research methods under the umbrella of ethnographic methodology.

First, displacement invokes the notion of distinct geographic-cum-cultural space, which today is a more problematic concept than ever. The ethnographer used to rely on an *out*sider's perspective on a presumably *in*sular group in order to produce theoretical statements free from the constraints of emic categories. Contemporary global ethnography, however, involves studying people and processes that are already enmeshed in the ethnographer's inherited web of meaning (cf. Riles 2000). The question becomes whether one can stand outside the sociocultural milieu in which one was socialized. Riles suggests that the answer is "yes" if the ethnographer focuses on "the aesthetics of bureaucratic practices" so as to uncover the designs that make information practices possible and ultimately turn "the network inside out" (16). Nonlocal ethnography starts from a different, though not incompatible, position. Following Clifford (1997, 218), ethnography is one manifestation of a long tradition of Western travel practices that have been understood as "more or less voluntary practices of leaving familiar ground in search of difference, wisdom, power, adventure, an altered perspective." On the one hand, his point reveals participant-observation's traditional empiricist assumptions and comparative aims: learning through direct personal experience and immersion in cultural difference. This view of displacement also shows the importance of developing critical perspectives on one's social reality through removal from it. On the other, Clifford also argues that "travel needs to be rethought in different traditions and historical predicaments" (218). From here we can ask if the desired displacement is achieved solely through entry into an ostensibly alien cultural setting. On the grounds that it is not, nonlocal ethnography recognizes "displacement" as any research (or personal) practice that dislodges the assumptions, discourses, and rationales which the researcher would otherwise take for granted. Nonlocal ethnographers, who might not necessarily travel to remote places, would thus not duplicate the observations of other commentators because their inquiry already aims to destabilize the received assumptions framing the matter in question. In contrast to journalists, for example, who speak "to existing publics in a language they already believe they understand . . . and so are rarely at odds with conventional wisdom," anthropologists have a duty not to be immediately accessible so that they can produce novel insights rather than reveal only unknown facts (Rabinow et al. 2008, 56–57). Displacement— the removal from familiarity and instant accessibility—need not be reduced to matters of crossing geographically demarcated cultural boundaries but, rather, deepened to include any experience in which discourse—the taken-for-granted assumptions that establish norms and deviation—is interrogated, problematized, or in a word, "situated." Ironically, to displace is to situate.

Second, participant-observation foregrounds the importance of historical contingency in human affairs, because "being there" shows the ethnographer what is actually happening in contested moments. It reveals that while the social may appear static (for example, the state), the putative stasis is only achieved through ongoing struggle, conflict, and violence. This perspective renders ethnography a genealogical methodology in the Nietzschean vein that sees history as the "story of petty malice, of violently imposed interpretations, of vicious intentions, of high sounding stories masking the lowest motives" (Dreyfus and Rabinow 1983, 108). It shows how moments of rupture, conflict, and discord result in power inequalities concealed through different political technologies. However, ethnography need not be reduced to participant-observation to achieve this kind of insight. Many methods can account for change through time in local, national, or global contexts. In fact, deep immersion might occlude views of other domains and modes in which conflict is performed, revealed, or concealed.

Nonlocal ethnography can show how an amorphous, polymorphous, and ungrounded apparatus emerges as a device of population management. It is quintessentially an ethnographic methodology because, like participant-observation, it critiques the hegemony of "common knowledge" and traces the role of contingency in human affairs. However, nonlocal ethnography is not constrained by the limits of participant-observation because it does not assume that the singularly most valuable type of evidence is found through direct sensory contact. It is an empirical methodology without the limitations of empiricism. Defined by the twin pillars of displacement and contingency, nonlocal ethnography prioritizes any method that suits the particular research design as long as it illuminates the rationales and fluid processes through which an apparatus materializes. Such an approach would help keep pace with the ephemerality of post/modern times, in which, as Arendt (1958, 304) observed,

> the emphasis shifted entirely away from the product and from the permanent, guiding model to the fabrication process, away from the question of what a thing is and what kind of thing was to be produced to the question of how and through which means and processes it had come into being and could be reproduced.

Nonlocal ethnography may seem to attribute agency to the migration apparatus over and above human intervention. To be sure, this book often describes
it as an active subject to help convey the pervasive role of abstract mediating
agents in human relations. Apparatuses, of course, do not inherently reduce
humans to automatons, but they do encourage the sacrifice of one's powers
of original thought for the cause of utility and efficiency. We risk sacrificing
our capacity for moral judgment on the contradictions that compose daily
life. The local/particular and the abstract/virtual become ever more difficult
to distinguish as the latter comes to enable the former. Stanley Kubrick (1968)
dramatized the point in *2001: A Space Odyssey* with the HAL computer. HAL is
certainly not a literal portrayal of the apparatus. Instead, it is a metaphor for the
apparatus's ostensibly affectionate disposition, which conceals its diversity of
economical and dispassionate modi operandi. For example, HAL's reassuring
voice masks its amoral decision-making criteria, as the liberal's universal humanitarianism is never fully distinguished from the cold logic of productivity,
security, and particularity:

> *Heuristically Programmed Algorithmic Computer aka HAL*: I enjoy working with
> people. I have a stimulating relationship with Dr. Poole and Dr. Bowman.
> My mission responsibilities range over the entire operation of the ship so
> I am constantly occupied. I am putting myself to the fullest possible use,
> which is all, I think, that any conscious entity can ever hope to do. . . .
>
> *BBC reporter*: Do you believe that HAL has genuine emotions?
>
> *Bowman*: Well, he acts like he has genuine emotions. Uh, of course, he's pro-
> grammed that way to make it easier for us to talk to him. But as to whether
> or not he has real feelings is something I don't think anyone can truthfully
> answer.

HAL later determines that Bowman wishes to sabotage the mission because
he has lost confidence in HAL's decision-making capability. HAL therefore attempts to terminate Bowman's life, but not by killing him with a direct assault
on his body. Instead, it shuts down the ship's life-support systems so that he
would die a bloodless, passive death. In self-defense, Bowman manages to dismantle HAL's operating systems to save himself. He not only keeps himself alive
in a strict biological sense but also restores his own agency. He recovers himself
as a unique person but only to sacrifice himself at a later point. As his journey
continues beyond Jupiter, he ultimately witnesses the completion of his own
aging process, thus standing external to himself. The film concludes with the

infant Bowman suspended in a luminous orb in outer space and staring back at a beautiful earth all aglow. This scene, famously enhanced by Strauss's *Also Sprach Zarathustra*, deceptively suggests the promise of a new beginning. However, it more likely represents in Arendtian terms (1958, ch. 6) the shrinkage of the Earth, for any practical human purpose, to an externalized orb-object and the concomitant dissipation of directly connected social life that it once sustained. The infant Bowman, enclosed in his own glowing orb, has become fully transparent and isolated, a literal world unto himself. He is alienated from the Earth as a natural entity and from the world as a social entity.

Understanding the conditions that facilitate our slide from active agents to passive technicians is the first step toward reversing that harrowing trajectory. The incumbent processes are structured by rationalized, generic, and abstract methods designed to manage globalization's apparent madness. Agamben (1998) seeks to explain the logic of these methods in his inquiry into the conditions that create *Homo sacer*: that dispensible soul who may be killed or neglected but categorically cannot be sacrificed. This strangely universal character includes everyone, not only migrants, refugees, and inmates (ibid., 115). While some people are still herded into delineated camps (the particular site through which Agamben demonstrated his original argument), this spatial category also functions in undefined areas: either physical spaces such as deserts and seas, where migrants anonymously perish, or the social spaces of mass society that work by breaking down social connections to leave people isolated, unconnected, confused, and ultimately disposable. Disturbingly, the vast inequalities that the migration apparatus sustains today perhaps result more from the violence of social indifference than the targeted, tangible brutality of collective hatred. In this age of right versus right, it takes its toll through the benign neglect of liberalism as much as through the sting of nationalism.

EPILOGUE
The Comparative Advantages of the Academic
and the Policymaker

The fact that apparatuses and nonlocal ethnography are wedded to policy processes raises the important issue of "policy engagement" in academic research. Anyone familiar with it knows that the relationship between the academic and the policymaker can be difficult and prone to misunderstanding. It easily stalls at two particular roadblocks. First, it can collapse into mutual antagonism: the academic dismisses the policymaker as an unenlightened creature of bureaucratic habit; or the policymaker tries to mold the academic into an advisor to the prince when searching for simplified, utilitarian input—"Give me research I can use!" Second, the academic's specific policy advice is often neither unique nor particularly helpful. My advice is obvious as well: "Level out global economic inequality so people can lead dignified lives wherever they are." Policymakers are often already aware of the academic's advice but find it impractical even if agreeable. They also quickly realize that their purposes are better served by think tanks, professional consultants, or in-house research units.

A possible way of improving this relationship would build off Foucault's notion of the "specific intellectual," who is an individual with "a direct and localised relation to scientific knowledge and institutions" (1980, 128; see 126–33 for a full discussion). The policymaker embodies the specific intellectual rather than the academic, because the former possesses unique knowledge in navigating the local technocratic terrain and is likely to avoid "major ideological polemics" by focusing on particular sectoral questions (Rabinow 1989, 251). In this situation, the role of the academic is to give the policymaker the opportunity to reflect upon the banality of bureaucratic work outside its particular epistemological and ethical frame. Many interviewees for this book seemed to enjoy these opportunities especially when scheduled after work hours and away from the office. Both partners have to make adjustments for this conversation to take hold. On the one hand, academics must communicate the insights of critical theory in ordinary terms during ethnographic fieldwork and in the written ethnography. Often a divisive term, "critical theory" can simply refer to investigations of social reality that start by questioning, rather than taking for granted, the conditions that enable dominant knowledge practices and the worldviews that they encourage. In any case, the ability to deconstruct human relations necessarily precedes the possibility to reconstruct them in more equitable forms. The academic must also stay attuned to how the policymaker articulates the contradictions that he or she regularly faces, and must show how "common sense" policy talk conceals the conditions necessary for their manifestation. On the other hand, policymakers must be prepared to call into question the assumptions on which their knowledge practices are built rather than dismiss the academic for not accepting their universal validity. Often the ethical conflicts that policymakers experience indicate dissatisfaction with tacit policy assumptions and a desire for genuine alternatives. The academic, as interlocutor, provides the opportunity for the policymaker to elaborate such alternatives. This type of dialogue may give rise to new and fairer approaches that policymakers could apply from their particular locations in the larger policy apparatus.

In sum, the academic and the policymaker must each draw on the unique capacities that they bring to their conversations about fairer policy measures. For the academic, it is the ability to articulate counterintuitive perspectives on the interface between social processes and public administration. For the policymaker, it is the skill and experience in manipulating that interface. If the proposition seems starry-eyed, then we need only recall what Margaret Mead once said about small groups of thoughtful people changing the world: "Indeed, it's the only thing that ever has."

REFERENCES

Abdou, Nyier. 2003. Italy and Egypt Meet Online. *Al-Ahram Weekly*, no. 660, 16–22 October. http://weekly.ahram.org.eg/2003/660/eg10.htm (accessed 28 August 2009).

Abrams, Philip. 1988. Notes on the Difficulty of Studying the State. *Journal of Historical Sociology* 1(1): 58–89.

Adnkronos International. 2008. Italy: Government Moves to Dismantle Gypsy Camp. http://www.adnkronos.com/AKI/English/CultureAndMedia/?id=1.0.2230802468 (accessed 15 February 2010).

Agamben, Giorgio. 1998. *Homo Sacer: Sovereign Power and Bare Life*. Stanford, CA: Stanford University Press.

———. 2009. *What Is an Apparatus? And Other Essays*. Stanford, CA: Stanford University Press.

Airport Technology. 2008. Schiphol Airport (AMS/EHAM), Amsterdam, Netherlands. Net Resources International. http://www.airport-technology.com/projects/schiphol (accessed 10 March 2008).

Amit, Vered, ed. 1999. *Constructing the Field: Ethnographic Fieldwork in the Contemporary World*. London: Routledge.

Anrys, Stefaan. 2008. EU Opens Migration Centre in Mali. Trans. Paul Ghysbrecht. *Mondiaal Nieuws*, 28 August. http://www.mo.be/index.php?id=63&tx_uwnews_pi2%5Bart_id%5D=22256&cHash=42ad1fb1d5 (accessed 3 December 2008).

Appadurai, Arjun. 1991. Global Ethnoscapes: Notes and Queries for a Transnational Anthropology. In *Recapturing Anthropology: Working in the Present*, ed. Richard Fox, 191–210. Santa Fe, NM: School of American Research.

———. 1996. *Modernity at Large: Cultural Dimension of Globalization*. Minneapolis: University of Minnesota Press.

Arendt, Hannah. 1958. *The Human Condition*. Chicago: University of Chicago Press.

———. 1966. *The Origins of Totalitarianism*. New York: Harcourt, Brace & World.

———. 2006. *Eichmann in Jerusalem: A Report on the Banality of Evil*. London: Penguin Books.

Arrighi, Giovanni. 1994. *The Long Twentieth Century: Money, Power, and the Origins of Our Times*. London: Verso.

————. 2005. Hegemony Unravelling—1. *New Left Review* 32: 23–80.

Bailey, Adrian J. 2010. Population Geographies, Gender, and the Migration-Development Nexus. *Progress in Human Geography* 34(3): 375–86.

Bauman, Zygmunt. 1991. *Modernity and Ambivalence.* Cambridge, UK: Polity Press.

Baumann, Gerd. 1996. *Contesting Culture: Discourses of Identity in Multi-Ethnic London.* Cambridge, UK: Cambridge University Press.

BBC. 2004a. Billy's Journey: Crossing the Sahara. *British Broadcasting Corporation,* 22 March. http://news.bbc.co.uk/2/hi/africa/3520404.stm (accessed 27 March 2007).

————. 2004b. Billy's Journey: Europe at Last. *British Broadcasting Corporation,* 30 March. http://news.bbc.co.uk/2/hi/africa/3520410.stm (accessed 27 March 2007).

————. 2004c. Guinea: Unstoppable Exodus. *British Broadcasting Corporation,* 18 May. http://news.bbc.co.uk/2/hi/africa/3568329.stm (accessed 27 March 2007).

————. 2010. EU Teams to Patrol Greek Border amid Migrant Surge. British Broadcasting Corporation, 25 October. http://www.bbc.co.uk/news/world-europe-11618094 (accessed 25 October 2010).

Benyon, John, Lynne Turnbull, Andrew Willis, Rachel Woodward, and Adrian Beck. 1993. *Police Co-operation in Europe: An Investigation.* Leicester, UK: University of Leicester, Centre for the Study of Public Order.

Berglund, Eric. n.d. Frontex: The Potential of UAS for European Border Surveillance. http://uasresearch.com/UserFiles/File/042_Contributing-Stakeholder_FRONTEX.pdf (accessed 5 March 2010).

Biao, Xiang. 2007. *Global "Body Shopping": An Indian Labor System in the Information Technology Industry.* Princeton, NJ: Princeton University Press.

Biometric Expertise Group. n.d. About. http://www.biometricexpertisegroup.com/mission.html (accessed 28 February 2008).

Boswell, Christina. 2003. The External Dimension of EU Immigration and Asylum Policy. *International Affairs* 79(3): 619–38.

Bourdieu, Pierre. 1984. *Distinction: A Social Critique of the Judgement of Taste.* Cambridge, MA: Harvard University Press.

Bowker, Geoffrey C., and Susan Leigh Star. 1999. *Sorting Things Out: Classification and Its Consequences.* Cambridge, MA: MIT Press.

Brenneis, Don. 1994. Discourse and Discipline at the National Research Council: A Bureaucratic *Bildungsroman. Cultural Anthropology* 9(1): 23–36.

————. 2006. Reforming Promise. In *Documents: Artifacts of Modern Knowledge,* ed. Annelise Riles, 41–70. Ann Arbor: University of Michigan Press.

Browne, Simone. 2009. Digital Epidermalization: Race, Identity and Biometrics. *Critical Sociology* 36(1): 131–50.

Burawoy, Michael. 2009. *The Extended Case Method: Four Countries, Four Decades, Four Great Transformations, and One Theoretical Tradition.* Berkeley: University of California Press.

Burawoy, Michael. 2000. Introduction: Reaching for the Global. In *Global Ethnography: Forces, Connections, and Imaginations in a Postmodern World*, ed. Michael Burawoy et al., 1–40. Berkeley: University of California Press.

Butler, Judith. 1990. *Gender Trouble: Feminism and the Subversion of Identity*. New York: Routledge.

Calavita, Kitty. 2005. *Immigrants at the Margins: Law, Race, and Exclusion in Southern Europe*. Cambridge, UK: Cambridge University Press.

Campbell, David. 1998. *Writing Security: United States Foreign Policy and the Politics of Identity*. Minneapolis: University of Minneapolis Press.

Cape Verde Property. 2009a. Cape Verde and the Mobility Partnership. *Cape Verde Property*. http://cape-verde-property-direct.com/index.php/Latest/Cape-Verde-and-the-Mobility-Partnership.html (accessed 8 September 2009).

———. 2009b. Why Cape Verde? *Cape Verde Property*. http://cape-verde-property-direct.com/index.php/Cape-Verde-Property-Direct/Why-Cape-Verde.html (accessed 8 September 2009).

Carrera, Sergio. 2007. The EU Border Management Strategy: Frontex and the Challenges of Irregular Immigration in the Canary Islands. CEPS Working Document No. 261, March 2007. Brussels: Centre for European Policy Studies.

Chalfin, Brenda. 2006. Global Customs Regimes and the Traffic in Sovereignty: Enlarging the Anthropology of the State. *Current Anthropology* 47(2): 243–76.

———. 2010. *Neoliberal Frontiers: An Ethnography of Sovereignty in West Africa*. Chicago: University of Chicago Press.

CIGEM. 2008. Centre for Migration Information and Management (CIGEM), Mali. Press Pack—Inauguration of CIGEM, 6 October. http://ec.europa.eu/europeaid/where/acp/country-cooperation/mali/documents/cigem_press_pack_en.pdf (accessed 15 April 2010).

Clifford, J. 1997. Spatial Practices: Fieldwork, Travel, and the Disciplining of Anthropology. In *Anthropological Locations: Boundaries and Grounds of a Field Science*, ed. A. Gupta and J. Ferguson, 185–222. Berkeley: University of California Press.

Cohn, Carol. 1987. Sex and Death in the Rational World of Defense Intellectuals. *Signs* 12(4): 687–718.

Collett, Elizabeth. 2009. Blue Cards and the "Global Battle for Talent." European Policy Centre, 28 May. http://www.epc.eu/en/pub.asp?TYP=TEWN&LV=187&see=y&t=&PG=TEWN/EN/detailpub&l=12&AI=967 (accessed 6 August 2009).

Collier, Stephen J., Andrew Lakoff, and Paul Rabinow. 2004. Biosecurity: Towards an Anthropology of the Contemporary. *Anthropology Today* 20(5): 3–7.

Collier, Stephen J., and Aihwa Ong. 2005. Global Assemblages, Anthropological Problems. In *Global Assemblages: Technology, Politics, and Ethics as Anthropological Problems*, ed. Aihwa Ong and Stephen J. Collier, 3–21. Malden, MA: Blackwell.

Comaroff, Jean, and John Comaroff, eds. 2001. *Millennial Capitalism and the Culture of Neoliberalism.* Durham, NC: Duke University Press.

———. 2003. Ethnography on an Awkward Scale: Postcolonial Anthropology and the Violence of Abstraction. *Ethnography* 4(2): 147–79.

———. 2009. *Ethnicity, Inc.* Chicago: University of Chicago Press.

Commission of the European Communities. 2004. Proposal for a Regulation of the European Parliament and of the Council Concerning the Visa Information System (VIS) and the Exchange of Data Between Member States on Short Stay-Visas. http://eur-lex .europa.eu/LexUriServ/site/en/com/2004/com2004_0835en01.pdf (accessed 31 March 2010).

Cotonou Agreement. 2000. Article 13. http://ec.europa.eu/development/icenter/reposi tory/agr01_en.pdf (accessed 15 April 2010).

Council of the European Union. 2003. Report of the Ad Hoc Group for the Study of the 3rd Pillar Information Systems. No. 8857/03. http://www.statewatch.org/news/2008/ aug/eu-databases-8857–03.pdf (accessed 8 April 2010).

———. 2007. Administrative and Technical Implementing Agreement to the Prüm Convention. No. 5473/07, 22 January. http://www.statewatch.org/news/2007/jan/prum -implementing-agreement.pdf (accessed 1 April 2010).

———. 2009. France Supports the Principle of Establishing the Agency in Strasbourg, to Ensure Continuity of the Existing Situation. No. 13305/09. http://www.statewatch .org/news/2010/jan/eu-sis-access-13305-09.pdf (accessed 20 June 2011).

Coutin, Susan Bibler. 2000. *Legalizing Moves: Salvadoran Immigrants' Struggle for U.S. Residency.* Ann Arbor: University of Michigan Press.

———. 2007. *Nations of Emigrants: Shifting Boundaries of Citizenship in El Salvador and the United States.* Ithaca, NY: Cornell University Press.

Cowan, Jane. 2003. Who's Afraid of Violent Language? Honour, Sovereignty and Claims-Making in the League of Nations. *Anthropological Theory* 3(3): 271–91.

Cowan, Jane, Marie-Bénédicte Dembour, and Richard Wilson, eds. 2001. *Culture and Rights: Anthropological Perspectives.* Cambridge, UK: Cambridge University Press.

Cresswell, Tim. 2006. *On the Move: Mobility in the Modern Western World.* New York: Routledge.

De Genova, Nicholas P. 2002. Migrant "Illegality" and Deportability in Everyday Life. *Annual Review of Anthropology* 31: 419–47.

De Genova, Nicholas, and Nathalie Peutz, eds. 2010. *The Deportation Regime: Sovereignty, Space, and the Freedom of Movement.* Durham, NC: Duke University Press.

De Haas, Hein. 2005. Morocco: From Emigration Country to Africa's Migration Passage to Europe. Migration Policy Institute, October 2005. http://www.migrationinforma tion.org/Profiles/display.cfm?ID=339 (accessed 8 June 2010).

———. 2006. Trans-Saharan Migration to North Africa and the EU: Historical Roots

and Current Trends. Migration Policy Institute, November 2006. http://www.migra
tioninformation.org/Feature/display.cfm?ID=484 (accessed 8 June 2010).

―――. 2008. Irregular Migration from West Africa to the Maghreb and the European
Union: An Overview of Recent Trends. IOM Migration Research Series No. 32, August 2008. Geneva: International Organization for Migration.

De Queiroz, Mario. 2008. Cape Verde-EU: Oiling the Wheels of Temporary Migration.
IPS [Lisbon], 12 June. http://ipsnews.net/news.asp?idnews=42769 (accessed 8 September 2009).

Debord, Guy. 1994. *The Society of the Spectacle.* New York: Zone Books.

Delegation of the European Union. 2009. The EU Blue Card Directive for Employment of
Highly Qualified Third-Country Nationals Enters into Force. Press Release, 18 June.
http://www.delrus.ec.europa.eu/en/news_1173.htm (accessed 8 September 2009).

Der Derian, James. 1987. *On Diplomacy: A Genealogy of Western Estrangement.* Oxford,
UK: Basil Blackwell.

Douglas, Mary. 1966. *Purity and Danger: An Analysis of Concepts of Pollution and Taboo.*
New York: Praeger.

Dreyfus, H., and P. Rabinow. 1983. *Michel Foucault: Beyond Structuralism and Herme-
neutics.* Chicago: University of Chicago Press.

Dunn, Elizabeth. 2003. Trojan Pig: Paradoxes of Food Safety Regulation. *Environment
and Planning A* 35(8): 1493–511.

―――. 2004. *Privatizing Poland: Baby Food, Big Business, and the Remaking of Labor.*
Ithaca, NY: Cornell University Press.

Egyptian Ministry of Manpower and Emigration. 2009a. Prevention of Irregular Migration Project: Job Seekers. http://www.emigration.gov.eg/JobSeekers/JobSeekerHow
ToFill.aspx (accessed 28 August 2009).

―――. 2009b. Prevention of Irregular Migration Project: Objectives. http://www.emi
gration.gov.eg/AboutUs/Objectives.aspx (accessed 28 August 2009).

―――. 2009c. Prevention of Irregular Migration Project: Vision. http://www.emigra
tion.gov.eg/AboutUs/Vision (accessed 28 August 2009).

Escobar, Arturo. 1995. *Encountering Development: The Making and Unmaking of the
Third World.* Princeton, NJ: Princeton University Press.

EurActiv. 2007a. Frattini Hints at "Selective" Immigration Policy. *EurActiv*, 17 January.
http://www.euractive.com/en/justice/frattini-hints-selective-immigration-policy/
article-160974?_print (accessed 17 May 2007).

―――. 2007b. RABIT to Run EU Border Patrols. *EurActiv*, 23 April. http://www.eur
active.com/en/security/rabit-run-eu-border-patrols/article-163429?_print (accessed
17 May 2007).

―――. 2008a. An EU "Blue Card" for High-Skilled Immigrants? *EurActiv*, 22 April.
http://www.euractiv.com/en/socialeurope/eu-blue-card-high-skilled-immigrants/
article-170986 (accessed 10 December 2008).

————. 2008b. Divided Parliament Approves EU Blue Card System. *EurActiv*, 21 November. http://www.euractiv.com/en/socialeurope/divided-parliament-approves-eu-blue -card-system/article-177380 (accessed 10 December 2008).

Euro-African Partnership on Migration and Development. 2006. Rabat Declaration. http://www.unhcr.org/refworld/category,POLICY,MAEC,,,4694d2ea2,0.html (accessed 15 April 2010).

Europa. 2008a. Examining the Creation of a European Border Surveillance System (EUROSUR). Memo/08/86. Brussels: *Europa*, 13 February. http://europa.eu/rapid/ press ReleasesAction.do?reference=MEMO/08/86&format=HTML&aged=0&lan guage=EN (accessed 6 June 2008).

————. 2008b. New Tools for an Integrated European Border Management Strategy. Memo/08/85. Brussels: *Europa*, 13 February. http://europa.eu/rapid/pressReleases Action.do?reference=MEMO/08/85&format=HTML&aged=0&language=EN&gui Language=en (accessed 29 March 2010).

————. 2009a. EU's Biometric Database Continues to Ensure Effective Management of the Common European Asylum System. IP/09/1357. Brussels: *Europa*, 25 September. http://europa.eu/rapid/pressReleasesAction.do?reference=IP/09/1357&format= HTML &aged=0&language=EN&guiLanguage=en (accessed 30 March 2010).

————. 2009b. Integration of Biometric Features in Passports and Travel Documents. Brussels: *Europa*, 2 September. http://europa.eu/legislation_summaries/justice_free dom_security/fight_against_terrorism/l14154_en.htm (accessed 26 May 2010).

Europafrica. 2008. EU Opens Migration Centre in Mali. Europafrica.net: News and Resources on the Joint Africa-EU Strategy, 25 September. http://europafrica.net/2008/ 09/25/eu-opens-migration-centre-in-mali/ (accessed 10 August 2009).

European Biometrics Forum. 2003. About the EBF. *European Biometrics Forum*, 29 October. http://www.eubiometricsforum.com/index.php?option=content&task=view&id =2&Itemid=28 (accessed 20 May 2008).

European Biometrics Portal. n.d. Frequently Asked Questions: Why Is Biometrics Becoming a Primary Concern of European Society? http://www.europeanbiometrics .info/faq/index.php (accessed 28 February 2008).

European Commission. 2005. The Hague Programme—Ten Priorities for the Next Five Years. http://ec.europa.eu/justice_home/news/information_dossiers/the_hague_prior ities/index_en.htm (accessed 24 May 2007).

————. 2006a. EU Immigration: Frontex Operation. European Commission—Audiovisual Services. Archive Video Stockshots, no. i052147. Video. http://ec.europa.eu/av services (accessed 12 June 2008).

————. 2006b. Amending the Common Consular Instructions on Visas for Diplomatic Missions and Consular Posts in Relation to the Introduction of Biometrics Including Provisions on the Organisation of the Reception and Processing of Visa Ap-

plications. COM(2006) 269 final. http://eur-lex.europa.eu/LexUriServ/site/en/com/
2006/com2006_0269en01.pdf (accessed 28 May 2010).

———. 2007. Circular Migration and Mobility Partnership Between the European
Union and Third Countries. Communication from the European Commission.
Memo07/197. Brussels, 16 May.

———. 2008. Mali: Migration Information and Management Centre. Video. http://ec
.europa.eu/europeaid/multimedia/videos/cigem/cigem_en.htm (accessed 10 August
2009).

———. 2010. Delivering an Area of Freedom, Security and Justice for Europe's Citizens—Action Plan Implementing the Stockholm Programme. http://ec.europa.eu/
justice_home/news/intro/doc/com_2010_171_en.pdf (accessed 28 May 2010).

European Commission—Audiovisual Services. 2010. European Border Guards Day and
5th Anniversary of the Establishment of FRONTEX: Conference on the Future of
Border Management in Europe with the Participation of Cecilia Malmström and Al-
fredo Pérez Rubalcaba, Spanish Minister for the Interior. Ref. I-066107, 25 May. Video.
http://ec.europa.eu/avservices/video/video_search_en.cfm?witch=1&keyword=&ref
=I&videoref=066107&search=smp&sitelang=en&LO (accessed 30 August 2010).

European Commission Joint Research Centre. 2009. The JRC-Acquis Multilingual Parallel Corpus. http://langtech.jrc.it/JRC-Acquis.html#Statistics (accessed 19 August
2010).

European Migration Network. 2010. *Asylum and Migration Glossary: A Tool for Better
Comparability*. Brussels: European Commission.

European Migration Policy Organization. 2004. Unpublished Report.

European Roma Rights Centre. 2008. *Security a la Italiana: Fingerprinting, Extreme Violence and Harassment of Roma in Italy*. Budapest: European Roma Rights Centre.

European Union Agency for Fundamental Rights. 2008. Incident Report: Violent Attacks
Against Roma in the Ponticelli District of Naples, Italy. http://fra.europa.eu/fraWeb
site/attachments/Incid-Report-Italy-08_en.pdf (accessed 15 February 2010).

Evens, T.M.S., and Don Handelman. 2006. Introduction: The Ethnographic Praxis of
the Theory of Practice. In *The Manchester School: Practice and Ethnographic Praxis
in Anthropology*, ed. T.M.S Evens and Don Handelman, 1–11. New York: Berghahn
Books.

Ewald, François. 1991a. Norms, Discipline, and the Law. In *Law and the Order of Culture*,
ed. Robert Post, 138–61. Berkeley: University of California Press.

———. 1991b. Insurance and Risk. In *The Foucault Effect: Studies in Governmentality*,
ed. Graham Burchell, Colin Gordon, and Peter Miller, 197–210. Chicago: University
of Chicago Press.

Faist, Thomas, and Andreas Ette, eds. 2007. *The Europeanization of National Immigration Policies: Between Autonomy and the European Union*. Houndmills, UK: Palgrave
Macmillan.

Fassin, Didier. 2005. Compassion and Repression: The Moral Economy of Immigration Policies in France. *Cultural Anthropology* 20(3): 362–87.

Faubion, James D., and George E. Marcus, eds. 2009. *Fieldwork Is Not What It Used to Be: Learning Anthropology's Method in a Time of Transition.* Ithaca, NY: Cornell University Press.

Feldman, Gregory. 2005a. Estranged States: Diplomacy and the Containment of National Minorities in Europe. *Anthropological Theory* 5(3): 219–45.

———. 2005b. Culture, State, and Security in Europe: The Case of Citizenship and Integration Policy in Estonia. *American Ethnologist* 32(4): 676–95.

———. 2005c. Essential Crises: A Performative Approach to Migrants, Minorities, and the European Nation-State. *Anthropological Quarterly* 78(1): 213–346.

———. 2008. The Trap of Abstract Space: Recomposing Russian-Speaking Immigrants in Post-Soviet Estonia. *Anthropological Quarterly* 81(2): 311–42.

———. 2011. Illuminating the Apparatus: Steps Toward a Nonlocal Ethnography of Global Governance. In *Policy Worlds: Anthropology and the Anatomy of Contemporary Power*, ed. Davide Però, Cris Shore, and Sue Wright. London: Berghahn Books.

Feldman, Martha. 1989. *Order Without Design: Information Production and Policy Making.* Stanford, CA: Stanford University Press.

Ferguson, James. 1994. *The Anti-Politics Machine: "Development," Depoliticization, and Bureaucratic Power in Lesotho.* Minneapolis: University of Minnesota Press.

Findley, Sally E. 2004. Mali: Seeking Opportunity Abroad. Migration Policy Institute, September. http://www.migrationinformation.org/Profiles/display.cfm?ID=247 (accessed 8 June 2010).

Foucault, Michel. 1977. *Discipline and Punish.* Harmondsworth, UK: Penguin.

———. 1980. *Power/Knowledge: Selected Interviews and Other Writings 1972–1977.* Ed. Colin Gordon. New York: Pantheon Books.

———. 1988. *Politics, Philosophy, Culture: Interviews and Other Writings 1977–1984.* Ed. Lawrence Kritzman. London: Routledge.

———. 1990. *The History of Sexuality: An Introduction, Volume I.* New York: Vintage Books.

———. 2007. *Security, Territory, Population: Lectures at the Collège de France, 1977–78.* Ed. Michael Senellart. Trans. Graham Burchell. New York: Palgrave Macmillan.

———. 2008. *The Birth of Biopolitics: Lectures at the Collège de France, 1978–79.* Ed. Michael Senellart. Trans. Graham Burchell. New York: Palgrave Macmillan.

Frattini, Franco. 2005. Commissioner Frattini's Speech on "The Commission's Policy Priorities in the Area of Freedom, Security and Justice." http://www.europa-eu-un.org/articles/fr/article_4361_fr.htm. (accessed 3 February 2010).

———. 2007. Enhanced Mobility, Vigorous Integration Strategy and Zero Tolerance on Illegal Employment: A Dynamic Approach to European Immigration Policies. Speech given in Lisbon, 13 September. http://europa.eu/rapid/pressReleasesAction

.do?reference=SPEECH/07/526&format=HTML&aged=1&language=EN&guiLang uage=en (accessed 15 April 2010).

Friedman, Jonathan, ed. 2003. *Globalization, the State, and Violence.* Walnut Creek, CA: Altamira Press.

Frontex. 2006a. BORTEC: Study on Technical Feasibility of Establishing a Surveillance System. Warsaw: Frontex.

———. 2006b. Feasibility Study on Mediterranean Coastal Patrols Network: MEDSEA. Warsaw: Frontex.

———. 2006c. Frequently Asked Questions. http://www.frontex.europa.eu/faq/ (accessed 3 March 2010).

———. 2006d. Longest Frontex Coordinated Operation—HERA, the Canary Islands. Frontex, 19 December. http://www.frontex.europa.eu/newsroom/news_releases/art8 .html (accessed 7 January 2007).

———. 2007a. Frontex Press Kit. Volume 2/11, issue 1. Warsaw: Frontex.

———. 2007b. Rapid Border Intervention Teams First Time in Action. 6 November. http:// www.frontex.europa.eu/newsroom/news_releases/art29.html (accessed 28 May 2010).

———. 2008. Rapid Border Intervention Teams First Time in Action. 6 November. http:// www.frontex.europa.eu/newsroom/news_releases/art45.html (accessed 28 May 2010).

———. 2009. General Report 2008. Warsaw: Frontex.

———. 2010. Greece RABIT 2010 Deployment. Frontex Press Kit. http://www.frontex .eu.int/rabit_2010/background_information/ (accessed 1 April 2011).

Geddes, Andrew. 2000. *Immigration and European Integration: Towards Fortress Europe?* Manchester, UK: Manchester University Press.

———. 2003. *The Politics of Immigration and Migration in Europe.* Cambridge, UK: Cambridge University Press.

Geertz, Clifford. 1973. *The Interpretation of Cultures.* New York: Basic Books.

Giles, Chris. 2006. Richest 2% Hold Half the World's Assets. *Financial Times,* 5 December, P8.

Gingrich, Andre. 2006. Nation, Status and Gender in Trouble? Exploring Some Contexts and Characteristics of Neo-nationalism in Western Europe. In *Neo-Nationalism in Europe and Beyond: Perspectives from Social Anthropology,* ed. Andre Gingrich and Marcus Banks, 29–49. New York: Berghahn Books.

Gleeson, Frances. 2003. Snags Hold Up Biometrics, Experts Say. *The Register,* 22 July. (Originally published on ElectricNews.net, 21 July.) http://www.theregister. co.uk/2003/07/22/snags_hold_up_biometrics_experts (accessed 10 April 2008).

Glick Schiller, Nina. 2005. Transnational Social Fields and Imperialism: Bringing a Theory of Power to Transnational Studies. *Anthropological Theory* 5(4): 439–61.

Glick Schiller, Nina, and Georges Eugene Fouron. 2001. *Georges Woke Up Laughing: Long-Distance Nationalism and the Search for Home.* Durham, NC: Duke University Press.

Global Commission on International Migration. 2005. *Migration in an Interconnected World: New Directions for Action.* http://www.gcim.org/attachements/gcim-complete -report-2005.pdf (accessed 13 April 2010).

Gluckman, Max. 1940. Analysis of a Social Situation in Modern Zululand. *Bantu Studies* 14: 1–30.

Goldirova, Renata. 2008. Italy Extends State of Emergency over Immigration. euobserver .com. http://euobserver.com/9/26551?print=1 (accessed 17 September 2008).

Goldman, Michael. 2005. *Imperial Nature: The World Bank and Struggles for Social Justice in an Age of Globalization.* New Haven, CT: Yale University Press.

González Enríquez, Carmen, and Miquel Reynés Ramón. 2010. Circular Migration Between Morocco and Spain. Metoikos Project. San Domenico di Fiesole, Italy: Robert Schuman Centre for Advanced Studies, European University Institute www.eui .eu/Project/METOIKOS/Documents/BackgroundReports/METOIKOSprojectBack grRepSpainMoroccoMay2010.pdf (accessed 22 June 2010).

Gramsci, Antonio. 1971. *Selections from the Prison Notebooks of Antonio Gramsci.* Ed. and trans. Quintin Hoare and Geoffrey Noell-Smith. London: Lawrence and Wishart.

Greenhalgh, Susan. 2003. Planned Births, Unplanned Persons: "Population" in the Making of Chinese Modernity. *American Ethnologist* 30(2): 196–215.

———. 2008. *Just One Child: Science and Policy in Deng's China.* Berkeley: University of California Press.

Grinker, Roy R. 1998. *Korea and Its Futures: Unification and the Unfinished War.* New York: St. Martin's Press.

Guild, Elspeth. 2003. The Border Abroad: Visas and Border Controls. In *In Search of Europe's Borders*, ed. Kees Groenendijk, Elspeth Guild, and Paul Minderhoud, 87–104. The Hague: Kluwer Law International.

———. 2005. *Danger: Borders Under Construction: Assessing the First Five Years of Border Policy in an Area of Freedom, Security and Justice.* Brussels: Centre for European Studies.

Gupta, Akhil, and James Ferguson. 1997. Discipline and Practice: "The Field" as Site, Method, and Location in Anthropology. In *Anthropological Locations: Boundaries and Grounds of a Field Science*, ed. Akhil Gupta and James Ferguson, 1–46. Berkeley: University of California Press.

Gusterson, Hugh. 1997. Studying Up Revisited. *Political and Legal Anthropology Review* 20(1): 114–19.

Hage, Ghassan. 2000. *White Nation: Fantasies of White Supremacy in a Multicultural Society.* New York: Routledge.

Hannerz, Ulf. 1996. *Transnational Connections: Culture, People, Places.* London: Routledge.

Hardt, Michael, and Antonio Negri. 2000. *Empire.* Cambridge, MA: Harvard University Press.

Harper, Richard. 1998. *Inside the IMF: An Ethnography of Documents, Technology and Organisational Action.* San Diego: Academic Press.

Harvey, David. 2003. *The New Imperialism.* Oxford, UK: Oxford University Press.

Hayes, Ben. 2005. SIS II: *Fait Accompli?* Construction of EU's Big Brother Database Underway. *Statewatch,* 5 May. www.statewatch.org/analyses/no-45-sisII-analysis-may05.pdf

Hervik, Peter. 2006. The Emergence of Neo-Nationalism in Denmark, 1992–2001. In *Neo-Nationalism Inside the EU: Anthropological Perspectives,* ed. Marcus Banks and Andre Gingrich, 92–106. Oxford, UK: Berghahn Books.

Herzfeld, Michael. 1992. *The Social Production of Indifference: Exploring the Symbolic Roots of Western Bureaucracy.* London: Berg.

Hess, Sabine. 2008. Migration and Development: A Governmental Twist of the EU Migration Management Policy. Paper presented at Sussex University, Brighton, UK, 18–19 September.

Heyman, Joshiah McC. 2000. Respect for Outsiders? Respect for the Law? The Moral Evaluation of High Scale Issues by US Immigration Officers. *Journal of the Royal Anthropological Institute* 6(4): 635–52.

———. 2008. Constructing a Virtual Wall: Race and Citizenship in US-Mexico Border Policing. *Journal of the Southwest* 50(3): 305–34.

Heyman, Josiah McC., and Howard Campbell. 2009. The Anthropology of Global Flows: A Critical Reading of Appadurai's "Disjuncture and Difference in the Global Cultural Economy." *Anthropological Theory* 9(2): 131–48.

Holmes, Douglas. 2000. *Integral Europe: Fast Capitalism, Multiculturalism, Neofascism.* Princeton, NJ: Princeton University Press.

Hyndman, Jennifer. 2000. *Managing Displacement: Refugees and the Politics of Humanitarianism.* Minneapolis: University of Minnesota Press.

ILO. 2009. Pagesos Solidaris (Farmers Solidarity Foundation). http://www.ilo.org/dyn/migpractice/migmain.showPractice?p_lang=en&p_practice_id=46 (accessed 24 June 2010).

Inda, Jonathan Xavier, and Renato Rosaldo. 2002. Introduction: A World in Motion. In *The Anthropology of Globalization: A Reader,* ed. Jonathan Xavier Inda and Renato Rosaldo, 1–35. Oxford, UK: Blackwell.

Information Technology Laboratory. 2007. Published International Standards Developed by ISO/IEC JTC 1/SC 37—Biometrics. U.S. National Institute for Standards and Technology, 6 April. http://www.itl.nist.gov/div893/biometrics/documents/April%206_FP_Published_ISO_Standards.pdf (accessed 12 March 2008).

Information Technology Standards. 2003a. Enterprise Workspace: ISO/IEC JTC 001. http://isotc.iso.org/livelink/livelink/fetch/2000/2122/327993/customview.html?func=ll&objId=327993 (accessed 12 March 2008).

————. 2003b. Enterprise Workspace: At a Glance. ISOTC Portal. http://isotc.iso.org/livelink/livelink/fetch/2000/2122/327993/755080/1054033/2314809/customview.html?func=ll&objId=2314809&objAction=browse&sort=name (accessed 12 March 2008).

International Centre for Migration Policy Development. 2008. The DG's Corner. *ICMPD Newsletter*, November, 2. http://www.icmpd.org/fileadmin/ICMPD-Website/ICMPD_General/Newsletters/ICMPD_NL_3_08_web.pdf (accessed 16 December 2008).

IOM. 2008. IMIS Project. UN-ESCWA: United Nations Economic and Social Commission for Western Asia. http://www.escwa.un.org/divisions/scu/migration/Session2_IOM_1.pdf (accessed 8 December 2008).

IRIN. 2008. MALI: Returnees Sceptical About New EU Information Centre. *Wow.gm*, 7 October. http://wow.gm/africa/mali/bamako/article/2008/10/7/mali-returnees-sceptical-about-new-eu-information-centre-1 (accessed 10 August 2009).

Islam in Europe. 2006. Denmark: Marriage Immigration Drops. http://islamineurope.blogspot.com/2006/10/denmark-marriage-immigration-drops.html (accessed 28 March 2011).

Joint Africa-EU Declaration on Migration and Development. 2006. Joint Africa-EU Declaration on Migration and Development. http://www.unhcr.org/refworld/category,POLICY,EU,,,47fdfb010,0.html (accessed 15 April 2010).

Joubert, Chantal, and Hans Bevers. 1996. *Schengen Investigated: A Comparative Interpretation of the Schengen Provisions on International Police Cooperation in the Light of the European Convention on Human Rights*. The Hague: Kluwer Law International.

Juchno, Piotr. 2007. Asylum Applications in the European Union. Eurostat. *Statistics in Focus: Population and Social Conditions*. No. 110/2007. Geneva: European Communities.

Kjærsgaard, Pia. 2001. Opening Remarks for the Debate of the Danish Parliament on 4 October. http://en.wikiquote.org/wiki/Danish_People's_Party#cite_note-1 (accessed 10 May 2010).

Kubrick, Stanley, dir. 1968. *2001: A Space Odyssey*. (film) MGM/Warner Bros.

Kuus, Merje. In press 2011. Policy and Geopolitics: Bounding Europe in EUrope. *Annals of the Association of American Geographers*.

Kymlicka, Will. 1995. *Multicultural Citizenship: A Liberal Theory of Minority Rights*. Oxford, UK: Oxford University Press.

Lahav, Gallya. 2008. *Immigration and Politics in the New Europe: Reinventing Borders*. Cambridge, UK: Cambridge University Press.

Latour, Bruno. 1990. Drawing Things Together. In *Representation in Scientific Practice*, ed. Michael Lynch and Steve Woolgar, 19–68. Cambridge, MA: MIT Press.

Lea, Tess. 2008. *Bureaucrats and Bleeding Hearts: Indigenous Health in Northern Australia*. Sydney: University of New South Wales Press.

Lefebvre, Henri. 1991. *The Production of Space*. Trans. Donald Nicholson-Smith. Malden, MA: Blackwell.

Leidel, Steffen. 2007. Spain's Border Surveillance System Remains Controversial. *Deutsche Welle*, 29 October. http://www.dw-world.de/dw/article/0,2144,2835465,00.html (accessed 23 June 2008).

Lewis, Paul. 2008. Rabit Run. *The Guardian*, 16 April. http://commentisfree.guardian.co .uk/paul_lewis/2008/04/rabit_run.html (accessed 4 June 2008).

Li, Tania. 2007. The Will to Improve: Governmentality, Development, and the Practice of Politics. Durham, NC: Duke University Press.

Lindquist, Johan A. 2009. *The Anxieties of Mobility: Migration and Tourism in the Indonesian Borderlands*. Honolulu: University of Hawaii Press.

Lobjakas, Ahto. 2005. EU: Brussels to Introduce Fingerprinting for Many Schengen Visitors by 2007. *Radio Free Europe*, 7 January. http://www.rferl.org/content/article/1056744.html (accessed 6 June 2006).

Löfgren, Orvar. 1989. The Nationalization of Culture. *Ethnologia Europaea* 19: 5–23.

Luhmann, Niklas. 1993. *Risk: A Sociological Theory*. New York: Aldine de Gruyter.

Lutz, Catherine, and Donald Nonini. 1999. The Economies of Violence and the Violence of Economies. In *Anthropological Theory*, ed. Henrietta Moore, 73–113. Cambridge, UK: Polity Press.

Lyon, David. 2001. *Surveillance Society: Monitoring Everyday Life*. Buckingham, UK: Open University Press.

Malkki, Liisa. 1995. Refugees and Exile: From "Refugee Studies" to the National Order of Things. *Annual Review of Anthropology* 24: 495–523.

Marcus, George. 1995. Ethnography in/of the World System: The Emergence of Multi-Sited Ethnography. *Annual Review of Anthropology* 24: 95–117.

MARISS. 2007. The Mariss Service Portfolio. *Mariss Newsletter* 2: 2–3.

Marrese, Emilio. 2002. Ramadan, sindaco nega lo spazio, Benetton concede il palazzetto. *La Repubblica*, 3 December. http://www.repubblica.it/online/cronaca/immitreviso/ramadan/ramadan.html (accessed 18 February 2010).

Mazower, Mark. 2000. *Dark Continent: Europe's Twentieth Century*. New York: Vintage.

Messina, Anthony. 2007. *The Logics and Politics of Post-WWII Migration to Western Europe*. Cambridge: Cambridge University Press.

MIDA. 2002. Self-Evaluation Report MIDA Great Lakes. http://www.iom.int/MIDA/pdf/GreatLakes1.pdf (accessed 29 December 2008).

Migration Policy Institute. 2010. MPI Data Hub: Migration Facts, Stats, and Maps. http://www.migrationinformation.org/datahub/remittances.cfm (accessed 15 April 2010).

Mitchell, Timothy. 2002. *Rule of Experts: Egypt, Techno-politics, Modernity*. Berkeley: University of California Press.

Miyazaki, Hirokazu. 2006. Documenting the Present. In *Documents: Artifacts of Modern Knowledge*, ed. Annelise Riles, 206–25. Ann Arbor: University of Michigan Press

Moch, Leslie Page. 1992. *Moving Europeans: Migration in Western Europe Since 1650*. Bloomington: Indiana University Press.

Moore, Sally Falk. 2005. Comparisons: Possible and Impossible. *Annual Review of Anthropology* 34: 1–11.

Mosse, David. 2004. *Cultivating Development: An Ethnography of Aid Policy and Practice.* London: Pluto.

Mosse, George. 1979. Introduction: Toward a General Theory of Fascism. In *International Fascism: New Thoughts and New Approaches*, ed. George Mosse, 1–41. London: Sage.

MSNBC. 2006. Film Exposes Immigrants to Dutch Liberalism. *MSNBC*, 16 March. http://www.msnbc.msn.com/id/11842116/ (accessed 1 March 2007).

Nader, Laura. 1972. Up the Anthropologist: Perspectives Gained from Studying Up. In *Reinventing Anthropology*, ed. D. Hymes, 285–311. New York: Pantheon Press.

Navaro-Yashin, Yael. 2003. "Life Is Dead Here": Sensing the Political in "No Man's Land." *Anthropological Theory* 3(1): 107–25.

Ndiaye, Mbalo. 2007. Senegal Agricultural Situation Country Report. No. SG7001. United States Department of Agriculture Foreign Agricultural Service. http://www.fas.usda.gov/gainfiles/200701/146279961.pdf (accessed 17 June 2010).

No-Racism. 2008. Station Bamako (Mali). *No-Racism.net*, 21 April. http://no-racism.net/article/2525/ (accessed 10 August 2009).

Ong, Aihwa. 1999. Clash of Civilizations or Asian Liberalism? An Anthropology of the State and Citizenship. In *Anthropological Theory Today*, ed. Henrietta Moore, 48–72. Cambridge, UK: Polity Press.

OSCE/IOM/ILO. 2006. *Handbook on Establishing Effective Labour Migration Policies in Countries of Origin and Destination.* Vienna and Geneva: OSCE/IOM/ILO.

Peck, Jamie. 2008. Remaking Laissez-Faire. *Progress in Human Geography* 32(1): 3–43.

Perry, Richard Warren, and Bill Maurer, eds. 2003. *Globalization Under Construction: Governmentality, Law, and Identity.* Minneapolis: University of Minnesota Press.

Peutz, Nathalie, and Nicholas De Genova. 2010. Introduction. In *The Deportation Regime: Sovereignty, Space, and the Freedom of Movement*, ed. Nicholas De Genova and Nathalie Peutz, 1–29. Durham, NC: Duke University Press.

Pilger, John. 2002. *The New Rulers of the World.* London and New York: Verso.

Pisa, Nick. 2008. Italy Declares State of Emergency over Roma Immigrants. *Telegraph*, 25 July. http://www.telegraph.co.uk/news/worldnews/europe/italy/2459968/Italy-declares-state-of-emergency-over-Roma-immigrants.html (accessed 15 February 2010).

Portuguese Consulate in Sydney. 2007. *Passaporte Electrónico Português.* Video. http://www.consulportugalsydney.org.au/video_eng.html (accessed 4 March 2008).

Poulantzas, Nicos. 1973. *Political Power and Social Classes.* Trans. Timothy O'Hagan. Norfolk, UK: Lowe and Bryndon. (Originally published as *Pouvoir politique et classes sociales de l'état capitaliste.* Paris: F. Maspero, 1968.)

Power, Michael. 1997. *The Audit Society: Rituals of Verification.* Oxford, UK: Oxford University Press.

Pritchett, Lant. 2006. *Let Their People Come: Breaking the Gridlock on Global Labor Mobility.* Washington, DC: Centre for Global Development.

Rabinow, Paul. 1989. *French Modern: Norms and Forms of the Social Environment.* Cambridge, MA: MIT Press.

———. 2003. *Anthropos Today: Reflections on Modern Equipment.* Princeton, NJ: Princeton University Press.

Rabinow, Paul, and George E. Marcus, with James D. Faubion and Tobias Rees. 2008. *Designs for an Anthropology of the Contemporary.* Durham, NC: Duke University Press.

Ramdas, Kavita N. 2007. No Fair Trade for Women. *Huffington Post,* 27 September. http://www.huffingtonpost.com/kavita-n-ramdas/no-fair-trade-for-women_b_66189.html (accessed 14 May 2008).

Republica Moldova. 2009. Mobility Partnership Between Moldova and European Union. Newsletter, no. 1, March 2009. http://soderkoping.org.ua/page23729.html (accessed 10 May 2010).

Riles, Annelise. 2000. *The Network Inside Out.* Ann Arbor: University of Michigan Press.

———. 2006a. Introduction: In Response. In *Documents: Artifacts of Modern Knowledge,* ed. Annelise Riles, 1–38. Ann Arbor: University of Michigan Press.

———, ed. 2006b. *Documents: Artifacts of Modern Knowledge.* Ann Arbor: University of Michigan Press.

Roman, Howaida. 2008. *Italian-Egyptian Model in Managing the Emigration from Egypt to Italy: Dimensions and Prospects.* CARIM Analytic and Synthetic Notes 2008/18. Circular Migration Series, Political and Social Module. http://cadmus.eui.eu/dspace/bitstream/1814/ . . . /CARIM_AS%26N_2008_18.pdf (accessed 22 June 2010).

———. 2009. Egypt: The Political and Social Dimension of Migration. In *Mediterranean Migration: 2008–2009 Report, October 2009,* ed. Philippe Fargues, 89–96. CARIM Mediterranean Migration Report 2008–2009. San Domenico di Fiesole, Italy: Robert Schuman Centre for Advanced Studies, European University Institute.

Rose, Nikolas. 1992. Governing the Enterprising Self. In *The Values of the Enterprise Culture: The Moral Debate,* ed. P. Heelas and P. Morris, 141–64. London: Routledge.

———. 1993. Government, Authority, and Expertise in Advanced Liberalism. *Economy and Society* 22(3): 283–300.

———. 1999. *The Powers of Freedom: Reframing Political Thought.* Cambridge, UK: Cambridge University Press.

Roy, Ananya. 2010. *Poverty Capital: Microfinance and the Making of Development.* New York: Routledge.

Sahlins, Marshall. 1995. *How "Natives" Think: About Captain Cook, For Example.* Chicago: University of Chicago Press.

Said, Edward. 1979. *Orientalism.* New York: Vintage Books.

Samers, Michael. 2004. An Emerging Geopolitics of "Illegal Migration" in the European Union. *European Journal of Migration and Law* 6: 27–45.

Sassen, Saskia. 1999. *Guests and Aliens.* New York: New Press.

———. 2008. Fear and Strange Arithmetics: When Powerful States Confront Powerless Immigrants. *Open Democracy.* http://www.opendemocracy.net/prinhttp://www.open democracy.net/print/45097t/45097 (accessed 25 June 2010).

SCADPlus. 2004. Integrated Management of External Borders. http://europa.eu/scad plus/leg/en/lvb/l33205.htm (accessed 6 June 2008).

Schiphol Airport. n.d. a. Privium: Fast Border Passage with Iris Scan. *Schiphol.* http://www.schiphol.nl/AtSchiphol/PriviumIrisscan/FastBorderPassageWithIrisScan.htm (accessed 12 May 2008).

———. n.d. b. Frequently Asked Questions: What Happens if the Iris Recognition Fails? *Schiphol.* http://www.schiphol.nl/AtSchiphol/PriviumIrisscan/FrequentlyAskedQues tions.htm (accessed 12 May 2008).

Schwegler, Tara. 2008. Take It from the Top (Down)? Rethinking Neoliberal Economic Knowledge and Political Hierarchy in Mexico. *American Ethnologist* 35(4): 682–700.

Scott, James. 1998. *Seeing Like a State: How Certain Schemes to Improve the Human Condition Have Failed.* New Haven, CT: Yale University Press.

———. 2005. Afterword to Moral Economies, State Spaces, and Categorical Violence. *American Anthropologist* 107(3): 395–402.

secunet. 2006. ePassport Interoperability Test Event. Final Report, Version 1.1. Berlin, 29 May–1 June. http://www.essen-group.org/download/InteropEvent_Final-Report _1-1.pdf (accessed 10 March 2008).

———. 2008. Essen Group. http://www.secunet.com/de/produkte-dienstleistungen/gov ernment/biometrie-hoheitliche-dokumente/essen-group/ (accessed 10 March 2008).

Shamir, Ronen. 2005. Without Borders? Notes on Globalization as a Mobility Regime. *Sociological Theory* 23(2): 197–217.

Shore, Cris. 2000. *Building Europe: The Cultural Politics of European Integration.* London: Routledge.

———. 2006. The Limits of Ethnography Versus the Poverty of Theory: Patron-Client Relations in Europe Re-Visited. *Sites: Journal of Social Anthropology and Cultural Studies* 3(2): 40–59.

Shore, Cris, and Susan Wright. 1997. Policy: A New Field of Anthropology. In *Anthropology of Policy: Critical Perspectives on Governance and Power,* ed. Cris Shore and Susan Wright, 3–39. London: Routledge.

Silverstein, Michael. 1976. Shifters, Linguistic Categories, and Cultural Description. In *Meaning in Anthropology,* ed. Keith H. Basso and Henry A. Selby, 11–55. Albuquerque: University of New Mexico Press.

Silverstein, Paul. 2005. Immigrant Racialization and the New Savage Slot: Race, Migration, and Immigration in the New Europe. *Annual Review of Anthropology* 34: 363–84.

Sirtori, Sonia, and Patricia Coelho. 2007. Defending Refugees' Access to Protection in

Europe. Report published by the European Council on Refugees and Exiles, December 2007.

Slovenian Presidency. 2008a. Illegal Migration in Slovenia (Statistical Data). Electronic document available at http://www.policija.si/portal_en/szj/2008/apr10-Rabit.php (accessed 4 June 2008).

————. 2008b. RABIT Exercise: Joint Exercise of the Slovenian and Other European Police Forces at the External Schengen Border. Press Release, 4 October. http://www.eu2008.si/en/News_and_Documents/Press_Releases/April/0410MNZ_Frontex.html (accessed 4 June 2008).

Smith, Gavin. 2006. When "the Logic of Capital Is the Real Which Lurks in the Background": Programme and Practice in European "Regional Economies." *Current Anthropology* 47(4): 621–39.

Snijder, Max. 2005. New Man at the Top for EBF. *Biometric Technology Today* 13(10, November/December): 7.

Spain—Out of Africa. 2007. Videorecording. Produced by Martin Butler, 20 min., 53 sec. Journeyman Pictures, 22 January 2007.

Statewatch. n.d. SIS II: *Fait Accompli?* Construction of EU's Big Brother Database Underway. http://www.statewatch.org/analyses/no-45-sisII-analysis-may05.pdf (accessed 15 October 2010).

Steinmetz, George. 2003. The State of Emergency and the Revival of American Imperialism: Toward an Authoritarian Post-Fordism. *Public Culture* 15(2): 323–45.

Stolcke, Verena. 1995. Talking Culture: New Boundaries, New Rhetorics of Exclusion in Europe. *Current Anthropology* 36(1): 1–24.

Strathern, Marilyn. 1995. Comment on "Talking Culture: New Boundaries, New Rhetorics of Exclusion in Europe." *Current Anthropology* 36(1): 16.

————. 2000. *Audit Cultures: Anthropological Studies in Accountability, Ethics, and the Academy*. London: Routledge.

Sunier, Thijl, and Rob van Ginkel. 2006. "At Your Service!": Reflections on the Rise of Neo-Nationalism in the Netherlands. In *Neo-Nationalism Inside the EU: Anthropological Perspectives*, ed. Marcus Banks and Andre Gingrich, 107–24. Oxford, UK: Berghahn Books.

Tape, Nurah. 2006. Dutch Immigration Test "Anti-Muslim." *Al Jazeera*, 22 March. http://english.aljazeera.net/News/archive/archive?ArchiveId=19363 (accessed 1 March 2007).

Tholen, Berry. 2005. The Europeanisation of Migration Policy—The Normative Issues. *European Journal of Migration and Law* 6: 323–51.

Thomas, Rebekah. 2005. Biometrics, International Migrants and Human Rights. *European Journal of Migration and Law* 7: 377–411.

Ticktin, Miriam. 2006. Where Ethics and Politics Meet: The Violence of Humanitarianism in France. *American Ethnologist* 33(1): 33–49.

Todorova, Maria. 1997. *Imagining the Balkans*. New York: Oxford University Press.

Touahri, Sarah. 2007. Employment Promotion Agency Helps Young People Enter the Labour Market. *Magharebia*. http://www.magharebia.com/cocoon/awi/print/fa/fea tures/awi/reportage/2007/04/20/reportage-01 (accessed 22 June 2010).

Trouillot, Michel-Rolph. 2001. The Anthropology of the State in the Age of Globalization: Close Encounters of the Deceptive Kind. *Current Anthropology* 42(1): 125–38.

Tsing, Anna. 2005. *Friction: An Ethnography of Global Connection*. Princeton, NJ: Princeton University Press.

Turner, Terence. 1995. Comment on "Talking Culture: New Boundaries, New Rhetorics of Exclusion in Europe." *Current Anthropology* 36(1): 16–18.

———. 2003. Class Projects, Social Consciousness, and the Contradictions of "Globalization." In *Globalization, the State, and Violence*, ed. Jonathan Friedman, 35–66. Walnut Creek, CA: Altamira Press.

Unisys. 2008. Unisys to Create New Web Portal on Immigration for European Commission. Unisys News Release 1003/8914. Brussels, 3 October. http://www.unisys.com/uni sys/news/detail.jsp?id=5800038 (accessed 10 September 2009).

———. 2009. Unisys Corporate Website. http://www.unisys.com (accessed 29 February 2008).

United Kingdom Home Office Press Office. n.d. Frequently Asked Questions: What Is eBorders? http://press.homeoffice.gov.uk/faqs/controlling-our-borders/ (accessed 15 May 2008).

United Kingdom Parliament. 2006. Memorandum by the European Commission, Directorate General, Justice, Freedom and Security. Select Committee on European Union, Minutes of Evidence. http://www.publications.parliament.uk/pa/1d200506/ldselect/ldeucom/166/6030209.htm (accessed 6 June 2006).

Urciuoli, Bonnie. 2008. Skills and Selves in the New Workplace. *American Ethnologist* 35(2): 211–28.

Van der Veer, Peter. 2006. Pim Fortuyn, Theo van Gogh, and the Politics of Tolerance in the Netherlands. *Public Culture* 18(1): 111–24.

Van Liempt, Ilse, and Jeroen Doomernik. 2006. Migrant's Agency in the Smuggling Process: The Perspectives of Smuggled Migrants in the Netherlands. *International Migration* 44(4): 165–90.

Vaughan-Williams, Nick. 2008. Borderwork Beyond Inside/Outside? Frontex, the Citizen-Detective and the War on Terror. *Space and Polity* 12(1): 63–79.

Vigneswaran, Darshan. 2008. Enduring Territoriality: South African Immigration Control. *Political Geography* 27(2): 783–801.

Wacquant, Loïc. 2002. The Curious Eclipse of Prison Ethnography in the Age of Mass Incarceration. *Ethnography* 3(4): 371–97.

Watson, Graham. 2007. Graham Watson on Immigration. Video. Speech posted on YouTube. 26 September. http://www.youtube.com/watch?v=EgNjQ-l8psY (accessed 1 April 2008).

Weber, Cynthia. 1995. *Simulating Sovereignty: Intervention, the State, and Symbolic Exchange.* Cambridge, UK: Cambridge University Press.

Webster's Third New International Dictionary. 1971. "Police." Springfield, MA: G&C Merriam.

Wedel, Janine. 1998. *Collision and Collusion: The Strange Case of Western Aid to Eastern Europe, 1989–1998.* New York: St. Martin's Press.

Wedel, Janine, Cris Shore, Gregory Feldman, and Stacy Lathrop. 2005. Toward an Anthropology of Public Policy. *Annals of the American Association of Political and Social Sciences* 600: 30–51.

Wedel, Janine, and Gregory Feldman. 2005. Why an Anthropology of Public Policy? *Anthropology Today* 21(1): 1–2.

Weldes, Jutta, Mark Laffey, Hugh Gusterson, and Raymond Duvall, eds. 1999. *Cultures of Insecurity: States, Communities and the Production of Danger.* Minneapolis: University of Minnesota Press.

Wikan, Unni. 2002. *Generous Betrayal: Politics of Culture in the New Europe.* Chicago: University of Chicago Press.

Wilkinson, Tracy. 2008. Italy's Right Targets Gypsies, Migrants. *Los Angeles Times,* 24 May. http://articles.latimes.com/2008/may/24/world/fg-right24 (accessed 15 February 2010).

Williams, Allan M. 2006. Lost in Translation? International Migration, Learning and Knowledge. *Progress in Human Geography* 30(5): 588–607.

World Bank. 2009. Cape Verde. Country Brief. http://web.worldbank.org/WBSITE/EXTERNAL/COUNTRIES/AFRICAEXT/CAPEVERDEEXTN/0,,menuPK:349633~pagePK:141132~piPK:141107~theSitePK:349623,00.html (accessed 8 September 2009).

Zabusky, Stacia E. 1995. *Launching Europe: An Ethnography of European Cooperation in Space Science.* Princeton, NJ: Princeton University Press.

Žižek, Slavoj. 2000. Why We Love to Hate Haider. *New Left Review* 2: 37–45.

———. 2002. *Welcome to the Desert of the Real.* London: Verso.

Zohry, Ayman. 2003. Contemporary Egyptian Migration. Cooperazione Italiana, Arab Republic of Egypt, International Organization for Migration. Electronic copy.

———. 2006. Attitudes of Egyptian Youth Towards Migration to Europe. Cooperazione Italiana, Arab Republic of Egypt, International Organization for Migration. Electronic copy.

———. 2007. Migration and Development in Egypt. Paper prepared for the Institute of Migration and Cultural Studies, Osnabrück University, Osnabrück, Germany, 16–17 December.

Zolberg, Aristide. 1983. The Formation of New States as a Refugee Generating Process. *Annals of the American Academy of Political and Social Sciences* 467: 24–38.

INDEX

2001: A Space Odyssey (film), 197–198

3MP (Mediterranean Managed Migration Project), 1, 5, 19–20, 27; abstract cooperation, 126, 152, 192; harmonizing policy guidelines, 71–76, 83; I-Map, 23, 69–71

Abstract cooperation, 122–126

Acquis (*Acquis Communitaire*), 60, 66, 87

ALDE (Alliance of Liberals and Democrats for Europe), 81

Apparatus, 5, 8, 14, 79, 109, 142, 164; constructedness of, 15–18; global inequality, 7, 13, 80, 82, 115, 116, 158, 164; human agency, 17, 77, 197–198; humanitarian rationales, 83, 93; knowledge practices, 29, 57–59, 68, 69, 86, 92, 116; nonlocal ethnography, 17–18, 180, 181, 186, 188–196; personal sentiments, 109, 113–114. See also *2001: A Space Odyssey*; Crisis; Mediation; Mediating agents/ devices; Network, network effect; Nonlocal ethnography; Normalization; Security

Assemblages, 15

Asylum and Migration Glossary, 22, 65–67, 152. See also EMN

Baltic Sea Region Border Control Cooperation, 89

BEG (Biometrics Expertise Group), 123

Berglund, Erik, 96

Biometrics: history of, 120; dactylography, 120. See also EBF; EURODAC; Identity; PEP; RT programs; Schengen, SIS; Virtuous traveler; VIS

Blue Card: compared to Green Card, 174; EU Parliament debate, 175–178

Boundary objects, 16, 124, 149, 189

Brussels, 9, 20, 41, 64, 65, 68

Brussels Interoperability Group, 125

Buñuel, Luis, 2. See also *The Discreet Charm of the Bourgeoisie*

Canary Islands: policy analysis, 70, 115, 147, 188; migration journeys, 81–82, 110; Operation Hera, 97, 99, 100–103

Cape Verde, 97, 101. See also Mobility partnerships

Cayucos, 80, 97, 101–103

Ceuster, Jan de, 118

China: migration and border control, 87, 113, 141, 142, 158, 165

CIGEM (Migration Information and Management Centre), 160–164, 167, 171

Circular migration: 8, 10, 23, 24, 46, 149; history of, 158; idea of, 50–52, 154–157, 178–179; policy, 152, 159–160. See also Blue Card; CIGEM; CNAI; IDOM; IMIS; IOM; Migration and development, MIDA; Mobility partnerships

CNAI (Centro Nacional de Apio ao Imigrante), 162–163

Communism, 8

Connections: compared to relations, 5, 40, 82, 198; in ephemeral social contexts, 13, 19, 35, 79, 85, 126; in ethnographic methodology, 12, 180, 183–185, 186, 189, 192. See also Apparatus; Mediation; Network; Nonlocal; Relations